Mothering the Self

The mother–daughter relationship has preoccupied feminist writers for decades, but typically the daughter's story has been set centre stage. *Mothering the Self* brings together maternal and daughterly stories through drawing on in-depth interviews with women who speak both as mothers and as daughters.

In analysing these narratives along with the relations of expertise which define both motherhood and daughterhood, Steph Lawler argues that Euro-american mothers are primarily positioned in terms of their responsibility for 'mothering the self' of their children. Yet this 'self' assumes a model of the 'normal person' – marked by specific class, gender and race locations – and reduces social location and identity to an individualized psychology engendered by the mother.

This study examines the ways in which mothers and daughters participate in these understandings, both using and resisting them. The result is a fresh start from which to consider the far-reaching implications of this relationship – not simply for mothers and daughters, but in terms of how we understand the shaping of the self and its place within the social world.

Steph Lawler is a Lecturer in sociology at the University of Durham.

Transformations: Thinking Through Feminism

Edited by:

Maureen McNeil
Institute of Women's Studies, Lancaster University
Lynne Pearce
Department of English, Lancaster University
Beverley Skeggs
Department of Sociology, Manchester University

Other books in the series include:

Transformations
Thinking Through Feminism
Edited by Sara Ahmed, Jane Kilby, Celia Lury, Maureen McNeil and Beverley Skeggs

Strange Encounters
Embodied Others in Post-Coloniality
Sara Ahmed

Advertising and Consumer Citizenship
Gender, Images and Rights
Anne M. Cronin

Mothering the Self

Mothers, daughters, subjects

Steph Lawler

London and New York

First published 2000
by Routledge
11 New Fetter Lane, London EC4P 4EE

Simultaneously published in the USA and Canada
by Routledge
29 West 35th Street, New York, NY 10001

Routledge is an imprint of the Taylor & Francis Group

© 2000 Steph Lawler

Typeset in Baskerville by Taylor & Francis Books Ltd
Printed and bound in Great Britain by TJ International Ltd,
Padstow, Cornwall

British Library Cataloguing in Publication Data
A catalogue record for this book is available from the British Library

Library of Congress Cataloging in Publication Data
Lawler, Steph, 1958–
Mothering the self: mothers, daughters, subjects/ Steph Lawler.
        p. cm. – (Transformations)
Includes bibliographical references and index.
1. Mothers and daughters. 2. Women–Interviews.
I. Title. II. Series.
HQ755.85 .L38 2000
306.8743–dc21   00–024898

ISBN 0–415–17083–4 (hbk)
ISBN 0–415–17084–2 (pbk)

to Rose Griffiths and Toby Griffiths

Contents

Series editors' preface

We are delighted to present Steph Lawler's *Mothering the Self* as one of our first titles in the *Transformations* series. We believe that this volume – the first to reflect upon the radical changes that have taken place within, and around, the discourse of motherhood from the perspective of the 1990s – exemplifies the aims and objectives of the series in general: namely, to offer bold and cutting edge engagements with some of the key debates in contemporary feminist scholarship and, at the same time, to register the wider transformative impact of feminist thought on theoretical and methodological enquiry.

Issues surrounding motherhood have, of course, long been at the centre of feminist enquiry, but Lawler's volume takes a major step forward with its focus on the mothers', as well as the daughters', psychological/cultural standpoint. As recent feminist theorists besides Lawler have noted, most of the extant theorizing of the mother–daughter relationship concentrates on the daughters' testimonies. Lawler's decision, then, to analyze the 'stories' of a group of women who are both 'daughters' and 'mothers' results in many new, and challenging, insights into a bond where investments (on both sides) invariably run high. Yet, it is equally striking that some of Lawler's most important insights into the changing nature of these relations takes its lead from theorists (such as Foucault and Bourdieu) located outside the usual psychoanalytical/feminist arena; in its focus on the importance of autonomy, in particular, it makes excellent use of recent theorizing around Foucault's work on 'technologies of the self'.

It will be seen then, that the innovation and scholarly distinction of this volume lies not only in its emerging thesis, but in its imaginative theorizing and methodology. Lawler is able to offer us the insights she does because of her readiness to interrogate, interpolate, and then appropriate a wide range of theories towards her own ends: a practice which results in further 'transformation' at an epistemological level. Like the other volumes in this series, *Mothering the Self* is as much concerned with 'how we know' as 'what we know', and this reflexivity should make it of particular interest to both student readers and fellow ethnographers.

Yet it is our hope, as editors, that this book will also find a readership outside academia. The interviews that form the core of Lawler's text make extraordinarily compelling reading. Re-read, through the lens of Lawler's sensitive and insightful hypotheses, these stories shed light on the traumas common to the mother–daughter relationship, as well as demonstrating new, and liberating, reconfigurations of *the ties that bind*.

Maureen McNeil
Lynne Pearce
(series editors)

Acknowledgements

Many people have been extraordinarily generous in their help with this book, and I am left with many debts. Primarily, I am indebted to the women who participated in the interviews, who gave up their time and shared their stories, and without whom none of this would have been possible. They taught me more than it has been possible to reproduce here.

Thanks, too, to my colleagues and students at the Department of Sociology, University of Durham, who have been supportive and inspiring. I especially want to thank David Chaney and Sue Parker, who read and commented on drafts, and Margaret Bell, who expertly typed part of the manuscript. Thanks, too, to Mari Shullaw at Routledge and Lynne Pearce and Beverley Skeggs, the series editors, for indefatigable patience and inspiring critique; to Tom Lawler, Maureen Lawler and Noreen Moore, for constant love and support through agreement and disagreement; to Knox Walton for discussions of social work theory and practice, and for emotional and practical support.

I owe a special thanks to Mariam Fraser, Steve Fuller, Paul Johnson and Celia Lury, who not only read drafts, discussed ideas and offered unstinting encouragement, but also helped me to keep going through some bleak times.

Finally, a very special thanks to Toby Griffiths and Rose Griffiths, to whom this book is dedicated. They were the inspiration in the first place, and their extraordinary humour and love have sustained me throughout the writing of this book, and, indeed, throughout their lives.

Introduction
Mothering the self

Not only is the self entwined in society; it owes society its existence in the most literal sense.

(Theodor Adorno, *Minima Moralia*, pp. 153–4)

This is a book about mothers and daughters, and about the relationship between them But it is also a book which turns centrally on a third subject – that of 'the self'. This is because the book is concerned with the question of what it *means* to be a mother, and to be a daughter. Issues of self and subjectivity are intrinsically bound up with these meanings, as mothers have become increasingly responsible for nurturing a specific type of self within the daughter (and the son) – in short, for mothering the self.

For contemporary Euroamericans,[1] the issue of what kinds of persons we are – what kinds of selves we have – has become increasingly significant (Rose, 1991, 1999; Strathern, 1992b). Tied to this is the belief – so powerful it might almost be said to be axiomatic – that our selves are, at least to some degree, 'produced' by our parents, and, especially, by our mothers. So, we scrutinize ourselves (and are scrutinized by others) for signs of 'health' or 'pathology', 'normality' or 'abnormality'. And, in this search, we look to childhood – and especially to the mother–child relation – as the grounds and the foundation of our adult psychologies. This search takes place across a range of sites – in academic debates, in the therapeutic encounter, as well as in more everyday places such as the doctor's surgery, the counsellor's room, magazines, films, and so on (Rose, 1991).

Although this is a book about meanings, and about how meanings are produced and negotiated, let me make it clear that this is about much more than language. Certainly, language – as a contested, changing and changeable medium – is implicated in how meanings get constructed, but meanings are also produced and reproduced through social *practices*. It is not only an issue of the way we talk about and understand things; it is also about what we do (and what we are constrained to do). This encompasses the practices of individuals in their everyday lives – as parents, as children, as teachers, social workers, etc. – as well as the practices through which populations are governed. Indeed, this is about a great deal more than an examination of individual selves. The very running of the social world is often assumed to hinge on citizens being well-adjusted selves living in harmony with other well-adjusted selves. And so governments, through the media of public policy, education, health provision and promotion, social work, law, take an explicit interest in what kinds of selves its citizens are, and hence, in what kind of selves mothers are producing. As Valerie Walkerdine and Helen Lucey put it, the mother has become 'the guarantor of the liberal [democratic] order' (Walkerdine and Lucey, 1989: 15). Her task is to produce the good, well-managed self, which will uphold democracy. Yet this is a vision of social harmony which is based on the radical expulsion and othering of groups deemed excessive, repulsive, threatening. In Britain and North America, single mothers have been the prime target here, but many groups of mothers are subject to suspicious scrutiny, with working-class mothers under especial suspicion. Very often, they are seen as producers of the children who are or who will be a threat to social order. And they are seen as doing this through inadequately nurturing the selves of those children.

It is true that this conceptualization of what selves are has been recently called into question by a focus on a genetic basis to the self. Yet the debate remains caught in terms of the old nature/nurture divide. That is to say, there are three positions usually presented, and all three revolve around a nature/nurture dualism. These positions are: that we are produced by our genes; that we are produced by the social world (and especially our relation with our parents); or that we are produced by some combination of the two. But, while this is not the place to go into detailed analysis of the issues, the terms of this debate seem to me fundamentally misconceived, for several reasons. Firstly, a divide is frequently suggested between genes (unalterable, natural) and socialization (alterable, artificial) in ways which both artificially 'fix' genes (Rose, 1997) and render the social world less 'real'. This divide also obscures the ways in which the very conceptualization of 'nature' is *socially* imagined. Secondly, insofar as the social world *is* considered, this is presented, in popular versions, as reducible to a kind of crude socialization approach in which we simply mimic (or are forced to mimic) our parents. A central premise of this book is that selves are indeed socially produced, but that they are not produced in a straightforward mimicry of our parents. In any event, and as we will see in the accounts of the women interviewed in this study, an understanding of the self as being unique and more or less fixed at birth, can be perfectly compatible with an understanding of the self as being produced by the mother.

Moreover, while stronger or weaker forms of genetic determinism have certainly become prominent, the idea that the self is (wholly or in part) produced through early parent–child interaction remains a compelling one. It underscores most of the ways in which the self gets conceptualized in everyday language and practice, with or without an accompanying genetic model. And since it is mothers who, notwithstanding the rhetoric of greater equality, continue to do most child-care, it is mothers who apparently have to bear most of the responsibility for the production of the 'good self'.

What this book seeks to do is to critique this conceptualization, this Truth, not by opposing it with other, 'truer' truths, but by examining its effectivity, the ways in which knowledges about the self, its relation with other selves, and the obligations which some selves owe to others, come to be used by people in their everyday practices of living and understanding the world and their place within it. I want to consider the ways in which apparently value-free and neutral knowledges embody social relations of inequality and hierarchy, at the same time that they promise an end to inequality. I want to ask, where does our knowledge about the 'healthy' self come from? or, our knowledge about the role of the mother in 'making' this self? How do we know, in other words, what is the 'good self' produced by the 'good mother'? And what does it *mean*, in late twentieth century/early twenty-first century Euroamerican societies, to be a mother? To be a daughter? How are maternal and daughterly selves produced? In this context, these are not questions of metaphysics, but of the workings of knowledge in the social world and in the lives of individuals. How is it that some knowledges in this area have the status of Truth – apparently 'inevitable, unquestionable, necessary', as Hacking (1995: 4) puts it – while others are apparently outside of sense? And what are the *effects* of these knowledge relations?

Knowledges about the self, about mothering, about childhood, about the mother–daughter relationship, do not, as it were, fall from the sky: rather, they are produced and reproduced in specific relations of social and political power, and in response to specific social and political preoccupations. Some knowledges gain their status as 'truths' through the 'expert' status of the individuals and the disciplines which produce them. While this is not in itself a contentious statement, it is surprising how little expert knowledges – especially those around childhood – have been subject to intellectual scrutiny.

Further, it is my argument here that these knowledges, while claiming to liberate us by revealing the 'truth' about human nature, actually tie us in ever more closely with the workings of power. Not only are Euroamericans increasingly incited to watch over and scrutinize themselves in search of the 'true self', but, as the book will show, only some people *can* count as 'healthy' individuals, 'good' mothers, 'good' children. Others are pathologized. And it is no accident that these pathologized others are *not* middle class and white.

Mothers and daughters

The book considers mothers and daughters, and not mothers and sons, not because mothers are seen as insignificant in the lives of sons, but for two main reasons. First, mothers and daughters are usually seen as having a closer social, psychic or emotional identification than mothers and sons. And secondly, 'mother' and 'daughter' may be the *same person*. All mothers are also daughters. Even if the mother is absent, her very absence is likely to assume significance in the daughter's life. And many daughters are also mothers, many of them mothers of daughters. But 'mother' and 'daughter' are radically different positions. Daughters are constituted as the holders of 'needs' and mothers as the meeters of those needs. What happens, then, when women are *both* mothers and daughters? As Marianne Hirsch asks, what if mother and daughter 'inhabit the same body, what if they are the same person, speaking with two voices?' (Hirsch, 1989: 199). What, then, do the two voices say? Do they speak in contradiction? This is another central question of the book.

It is, above all, feminist literature which has brought the mother–daughter relationship into the public arena and which has made it a legitimate topic of study. We can no longer say, as Adrienne Rich did in 1976, that the mother–daughter relationship is 'the great unwritten story' (Rich, 1977: 225). But there are issues which remain relatively unexplored, and which I set out to examine here. First, there is the issue, outlined above, of the meanings, or truths, attached to the relationship – truths which themselves rest on truths about what the self is, how it is made, how it relates to other selves, and so on. As Boulton (1983) observed, most analyses of mothering have separated out the work which comes with mothering from the relationship with children – a relationship which is generally assumed to be innately fulfilling. Indeed, in general, analyses of both mothering and of the mother–daughter relationship have proceeded on the assumption that childhood is a 'given'; that it does not need to be subject to intellectual scrutiny. The issue then becomes one of considering how mothering might be divested of its 'superfluous' elements, such as housework and cleaning (as if the activity of mothering did not itself entail work!); or, of setting out how mothers should behave in order to produce whatever characteristics are deemed desirable in children. While the category 'mother' has been subject to scrutiny, the category 'child', at least in this context, rarely has. Yet a radical analysis of the mother–daughter relationship *must* entail an analysis of both motherhood and daughterhood/childhood, as well as an examination of self and subjectivity. 'Mother' as a social category is constituted in relation to the *prior* category 'child': what children are considered to need for development is used to define 'good mothering' (Woollett and Phoenix, 1991a). In turn, what children are considered to need rests on (historically and socially specific) conceptualizations of what counts as the (good) self. Knowledges around selfhood and subjectivity, around being a daughter, around being a mother, are interlinked, drawing upon each other to produce a set of seemingly intractable truths around the person, the mother and the daughter. These sets of knowledges, though always contested and never finalized, are a means through which power works on the human subject. Mothers and daughters situate themselves in relation to these knowledges and (in however contingent and fragmented a way) forge identities in relation to them.

Although not all daughters are 'children' in the sense that 'child' means 'not adult', all daughters are children in the sense that they stand in a specific kin relationship. As La Fontaine (1986) points out, the term 'child' is both an age category and a kinship category. However, it is important to note the ways in which the two senses of the term can become conflated. If the (age category) 'child' has needs which it is the mother's responsibility to meet, the relationship between mother and child can be structured by these needs and this responsibility, so that even relationships between mothers and adult children are constituted in terms of what the child needs and what the mother should provide. This has a particular significance in the mother–daughter relationship, because women's (daughters') selves are often held to be especially vulnerable, and especially 'needy'.[2]

Secondly, the perspective of the mother has rarely been explored. It is the daughter's voice which has, almost always, been heard. Even when mothers have spoken, they have usually done so as daughters, rather than as mothers. It is extremely rare for anyone to actually ask mothers about the relationship; rarer still to take them seriously.[3] The subject of feminist analyses, then, has largely been the daughter, against whom the mother is 'other' (Hirsch, 1989). So, this book analyses the position of the mother, as well as that of the daughter, and considers the tensions between the two voices.

Finding out ...

The study on which this book is based is an attempt to address all of the issues outlined above. It examines the accounts of fourteen white women, all of whom are daughters of mothers and mothers of daughters.[4] I collected these accounts through individual interviews and a group discussion (in which five women participated) conducted in 1992 and 1993.[5]

This work was motivated by a commitment to 'finding out' – finding out what mothers and daughters themselves say about the relationship, and about the truths in which it is embedded; finding out how they make sense of it and nego- tiate it. Gayle Rubin (1994) has noted how empirical work is often seen as inferior to work which might be termed purely theoretical – a 'low-status, even stigmatized activity' (Rubin, 1994: 92). As she argues:

> There is a disturbing trend to treat with condescension or contempt any work that bothers to wrestle with data. This comes, in part, from the quite justified critiques of positivism and crude empiricism. But such critiques should sharpen the techniques for gathering and evaluating information rather than becoming a rationalization for failing to gather information at all.
>
> (Rubin, 1994: 92)

Certainly, data do not 'speak for themselves': there are, at every stage, processes of selection and interpretation going on. But, from a sociological perspective at least, there are things we cannot know without actually going and looking for them. It is not, in any case, a question of the empirical *or* the theoretical: within social science work, there is no empirical work devoid of theory and no theoret- ical work devoid of some reference (however oblique) to the empirical. What is problematic, though, is when claims are made about how people live, or under- stand, or make sense of their lives, without any attempt to find out if the claims made have any purchase beyond that of the writer. To be sure, empirical work is difficult work which is full of pitfalls, some of which I discuss in this chapter. But without it, what we can claim to 'know' is going to be very limited indeed. I myself entered into this research attempting to recoup the mother–daughter relationship, to highlight (what I then saw as) its hidden support for women. It was the women I interviewed who made me see the deep ambivalence and complexity of the relationship, the ways in which a desire for a 'bonding' between mother and daughter simply does not hold. And their emphasis on the significance of the self in the mother–daughter relationship changed the course of the research, as they made me see the centrality of this category. But it is not just the 'doing' of empirical work which is significant, but the ways in which we do it, as the next section discusses.

Power and responsibility in the research process

> Most of the academic work we read is the end product of a long process, but we rarely have any understanding of this process. The representations of knowledge as a final product mask the conditions of its production. … If we have done research we all know that it is a difficult, messy, fraught, emotional, tiring and yet rewarding process; we know all about the elements involved, but how does anyone else get to know? All they usually see is the clean, crisp, neatly finished product. Intellectuals may excel in describing other people's implicit assumptions, but they are as implicit as anyone else when it comes to their own.
>
> (Skeggs, 'Introduction: processes in feminist cultural theory', p. 2)

Attention to the power relations inherent within empirical research have driven many, if not most, feminist critiques of research over the last two decades, and these issues can no longer be passed over without interrogation and explanation. This research, like others, raises issues of power and responsibility. The doing of the research taught me a great deal about these issues, leading me to the conclusion, outlined here, that these issues are considerably more complex than they might appear.

Some feminist analyses of methodology, attentive to the hierarchy of the research process, have proposed a breaking down of this hierarchy through a minimizing of the researcher's 'superior' status. Oakley (1990), for example, argues that the traditional, masculine, research model, in which the researcher gives nothing away about her/himself, or about the purpose of the interviews, objectifies and depersonalizes research subjects, and reinforces the power held by the researcher. To avoid this, Oakley proposes a reciprocal relationship, akin to friendship, between feminist researchers and women they research (cf. Finch, 1984). Against the conventional advice to forge a kind of bogus intimacy with one's research participants, Oakley's line is, 'No intimacy without reciprocity' (1990: 49): in other words, feminist researchers must be prepared to answer questions and to provide support.

Oakley's argument has been an important one. For example, her observation that there is no 'neutral' presentation of self and her emphasis on the importance of engaging in the research process remain significant and influential both inside and outside of feminist research. But her argument also raises a number of issues of its own. In this research, I was often asked questions which I could answer honestly and straightforwardly – questions about my opinions, or about problems with my children, for example. But some questions are more difficult to negotiate – not only those which invest the researcher with a professional expertise s/he does not have, but questions to which the researcher does not (yet) know the answer ('What are you going to do with this?' or 'What's your overall argument?').

As well, Oakley's argument presupposes that women research subjects *want* to know about the feminist researcher's life, or *want* to be 'friends' with her. But an interview situation may be a rare opportunity for women to talk at length about themselves and their preoccupations and the interviewer's sharing of her thoughts/experiences/feelings may therefore be experienced as intrusive. And there is no *a priori* reason why women should want to be friends with a feminist researcher. Shared gender does not necessarily lead to friendship in any other scenario, after all.

This is not to say that there can be no rapport within the research setting. Within this research, I think it is fair to say that there was often an ease between myself and the women which undoubtedly made the interviews go more smoothly. This may be an effect of what we had in common – being white, being women, being mothers of daughters. Certainly, one question every woman asked me during the course of the research (and usually at the outset) was, 'Are you a mother?' and I doubt whether most of the women would have talked to me so openly or so willingly had I not been – perhaps because of a belief that another mother might be less likely to subject them to the judgements routinely passed on mothers. The issue of a shared identification was an important one here, for both myself as researcher, and for the women I interviewed. With some women in particular, I felt a tremendous amount of identification because of our shared class 'movement' from being a working-class girl to being a woman in a position regarded as middle class.

But there was also much to separate us, and what separated us was inevitably linked to issues of power and inequality. No matter how powerless I felt at this stage of the research, I was still invested with some status as a Ph.D. student at a university, and I would still be able to take away what the women said to me and use it for my research. As Ruth Frankenberg observes:

> [T]here is in general a power imbalance between a researcher and the subjects of research in the sense that the researcher sets the agenda and edits the material, analyzes it, publishes it, and thereby takes both credit and blame for the overall result.
>
> (Frankenberg, 1993: 29)

This control over the research process cut across the advantages which I felt the majority of the women had over me in terms of age, wealth, status and self-confidence. This was brought home to me rather sharply when women made it clear that they saw me as possessing an expertise I did not feel myself to have (often quite justifiably so). For instance, one woman asked my advice on how to deal with a crying baby – should she be picked up, or left?.[6] I wanted to resist answering this question and I gave some non-committal response. This is the type of response critiqued by Oakley (1990) as belonging to the world of 'objective' (and patriarchal) knowledge-gathering. However, I was not worried about my replies 'polluting the data'; rather, I was anxious not to present myself as possessing a knowledge I did not have (i.e. the best way to bring up babies). Another woman countered some of my questions with, 'Well you're the sociologist!' which is reasonable enough, but, again, brought home to me the distance between the women's perception of me and my perception of myself: I was invested with 'knowledge' whether or not I felt knowledgeable.

It seems to me that the relations of power in the research setting are usually more complex than they might appear, and certainly are more complex than they have conventionally been theorized. Women participating in research are not necessarily powerless: research subjects usually can back out of the research at any point; they can refuse to answer questions; and they can withdraw their permission for material to be used.[7] Research subjects will often get what they can out of the research. This may just be time to talk about themselves and their preoccupations, or it may be the pleasure of participating in wider social processes – of being important enough to be the subjects of research. Women's expressions of their own insignificance in the research process are well documented (Oakley, 1990; McRobbie, 1982) and I myself found this to be the case, with women making comments like, 'I don't suppose I'll have anything interesting to tell you.' Participating in a process of knowledge production, no matter how problematic that process is, may enhance research subjects' belief in their own self-worth. As well, the interview process provided reassurance for some women, as in the following exchange at the end of one set of interviews:

PAULINE: I feel like I've been very negative. My relationship with my mother just seems – I just seem to have said a lot of negative things.
S.L.: Well – but that's incredibly common.
PAULINE: Is it? Oh good! …… I thought it was just me [laughs].[8]

As a result of talking about difficult and often painful matters, some women clearly felt distress during parts of the interviews. But they also seemed to gain some pleasure from the process – all of the women said that they had enjoyed it, and most said that they had got something from it. Some women also actively participated in the research process in other ways; for example, by writing notes between interviews, by showing me letters, or by 'saving' things to tell me at the next interview. It is sometimes suggested that feminist researchers should seek to increase women's participation in research, for example by inviting research subjects to collaborate in the analysis (Mies, 1991). However, this can be a thorny issue and raises a number of questions: what happens about confidentiality?

What if research subjects disagree with each other? with the researcher? More fundamentally, it may be exploitative. As Kelly *et al.* comment:

> Simplistic notions of participation and empowerment … mask other aspects of the power and responsibility of the researcher. It is we who have the time, resources and skills to conduct methodical work, to make sense of experience and to locate individuals in historic and social contexts.
>
> (Kelly *et al.*, 1994: 37)

Overall, it is clear that there are inequalities between researcher and research subjects, but the exercise of power is neither straightforward nor one-way. McRobbie (1982) draws parallels between the research relationship and that between teacher and pupil, or social worker and client. But both teachers and social workers have the backing of the law and relationships with pupils/clients are not usually voluntary on the latter's part. On the other hand, and as Walkerdine (1985e) argues, the researcher may be experienced as the 'Surveillant other'; I am aware, for example, that my visits to the women's homes might have provoked resonances of the visits of other middle-class professionals who also ask questions.

Perhaps there are no simple solutions to these issues; perhaps, as Janet Finch (1984) argues, it comes down to which side you are on. Feminist researchers probably do need to be 'on the side of' the women who are their research subjects, in some senses, but even taking a partisan stance is not without problems of its own. What do we do when women research subjects express homophobic or racist or classist sentiments? (See Kelly *et al.*, 1994.) And in this research, there were often a number of competing 'sides' to be on: the women's, their mothers' and their daughters'.

But there is no research practice which is devoid of pitfalls, nor any research space which is outside of social relations. Feminist research should surely further feminist aims, but these aims will not necessarily be achieved within the immediate setting of the research interaction. This is not to claim that it does not matter what researchers do whilst researching; I think it does matter, and that two decades of feminist theorizing about research practice have underlined how much it matters. Rather, it is to argue that the search for a 'pure' feminist methodology can be the search for an asocial research 'space' which is free from the workings of power. This can lead to a romanticization of the research process and an occlusion of differences between women.

Further, as Kelly *et al.* (1994) suggest, as feminist researchers, we need to be aware of our limitations. Although we can offer women research subjects support, we are unlikely, in most situations, to be able to give many women other things they may want or need – which may include decent housing, a job, a reasonable income, and so on. This does not mean, though, that feminist research is worthless; simply that its impact is likely to be neither straightforward nor immediate. As Miriam Glucksmann comments:

[T]he onus falls on feminist researchers neither, on the one hand, to succumb to defeatism nor, on the other, to confuse research practice for feminist politics, but to recognize the more attenuated relation between the theoretical work we do and any social transformation for what it is.

(Glucksmann, 1994: 164)

Values

However much feminist researchers try to minimize the hierarchy of the research situation, inequalities cannot simply be wished away. Indeed, the desire to be part of the group researched may itself be a product of the researcher's desire to divest herself of power (or not to take responsibility) (Kelly *et al.*, 1994), or for others to see her as she sees herself. Valerie Walkerdine (1985e) writes of the researcher's simultaneous 'desire to know' and attempts to get 'beyond power' in the relationship with her/his research subjects. Of her own research with a working-class family, she writes:

> I was struck by the fantasies, anxieties and pain triggered in me by being perceived as a middle-class academic confronting a working-class family. Although I invested considerable desire in wanting to be 'one of them' at the same time as 'being different', no amount of humanistic seeking for the 'beyond ideology' would get them to see in me a working-class girl 'like them'.
>
> (Walkerdine, 1985e: 195–6)

I found myself confronted with similar anxieties when speaking to working-class women; I wanted them to 'know' that I was not what I appeared to be – that I had been a working-class girl and that I experienced my role as a would-be academic with a mixture of pride and embarrassment. But why should they? For their purposes, I *was* what I appeared to be – a middle-class academic asking questions about their lives. The crisis was for me, not for them.

These desires and anxieties are part of the research process, and have to be acknowledged as such. For example, when speaking to working-class women, I think I had a sense of nostalgia for what I (secretly) felt to be the greater authenticity of working-class life. No doubt this is part of a nostalgia for my childhood, but for a while I was in danger of romanticizing working-class women. When I spoke to the middle-class women, there were times when I frankly envied some of them and saw them as having tremendous self-confidence and very few problems. During some interviews, I felt what I can only describe as rage (prompted, no doubt, by envy) towards the middle-class women. They seemed so self-possessed, so certain.

This kind of negative emotion can be very difficult to acknowledge, particularly in a piece of feminist research. Yet it is as much part of the research process as more positive (and more acceptable?) emotions of empathy, tenderness, and so on. Alison Jaggar (1997) has written of the ways in which emotions in general are 'outlawed' within mainstream research. But perhaps, as feminists, we need to be wary that we do not only look for positive relations between women and thus 'outlaw' certain 'negative' emotions between them. For myself as researcher, it was only by acknowledging my own envy and rage that I was able to see the pain, the lack of confidence, and the fears being expressed by middle-class women, and to understand that being born middle class can bring its own pain. Before confronting my own negative feelings, I was literally unable to see these things.

Valerie Walkerdine (1997) has examined the issue of emotion in the research process, arguing that the researcher's response to empirical material is likely to arise, in however complex and attenuated a way, out of her/his own autobiography. Rather than seeing this as an obstacle to be overcome, she argues that:

> instead of making futile attempts to avoid something that cannot be avoided [i.e. subjectivity in social research], we should think more carefully about how to utilise our subjectivity as part of the research process.
>
> (Walkerdine, 1997: 59)

For Walkerdine, it is through the researcher examining her/his own motivations and emotions that a fuller understanding of research material can be reached. As she herself notes, this can be a painful and embarrassing process, and it is one which opens up the researcher to charges of emotionality and 'bias'. Yet who is really producing value-free research? Who is researching without any engagement of their politics, their beliefs, or their emotions? All knowers are 'situated' (Haraway, 1986) in space, in time, in social relations, in politics. In many accounts, though, these things are written out (Skeggs, 1995).

Skeggs (1994, 1995, 1997) points to the onus on feminist researchers to make the research process as transparent as possible; to take responsibility for the process of knowledge production, and to expose the conditions in which knowledge is produced. Otherwise, we risk representing our research as a 'pure' form of knowledge, obscuring the relations of its production. Knowledge is produced under specific social relations, by specifically located, interested and embodied 'knowers'. To obscure the researcher's located-ness, her/his subjectivity and motivations, is to produce *less* rigorous research, rather than, as commonly thought, more rigorous research. As Skeggs notes, there are two meanings of 'objectivity' which are often collapsed together: firstly, objectivity refers to the 'practical adequacy' of accounts – how full and rigorous the research account is – and, secondly, it refers to the values of the researcher within the research (Skeggs, 1997: 33). She notes that it is impossible not to bring values to the research: indeed, at every stage of the research process, from the selection of the subject to the writing of the analysis, the researcher's values inform the account. But:

> Just because we value something does not mean that we cannot come up with an objective (in the first sense) account. Also, values may enable us to

recognize things that others would prefer to overlook (gender, race, class, etc.).

(Skeggs, 1997: 33)

Like Skeggs, I brought values to the research: some of these values (for example, an attachment to working-class 'authenticity', a desire to paint the mother–daughter relationship in wholly positive terms) were overturned *by* the research, others (such as a commitment to feminist analysis, and to an examination of the intersection of class and gender) remain, and indeed, the research, for me, underlined the continuing significance of these values.

As well as values, I brought a set of theoretical perspectives to the research. It would simply not have been possible for me to approach the interviews without some kind of theoretical framework in mind (even had I wanted to). This is not to say that the interview material was something to be 'tested' against a pre-formed set of theoretical assumptions. Rather, in analysing the interview material, I tried to move backward and forward between theoretical material and 'data', using the latter to inflect the former and the former to make sense of the latter. One effect of this approach was that the women's own interest in, and emphasis on, the self, became more and more central to the research as I began to see its significance for them and to look for theoretical perspectives which would explain this. In turn, the process of analysing the women's own perspectives enabled me to examine, and at times to critique, the theories themselves.

Storied lives

A beginning is an artifice, and what recommends one over another is how much sense it makes of what follows.

(Ian McEwan, *Enduring Love*, pp. 17–18)

We 'write' a running biography with life-language rather than word-language in order to 'be'. Call this identity!

(Spivak, 'In a word: interview', p. 359)

We all tell stories about our lives, both to ourselves and to others; and it is through such stories that we make sense of our selves, of the world, and of our relationship to others. Stories, or narratives, are a means by which people make sense of, understand, and live their lives. Henrietta Moore argues, 'narrative is a strategy for placing us within a historically constituted world. ... If narrative makes the world intelligible, it also makes ourselves intelligible' (Moore, 1994: 119).

In some ways, the word, 'stories' is a misleading one. While it captures the ways in which social actors arrange heterogeneous components – fragments of lives, events, episodes – into a more or less coherent 'life story', it also carries overtones of fiction, or even of duplicity. Yet the truth or falsity of such accounts is not the point: what is at issue is the *ways in which* the self and its relation with others is 'storied' – the ways in which what we know as 'experience' is an interpretive process.

'Experience' is neither a straightforward nor an unproblematic category. Carolyn Steedman (1996) points out the obvious, but little-noted, fact that the past is no longer here: 'The search is for a lost object, which really cannot be found, for the object is altered and changed by the very search for it, into something quite different and strange' (Steedman, 1996: 103). We must constantly engage in recall, re-telling, interpretation, in order to conjure up the past: we must engage in what Ian Hacking (1994, 1995) has called 'memero-politics' – a process by which the past is interpreted in light of the knowledge and understanding of the subject's 'present'. There is no unmediated access to the 'reality' of (in this case) the mother–daughter relationship. As Steedman (1986) notes, we interpret the past 'through the agency of social information':

> We all return to memories and dreams … again and again; the story we tell
> of our life is reshaped around them. But the point doesn't lie there, back in
> the past, back in the lost time at which they happened; the only point lies in
> interpretation. The past is re-used through the agency of social information,
> and that interpretation of it can only be made with what people know of a
> social world and their place within it.
>
> (Steedman, 1986: 5)

What we make of experiences depends on what we know about the ways in which those experiences relate to the wider social circumstances of our lives. This knowledge is not free-floating: the narratives which make up people's stories, and through which people make sense of their lives, do not originate within them; personal narratives are linked with broader, social narratives (Somers and Gibson, 1994). In this sense, as Paul Ricoeur (1991a) argues, people are the heroes, but not the authors, of their own lives.

Narrative works by synthesizing heterogeneous components into a more or less coherent 'story' (Ricoeur, 1991a; Somers and Gibson, 1994); it renders individual lives intelligible both in linking together disparate elements and in connecting individual lives to broader narratives of 'humanity'. In this way, narrative provides a framework for interpreting both past and present, a means of linking together past, present and future, and a way of understanding personal lives in the context of social contexts and social interaction.

In this sense, then, narrative is an ontological category (Hankiss, 1981; Somers and Gibson, 1994): it structures our being, as we tell stories (to ourselves and to others) about our selves, our being, our place in the scheme of things. Lives are understood through being 'emplotted'. But personal narratives cannot be seen in isolation; they are linked with social narratives which also tell stories about individuals and their place in the world. Childhood, for example, is emplotted through a number of different stories which claim to tell us what childhood *is*: a state of innocence or a state of depravity, for example (Stainton Rogers and Stainton Rogers, 1992). These stories of childhood provide a means for structuring people's understandings of their own childhood, and hence their personal histories.

Social narratives, and hence personal narratives, are socially and historically specific: they are inevitably related to what is 'known' and what can be said. Hence, as well as being an ontological category, narrative is an epistemological category. It is a means by which we not only live in the world but also understand and 'know' that world. For example, 'developmental' narratives of childhood rely on, and employ, psychological and medical expertise about the nature of children's development. As Gergen and Gergen argue:

> We would not accept a developmental account in which the child showed decline until the age of six and then demonstrated miraculous recovery at the age of seven. Or, a developmental story in which odd years were progressive while even years were regressive would be equally untenable – not because such accounts are manifestly false but because the narrative forms are not constituents of current intelligibility norms.
>
> (Gergen and Gergen, 1986: 38–9)

The narrative of 'development' brings together different interpretations of what development is (Gergen and Gergen, 1986; Stainton Rogers and Stainton Rogers, 1992) but it must necessarily rely on certain assumptions about what is to count as 'true' and 'reasonable'. Narrative is inevitably linked with authoritative, expert knowledges, but this link is obscured through narrative's use of the inclusive voice of the story-teller, rather than the authoritative voice of the expert (Franklin, 1990). Hence 'we' can be drawn in to the story, using its framework as a schema of self-understanding.

If there is no unmediated relationship to the 'reality' of personal histories, then this piece of research cannot provide a privileged account of what the mother–daughter relationship is 'really' like. What it can do, however, is to examine some of the stories that women tell about the relationship, to look at the ways in which these stories are connected with social narratives and with authoritative knowledges, and to consider some of the effects on women's lives of these personal and social understandings of the mother–daughter relationship.

There is, though, a second reason for considering the women's accounts in terms of the stories they tell. Such a focus draws attention to the *other* stories which hover on the margins of the one being told. In particular, I want to draw attention to the stories of these women's mothers and daughters, which, although they are incorporated into the women's own accounts, cannot 'speak for themselves'. As Adrienne Rich writes:

> Whatever I write, it is my story I am telling, my version of the past. If [my mother] were to tell her own story other landscapes would be revealed. But in my landscape or hers, there would be old, smoldering patches of deep-burning anger.
>
> (Rich, 1977: 221)

These other('s) stories might well tell the story differently, interpreting events differently, or assembling different events to make up the coherence of *their* stories.

Although this point may sound an obvious one, I make it because so many analyses of the mother–daughter relationship collapse the mother's story into that of the daughter: the daughter is seen as possessing a privileged insight into the relationship, and her account is seen as giving a 'true' representation of the mother.[9] I noted earlier that much feminist work to date has been a 'daughter's story' (Hirsch, 1989), in which mothers have often been constituted as other to the daughterly (feminist) self. Within many of these accounts, mothers are represented as the guarantors of a patriarchal social order: the daughter must struggle against the mother's influence if she is to achieve 'autonomy' (Gilbert and Webster, 1982). As a (willing or unwilling) representative of patriarchy, the mother becomes 'other' to the daughter's feminist 'self' . Thus, the subjectivity of mothers can be effaced in feminist accounts, as it so often is in 'mainstream' analyses. It is not (*pace* the claims of writers like Freely, 1996) that mothers have been 'ignored' or 'forgotten' in feminist work. Rather, it is that a contemporary (Euroamerican) focus on child-centredness has privileged the daughter's story over the mother's. Instead of two voices, we have so often been left with one voice which claims to tell the whole story. This study aims to analyse the two voices of mother and daughter, speaking from women who are both mothers and daughters, negotiating a maze of knowledges to forge identities within and across these often contradictory categories.

Chapter 1 examines one of the three categories which are the focus of the book – the self – and discusses how sets of 'truths' have grown up around this category. These truths, while they apparently *describe* pre-existing entities, are engaged in *producing* the entities of which they speak. This chapter will also consider how contemporary Euroamericans, in engaging in projects of self-fulfilment and self-awareness, are bound up in power relations which are all the more insidious for being hidden – for masquerading as the pursuit of 'freedom'. Apparently liberating knowledges engage the human subject in relations of power by which the self, in making itself 'free', is engaged in a project of working *on* the self. Chapter 2 continues this theme in its discussion of the ways in which the categories 'child' and 'mother' are produced through sites of truths which claim to be describing the categories.

Chapter 3 continues with a discussion of selves and subjectivity through a consideration of the ways in which the fourteen women interviewed for the research conceptualized the kinds of selves 'owned' by daughters, within the mother–daughter relationship. This chapter looks at how the self is conceptualized, by the women I spoke to, as biologically inherited, as shaped in the social arena, and as an essence, belonging to each person and to no-one else. Chapter 4 specifically takes up the theme of the 'intrinsic self' of the daughter within the accounts of the women who took part in the study. This chapter examines mothers' felt responsibility for nurturing 'autonomy' within the daughter, and also examines some of the contradictions involved in this construction of the self as 'autonomous'. I argue in this chapter that the daughter's adult identity is constituted on the basis of a feminized and heterosexualized identity which is at odds with the concept of 'autonomy'.

In Chapter 5, I look specifically at the women's fears and desires in their relationships with their mothers, especially at the fear, expressed by many women, of *becoming* their mothers. This chapter considers one way in which personal narratives may be constructed on the basis of unconscious desires and fantasies: I draw here on Freud's notion of the 'family romance' (Freud, 1909) – his argument that children believe themselves to be the children of more noble parents then the 'real' parents. I link this desire to gender and to class position, examining the ways in which the daughter's social mobility may inflect the stories she tells about her relationship with her mother.

Chapter 6 turns to a consideration of maternal selves and analyses the ways in which the women's maternity is seen to impact on their sense of 'self'. I consider here the links between constructions of children's 'needs' and constructions of the (good) mother, arguing that, however children's needs are defined, it is the mother who is primarily held to be the one who meets them. Chapter 7 continues this theme, arguing that children's 'needs' have come to be one means by which mothers are governed. I consider here the ways in which constructions of children's needs efface any claims to 'need' on the part of the mother.

The book as a whole represents my attempt to theorize the ways in which relations of expertise are lived, understood and communicated. Generation is important here, as mothers and daughters occupy different generational positions and relate to each other across them. Gender, clearly, is central, since the lives of both mothers and daughters are, at least in part, structured in terms of gender positioning and gender identity. And class, too – often theorized in terms of 'objective' markers alone – is important, as classed existences shape people's subjectivities and position them as 'right' or 'wrong'. Some of the women in this study occupy the same class position as their mothers; others do not. But for all of them, their class is central to their stories.

Perhaps more than anything, though, this book is concerned with power – the power to name and to define, to normalize and pathologize. And power, in its complexity, is the subject of the next chapter.

The women in the study[10]

Anna   Aged 41. Middle class, from a middle-class birth family. Has a degree and a postgraduate professional qualification, and works full time in a 'caring profession'. She has two children: Matthew (16) and Heather (15). Son lives with his father (Anna's ex-husband); daughter lives with Anna. Mother is still living.

Barbara   Aged 50. Middle class, working-class birth family. Left school after 'O' Levels; has a professional qualification; now works part-time as a craft worker. Married, with one daughter, Julia (20), at university. Husband employed as senior administrator. Both parents are dead.

Caroline   Aged 41. Middle class, middle-class birth family. Has a degree and a postgraduate qualification. Works full time in education. Married, with three daughters, Sophie (19), Faye (18) and Miriam (13), and one grandchild. Two younger daughters live at home; husband also works in education. Mother is still living.

Dawn   Aged 38. Middle class, with working-class birth family. Has a degree and a postgraduate qualification. Works full time in education. Married, with two daughters, Andy (13) and Jude (10), both living with her. Husband not employed; described as a 'house-husband'. Father is still living.

Elizabeth   Aged 52. Middle class, with middle-class birth family. Left school after 'O' Levels, and is currently working towards a professional qualification. Has one daughter, Karen (29), and one son, Andrew (24); also two grandchildren (daughter's children). Both parents are alive. Works full time in administration. Divorced after children were grown up and had left home; currently lives alone.

Frances   Aged 48. Middle class, with working-class birth family. Has a degree and a postgraduate qualification. Currently unemployed. Has one daughter, Chloe (23); divorced from Chloe's father and lives with second husband. Father is still living.

Gina   Aged 45. Working class, with working-class birth family. Left school after 'O' Levels; employed part time in welfare work. Divorced, with three children, Abigail (19), James (16) and Tom (14). Lives with a friend; sons live at home; daughter is at university. Both parents are living.

Hazel   Aged 43. Middle class, with working-class birth family. Has a professional qualification; employed full time in welfare work. Has one daughter, Leah (16), and one son, Adam (12). Lives with friends; children live with their father. Both parents are dead.

Janet   Aged 42. Working class, with working-class birth family. Left school at 16; employed full time in retail work. Widowed, with three daughters, Alison, (22), Laura (19), and Clare (16); younger two daughters living at home. Mother is still living.

Kate   Aged 47. Middle class, with working-class birth family. Has a degree and a postgraduate qualification. Part-time voluntary worker. Has one son, John (21), and one daughter, Louise (19). Son at home; daughter is at university. Married; husband employed in education. Both parents are dead.

Lynne   Aged 42. Middle class, with working-class birth family. Has a degree; employed full time in education. Has four children; Nicholas (15), Naomi (14), Luke (12) and Joe (7). Divorced; lives with children. Mother is still living.

Margaret   Aged 38. Working class, with working-class birth family. Left school at sixteen; employed part time in catering. Has one son, Anthony (12), and one daughter, Nicola (10). Separated from children's father; lives with children. Both parents are alive.

Pauline   Aged 55. Middle class, from lower-middle-class birth family. Has a degree and a postgraduate qualification; employed full time in education. Has two daughters; Deborah (29) and Lisa (26). Married; lives with husband (a businessman); both daughters have left home. Both parents are dead.

Rachel   Aged 44. Middle class, with middle-class birth family. Has a degree and a postgraduate qualification; employed part time in education. Has one son, Martin (15), and one daughter, Olivia (12). Married; husband employed in education. Lives with husband and children. Mother is still living.

1   Being and knowing
The social relations of truth

> We must accept that it is relations that define truth, not truth that defines relations.
>
> > (Roy Boyne, 'War and desire', p. 35)

The last chapter indicated some of the ways in which mothers are placed under an obligation to nurture the selves of their daughters – a theme which will be developed throughout the book. But what should these selves be like? and how do we come to know what they should be like? This chapter examines the kinds of self which mothers are meant to be nurturing – and the kinds of self which are assumed to be 'healthy' and 'normal' among late-twentieth-century/early twenty-first century Euroamericans. The aim here is to destabilize taken-for-granted assumptions about the self, and, in this way, to destabilize assumptions around mothering and childhood. The chapter explores the ways in which the self is forged on the basis of truths which, while claiming to speak *about* the self, work to *produce* specific forms of self. In this way, *who we are* is an effect of what (or who) we *know* ourselves to be. And in this being and knowing, power is at work.

Relations of expertise

In many ways, the late twentieth century *looks like* a period of deep uncertainty around both motherhood and childhood, for a number of reasons. The advent of new reproductive technologies potentially destabilizes the category 'mother' (Stanworth, 1987), the proliferation of family forms suggests that the nuclear family is increasingly unstable,[1] the British media's attention to so-called 'crises in childhood' and 'crises in parenthood' suggests that there is a pluralization in knowledges about what children are and about how they should be brought up. All this would suggest that authoritative, expert knowledges are losing their ground as people 'choose' their familial lifestyles without recourse to any other imperatives than their own beliefs, or, that the proliferation of expertise and various forms of contestation between experts means that 'expertise' is itself breaking down (Beck, 1992).

However, these crises may be more apparent than real. Firstly, and at least so far as child-care is concerned, the intervention of law means that some beliefs will just not be tolerated.[2] Secondly, there seems little evidence that there has been a loosening of surveillance of mothers and their children. Mothers of infants and young children are routinely handed out charts of child development against which they are meant to monitor their child's physical and psychological 'progress'. Health visitors and schools also routinely monitor this progress; popular advice manuals reinforce the authoritative knowledge claims of psychological expertise at every stage of the child's development from pre-birth to adulthood; and consumer culture is increasingly incorporating this expertise into its marketing – for example in the 'age scales' marked on children's toys and in advertising which appeals to the 'educational' value of consumer goods.

But this surveillance is increasingly bound up with processes of *self*-surveillance. Hence mothers, for example, are incited to take pleasure from their subjection to expertise: their monitoring of their child's development is a means by which they can enhance both their own self and that of the child – they can become good mothers producing good children (Urwin, 1985). In this way, the expertise which generates these discourses of 'normality' becomes obscured. The conditions of its production are lost in the rhetoric of 'choice' (Strathern, 1992a; Rose, 1992b) as people are incited to 'choose' to seek out and realize both their own selves and the selves of their children. But neither pleasure nor choice indicate an absence of authority or of the operation of power.

Certainly, there is always a 'struggle for meaning' (Walkerdine, 1987); people do not necessarily swallow whole the dictates of experts, and experts disagree among themselves. But there is a common ground on which competing discourses of childhood meet. This common ground is the 'needs' or the 'best interests' of the child. Since children's 'needs' or 'best interests' are rarely spelled out and even more rarely problematized, hardly any conceptual space is opened up within which questions can be asked about the meanings of these needs, of childhood in general, or of the motherhood which is held to meet the child's needs, let alone answers provided. So, changes in family form (for example) may have led to an uncertainty about what 'the family' is; but there is little corresponding uncertainty about what mothering is, or what childhood is. Indeed, as the next chapter will show, concepts of normality – of what constitutes the 'normal' child and the 'normal' mother – are at the very heart of public debate around childhood, motherhood and the family.

What is at stake here is the status of the truth statements generated by experts, not only in the mother–child relationship but in all areas of everyday Euroamerican life. A central argument of this book is that, far from such truths having the status of objective, disinterested 'facts', they are produced in the context of social and political preoccupations. Further, they are bound up with mechanisms of power and with the government of populations. In other words, the generation of knowledge is linked with the workings of power.

Power, knowledge and surveillance

A commonplace view of power is that of a prohibitive, denying force, working from outside the 'true' person who stands outside of the workings of power (Rose, 1992b). Knowledge, by contrast, is conventionally seen as that which will release us from the workings of power, and, indeed, as antithetical to the workings of power. If 'true' knowledge can be achieved, power will lose its hold as people learn to 'see through' power. A legacy of the Enlightenment, this conceptualization assumes a true self which lies outside of or beyond power (and, indeed, outside of the social world). This self is knowable through reason and through self-reflection, and its actualization through self-knowledge will release us from the workings of power (Flax, 1990). Autonomy, in this formulation, is at the opposite pole to regulation and government, and, indeed, to the workings of power.

The question is whether this is the best or most productive way to theorize the workings of power, or whether, indeed, its formulation is another manifestation of the workings of power itself. When we are incited to make our selves autonomous, to 'be who we really are', to realize and to express our 'true selves', what kinds of knowledges about the nature of the self are brought into play? Are these knowledges neutral, foundational and transcendent, or are they bound up with regimes of governing persons and populations? When we are most incited to be 'free', and to seek out the truth of our freedom, are we then most subjected to the workings of power? In other words, is power at its most powerful when it is least apparent, when it is working through our desires, when, as Rose puts it, it is 'governing through the freedom and aspirations of liberal subjects rather than in spite of them' (Rose, 1992b: 147)? As Michel Foucault, from whose work this concept of power derives, puts it, 'if power were never anything but repressive, if it never did anything but to say no, do you really think one would be brought to obey it?' (Foucault, 1980: 119).

Foucault's work has been the object of much criticism from feminists, not least because of his almost total neglect of issues of gender (Bordo, 1990; Hartsock, 1990; Jackson, 1992/3; Ramazanoglu, 1993). However, his insight into the ways in which power is deployed through meaning, is extremely useful as a basis from which to analyse the meanings which structure all of our lives and relationships. These meanings articulate with social practices. Foucault uses the term 'discourse' to elaborate the ways in which meaning and practice coalesce. For Foucault, discourses are not only linguistic representations: they produce meaning, create categories, and form 'objects' (including 'subjects'). In this sense, then, discourses are not distinct from *practices*. Part of his task, as he saw it, consisted in:

> not ... treating discourses as groups of signs (signifying elements referring to contents or representations) but as practices that systematically form the objects of which they speak. Of course, discourses are composed of signs; but what they do is more than use these signs to designate things. It is this more that renders them irreducible to language (*langue*) and to speech. It is this 'more' that we must reveal and describe.
>
> (Foucault, 1992: 48–9)

This perspective highlights the ways in which nothing evades (social) meaning; these meanings produce our understanding of the world. Discourses become, as Edward Said (1991: 10) puts it, 'epistemological enforcers' of *what* can be said, thought and lived, as well as of *how* it can be said, thought and lived. There are certain statements, propositions, actions, which are, as Foucault puts it, 'within the true' of any particular culture, and others which are 'outside of sense' (Foucault, 1981; see also Weedon, 1989; Barrett, 1991). As Henriques *et al.* argue:

> the argument is not that words determine but that those practices which constitute our everyday lives are produced and reproduced as an integral part of the production of signs and signifying systems.
>
> (1984: 99)

Discourses, then, cannot be separated from material practices or from the workings of societal institutions. According to Lois McNay, Foucault's work links together 'the material and the non-material in a theory of discourse' (McNay, 1992: 27). Foucault formulates this symbiosis through his conceptualization of the power–knowledge nexus:

> We should abandon a whole tradition that allows us to imagine that knowledge can exist only where the power relations are suspended and that knowledge can develop only outside its injunctions, its demands and its interests. ... We should admit rather that power produces knowledge ... that power and knowledge directly imply one another; ... there is no power relationship without the correlative constitution of a field of knowledge, nor any knowledge that does not presuppose and constitute at the same time power relations.
>
> (Foucault, 1979: 27)

Power, then, is not (only) a forbidding and denying force; nor is it a force which conceals or distorts a 'truth', the revelation of which will free us from the workings of power.[3] Rather, power can be seen as something which works productively – producing truths, forms of pleasure, categories of normality. Rather than *concealing* the 'true' situation, the operation of power *produces* (what is held to be) the truth of a situation. Conversely, knowledge, far from being the innocent and transparent representation of objective truth, is intrinsically bound up with the workings of power. The truth-status of 'truths' derives, not from some transcendent quality of the knowledges themselves, but from specific social and political preoccupations. Rather than *representing* truth, knowledges create and constitute the Truths by which contemporary Euroamericans have increasingly come to know and to act upon the self, both in relation *to* itself, and in relations with others. Categories of human subject – the categories 'mother' and 'daughter' for example – are not only understood through the meanings put on to them; rather, they are *produced* within discourse.

Increasingly significant in this context is the matrix of knowledges which produces truths about the self and its relations with others and which has been coined the 'psy complex' (Ingleby, 1985; see also Rose, 1991). The reference here is to knowledges generated through medicine, psychology, psychiatry, pedagogy, and so on, which several commentators have seen as gaining ascendance in the contemporary world, to such a degree that they inevitably inform the self-perceptions and self-consciousness of contemporary Euroamericans.

Psy knowledges are not confined to professional practice or statements within their own fields, but 'escape' from their specialist enclaves (Fraser, 1989) to inform the workings of other types of professionals (social workers, teachers, health visitors, counsellors, and so on), and to inform, too, a host of fields which are currently 'growth markets' in Euroamerican cultures – self-help literature, 'personal growth', child-care advice. And, significantly, these knowledges are reiterated in the minutiae of daily life – in doctors' surgeries, on chat shows, on 'the radio call-in, the weekly magazine column' – and inform the relationship of the self to itself, through 'the unceasing reflexive gaze of our own psychologically educated self-scrutiny' (Rose, 1991: 208). The self is increasingly becoming a project to be worked on, in pursuit of the 'real self'.

Psy knowledges are endlessly repeated across a range of sites, and, as we will see, they are embedded in law and other state processes. This makes them particularly intractable. The knowledges generated by psy are not normally represented as *theories*, open to contestation, but as truths about 'human nature', to such a degree, Rose claims, that 'it has become impossible to conceive of personhood, to experience one's own or another's personhood, or to govern oneself or others without "psy"' (1996a: 139).

The self and subjectivity

> As a form of power, subjection is paradoxical. To be dominated by a power external to oneself is a familiar and agonizing form power takes. To find, however, that what 'one' is, one's very formation as a subject, is in some sense dependent on that very power is quite another.
>
> (Butler, *The Psychic Life of Power*, pp. 1–2)

Such truths, such meanings, have far-reaching consequences in the lives of mothers and daughters. Truths about the self and its development within childhood, its relations with others, and the various obligations which some selves consequently owe to other selves, are the means by which the categories 'mother' and 'daughter' are constituted. They are the means by which mothers, in particular, are scrutinized, monitored and regulated, and through which both mothers and daughters may scrutinize and regulate themselves. In becoming (maternal and daughterly) *subjects*, women become *subjectivated* in the dual sense identified by Foucault:

This form of power applies itself to immediate everyday life which catego-
rizes the individual, marks him [*sic*] by his own individuality, attaches him to
his own identity, imposes a law of truth on him which he must recognize
and which others recognize in him. It is a form of power which makes individuals subjects. There are two meanings of the word *subject*: subject to
someone else by control and dependence, and tied to his own identity by a
conscience or self-knowledge. Both meanings suggest a form of power which
subjugates and makes subject to.

(Foucault, 1982: 212; emphasis in original)

Through subjectivation (*assujettissement*), mothers and daughters become tied to
the identities 'mother' and 'daughter' through these relations of power and
knowledge; they become (maternal and daughterly) *subjects*. But also, they
become *subjected* to the rules and norms engendered by a set of knowledges about
the mother, the daughter, the relationship between the two, and, in particular,
the role of the mother in producing the daughter's self. The self, itself – an entity
which seems (and perhaps feels) so idiosyncratic, so natural – is forged through
the workings of power. There is no 'natural' self which the social world shapes:
rather, the self, itself, is produced within a set of social relations which themselves
have relations of power/knowledge at their core.[4] The most apparently personal
and intimate parts of our lives, our desires and pleasures, are produced within
systems of regulation, including (and increasingly) self-regulation. As Butler puts
it, 'one inhabits the figure of autonomy only by becoming subjected to a power,
a subjection which implies a radical dependency' (Butler, 1997: 83).

Indeed, autonomy is at the heart both of the project of becoming a subject
and of being subjectified. It is through an appeal to autonomy that Euroamerican
persons are incited both to understand the self, and to work on, to perfect the
self. This project of autonomy has become increasingly significant in the shaping
of the self (Rose, 1991, 1993, 1996b) and, as we will see, it was a common theme
in many of the accounts of the women in this study, who strove for both their
own autonomy and that of their daughters. As Rose argues, the increasing significance of psy knowledges has led to a situation in which autonomy, as a
psychological state, takes on an overwhelming significance. Autonomy is what
lies behind projects of assertiveness training, self-help, therapy and counselling,
and the general discourse of psy which permeates the everyday lives of contemporary Euroamericans.

The knowledges of psy promise freedom through an actualizing of the self –
through uncovering the truth about the self and enabling persons to achieve the
'real self'. Increasingly, the Euroamerican self is incited to act on itself, relent-
lessly scrutinizing itself in the search for the truth *of* the self. Normality and
healthiness are established through the successful actualization of the project.
The autonomy promised through these processes appears as the very opposite to
government and regulation. Yet government and regulation are inherent in these
meanings and these practices.

In becoming autonomous subjects, we are subjected to the workings of power.

And it is, at least in part, through the relationship of the self *to* itself that governmentality is brought into play. In not (apparently) being regulated, contemporary Euroamericans are increasingly regulating themselves. According to Foucault, modern[5] forms of government increasingly operate on the basis of managing populations, rather than punishing them; the demand is for 'normality' rather than obedience to a sovereign power. Hence, 'techniques of normalization' have become the preferred means of government.

This is not to say that the juridical power of the law has ceased to exist, or even, necessarily, that it has diminished in its application or its influence. While Foucault saw the coercive power of the law as likely to diminish in the face of the normalizing power of 'psy' discourses, Carol Smart, in contrast, points to a 'merger' between law and psy, such that law is able to extend its juridical power through its incorporation of psy knowledges:

> Law is now the accepted mechanism for resolving social and individual conflicts. ... In this context law's colonization by the mechanisms of discipline should be seen in a new light rather than in terms of a form of power which is withering away. There is indeed a struggle going on, but at the same time law is extending its terrain in every direction. Moreover, whilst we can see a symbiotic relationship developing between law and the 'psy' professions, law is hardly challenged by other discourses, e.g. feminism.
>
> (Smart, 1989: 20)

For my purposes, one particularly apposite example of this 'merger' is the 1989 Children Act (England and Wales). This Act follows the child-centredness of contemporary psychological discourse in a number of ways: it replaces the notion of parental 'rights' with that of parental 'responsibilities', it enshrines the 'Gillick principle' by specifying the need for courts to take account of a child's maturity in determining her/his right to make decisions regarding her/his welfare;[6] it reiterates the paramountcy of 'the best interests of the child'; it refers to children's (physical, emotional and educational) 'needs'; and it places the wishes and feelings of the child at the top of the checklist of criteria which courts are obliged to consider when enacting the legislation (for example, when making a residence or care order) – a positioning which Bainham (1992: 14) regards as 'psychologically significant'.[7] Further, while the Act specifies that the paramount consideration of courts shall be the best interests of the child, it does not seek to establish what those 'best interests' are. This creates a gap which will inevitably be filled by 'psy' discourses.

However, although this piece of legislation is congruent with contemporary psychological expertise, this does not represent an imperialistic takeover of law by psychology. For one thing, law is not necessarily unified, even in its dealings with children. For example, the introduction in England and Wales of 'child jails' for persistent young offenders between the ages of twelve and fourteen (Dyer, 1994; Levy, 1994) indicates the continuing exercise of a coercive, rather than regulatory, form of power, and Levy (1994) argues that these institutions' rules governing punishment, parental visiting and so on are at odds with the 1989 Children Act.

Secondly, when law does incorporate the normalizing and regulatory discourses of the 'psy' professions, it *extends* its terrain, reinforcing its coercive mechanisms. For example, the notion of parental 'responsibilities' (rather than rights) extends the jurisdiction of law, absent parents must now legally maintain a link with their biological children. Parental 'responsibility' can now be juridically enforced through the courts; thus law extends its ground while legitimating normalizing apparatuses. And the professionals who work within the normalizing and regulatory paradigms of psy (health visitors, social workers and so on) operate with the force of the law behind them.

The 'symbiotic relationship' between law and normalization means that both types of power are able to extend their terrain: not only does law do so, but 'psy' discourses which rely on self-discipline and self-normalization are reinforced by their backing in law, even if this backing is not absolute. Hence, not only are 'psy' discourses grounded in the truth claims of scientific knowledge, but they are also legitimated by the truth claims of law itself. Further, they are able to rely upon more coercive mechanisms of power if the appeal to normalization 'fails'. Nevertheless, appeals to changes in the self are the preferred mechanism for effecting change. Even strategies of coercion – for example, social work intervention – have themselves come to rely on changing clients' understandings of themselves, and therefore rely on an encouragement to practise the preferred 'techniques of the self'.[8] Although these techniques are potentially coercive, their coercion incorporates practices of *self*-understanding and *self*-change. However, the subjectivation – in both senses – of the self is never accomplished once and for all; it is never finalized. It is iterated and reiterated in texts, in scrutiny, in self-scrutiny. Being a self is, as Butler puts it, 'no simple or continuous affair, but an uneasy practice of repetition and its risks, compelled yet incomplete, wavering on the horizon of social being' (Butler, 1997: 30). And through the repetition of these processes, there is room for change and for resistance (Butler, 1993, 1997).

It is important to note, however, that not everyone stands in the same relationship to the knowledges generated by psy. Those 'in the know' – those, for example, who have been trained within the psy professions – have access to forms of knowledge culturally marked as superior to other forms of knowledge. Different forms of knowledge here are emphatically *not* seen as 'equal but different'. So, for example, the 'child-centred' discourse of psy is marked as 'superior' to (and more forward-looking than) forms of child-care which rest on the mother invoking her own authority. Further, many of those 'in the know' routinely monitor and regulate those who are not 'in the know'. Among the women in this study, some could claim an easy familiarity with the knowledges of psy and had, to a large extent, incorporated them into their lives. Others had a much more attenuated relationship with them. This is no arbitrary division of the population, but a means by which class relations are produced and reproduced.

Classed knowledges

Although the existence of material inequalities between different groups of people is not, generally speaking, contested,[9] the question of whether 'class' remains a useful conceptual category *is* contested. Some theorists have argued that changes in the industrial structure, in political organizing, in property ownership, and in family form, for example, have led to the ailing, if not the death, of class as a meaningful conceptual tool (Giddens, 1990; Beck, 1992; Clark and Lipset, 1996). Others, however, argue that *changes* in class structures do not signal the demise of class as a significant mechanism of social inequality, and of inclusion/exclusion. Hout *et al.* (1996), for example, suggest that those theorists who signal the 'death of class' are working from an assumption that the class structure was once a stable and unitary phenomenon which relied on specific configurations of industry, employment, family, politics, etc. Hence, changes in these forms of social organization are taken as an indicator of the demise of class. Against this, Hout *et al.* argue:

> Class never was the all-powerful explanatory variable that some intellectual traditions assumed in earlier periods; class was always only one source of political identity and action alongside race, religion, nationality, gender and others. To say that class matters less now than it used to requires that one exaggerate its importance in the past and understate its importance at present. Class is important for politics to the extent that political organizations actively organize around class themes. Hence, in some periods the political consequence of class may appear latent, even if the underlying logic of class is unchanged. We would suggest that the same is true of other sources of social inequality [e.g. 'race' and gender].
>
> (Hout *et al.*, 1996: 56)

One trend in the 'death of class' thesis rests on the argument that the 'old categories' of class are being upstaged or replaced by 'new categories' of gender, 'race', nationality and so on (see, e.g. Pakula, 1996). These categories are deemed to be new, not in the sense that they are newly arisen, but, rather, that they have newly acquired significance. The argument here is that class as an identity is declining in the face of other identities on offer.[10]

But this argument relies on a curiously 'additive' model of identity and subjectivity (Smith, 1983; Spelman, 1988; Brah, 1992). It suggests, in other words, that the category 'woman' (or 'man'), black (or white), and so on, can take the place of an identity as working- or middle-class. But if there is one thing feminist debates around the category 'woman' have taught us, it is that these categories of identity and subjectivity are always cross-cutting, multilayered and multivalent. Gender, is, and always has been, classed, as it always has been raced, sexualized, nationalized. Conversely, class is and always has been gendered, raced, sexualized and nationalized. This important insight seems to be missing from many 'mainstream' discussions of class, perhaps because the focus of analysis remains (implicitly) the white, male worker. Similarly, the relational aspects of class seem at times to have slipped from sight. Yet as Walkerdine and others have shown, the category 'working class' is a category produced and reproduced in terms of its position as 'other' to a middle-class 'self'; it is marked as pathological to a middle-class 'normality'. An exclusive emphasis on economistic processes, on the measurement of class categories, and a categorizing of 'cultural' analyses only in terms of the 'underclass' work of writers like Murray (Murray, 1994a and b) means that these subjectivist and dialogic aspects of class become obscured.

Noting what she calls 'a retreat from class', Skeggs (1997) asks what lies behind such a retreat: is it because class is difficult to measure accurately? (in which case, it must be asked why measurement has become so all-encompassing a device for theorizing class); or is it because those who theorize about identity and social positioning generally have the privilege to ignore class? She asks:

> When a retreat [from class] is mounted, we need to ask whose experiences are being silenced, whose lives are being ignored and whose lives are considered worthy of study.
>
> (Skeggs, 1997: 7)

Yet class has indeed largely fallen out of favour in 'mainstream' analyses and it has been one of the most undertheorized areas of feminist analyses (Skeggs, 1997): it is only recently that a body of feminist work has begun to emerge which investigates the important links between gender and class.[11] One important insight which has been taken up within these analyses is that the inequalities of a class society cannot be reduced to economic inequality; indeed, economics may not be the most meaningful way to talk about class. While class is not *reducible* to symbolic systems, one of the ways in which it is made 'real' is through cultural mechanisms of inclusion and exclusion, of normalization and pathologization.[12] Where many writers have placed symbolic and cultural factors largely outside the realm of the political (see, e.g. Coole, 1996), I want to foreground the ways in which such factors are deeply embedded in political struggle and political inequality.

As Walkerdine and Lucey argue, the idea of a coherent, unitary and easily definable 'working class' may be a fiction, but is a fiction which is constantly produced and reproduced, and it is a fiction which has real effects. As they say:

> [T]he working class is constantly produced and reproduced as necessary, different, disgusting, Other – constantly told they are different in an order which ultimately depends upon their acceptance of oppression, exploitation and inequality as normal.
>
> (Walkerdine and Lucey, 1989: 30)

As part of this process, working-class people are constituted and reconstituted as getting it wrong – they do not *know* the right things, they do not *want* the right things, they do not *value* the right things. At the same time that they can be glamourized as 'the salt of the earth', they can be pathologized as ignorant, wasteful, dominating. And, as Walkerdine argues, 'the working classes' have come to be the repository for the fears and horrors, as well as the desires and hopes, of the middle-class observers who study them. In this role, they are a constant disappointment: they have not overthrown capitalism; they seem unwilling to take up a role as the 'noble poor'; and, at the same time, they are continually constituted as rigid and authoritarian, as laden with sexuality and dirt, as neglectful or overbearing mothers (Walkerdine and Lucey, 1989; Walkerdine, 1990, 1997; Roberts, 1999). They are the 'others' who define the parameters of normal (middle-class) life.

They are constituted as a group which has to be continually watched and monitored by those 'in the know'. As both Valerie Walkerdine (1997) and Ian Roberts (1999) have noted, the aim of much of this monitoring and surveillance has been part of an attempt to make working-class people more like their middle-class counterparts. Yet it seems that they even get this wrong:

> Implicitly their salvation would seem to lie in adopting middle-class attitudes and behaviour. On the other hand insofar as they have been seen to be making these changes they are seen as becoming enmeshed in a faceless culture or impoverished in the presence of unexampled wealth.
>
> (Roberts, 1999: 148; references omitted)

What is at issue here are the cultural and symbolic artefacts of class which Bourdieu has metaphorized as cultural and symbolic capital (Bourdieu, 1977, 1984, 1993). Cultural capital refers to a specific form of knowledge which, as Johnson puts it:

> equips the social agent with empathy towards, appreciation for or competence in deciphering cultural relations and cultural artefacts. ... The possession of ... cultural capital is accumulated through a long process of acquisition or inculcation which includes the pedagogical action of the family or group's members (family education), educated members of the social formation (diffuse education) and social institutions (institutionalized education).
>
> (Johnson, 1993: 7)

Not all cultural capital can be 'traded' on equal terms, however (Skeggs, 1997). It is only when cultural capital is sufficiently legitimated that it can be converted into symbolic capital – the prestige or recognition which various capitals acquire by virtue of *being* recognized and 'known' as legitimate. For Bourdieu, it is only the cultural capital of the middle classes which is legitimated in this way: their tastes, knowledges and dispositions are coded as *inherently* 'tasteful', *inherently* knowledgeable, *inherently* 'right'. In this way, class distinctions are simultaneously at work and obscured: they are at work through the distinctions drawn between the cultural competencies attached to different social class positions, and they are obscured because they become, not a matter of inequality in legitimated forms of knowledge and aesthetics, but, precisely, knowledge and aesthetics themselves. To not possess symbolic capital is to 'fail' in the games of aesthetic judgement, of knowledge, and of cultural competence. Working-class and middle-class cultural capital is not 'equal but different': rather the 'difference' which working-class people display is *made into* inequality (Walkerdine and Lucey, 1989). Because the cultural capital of the middle classes is marked as 'normal', its classed location is obscured.

Bourdieu's analysis both highlights and overturns conventional assumptions about cultural competencies and cultural knowledges. These competencies and knowledges are not usually seen as social mechanisms: rather, they are assumed to inhere within the self, and this in itself has specific social and cultural effects. In this sense, then, class is not simply an 'objective' position which one occupies, but becomes configured into a self.[13]

Dreams, fantasies and desires

If relations of power/knowledge come to inhere 'within' the self, this raises questions about the constitution of that self in terms of conscious and unconscious processes – the ground, in short, occupied by psychoanalysis. Although psychoanalytic analyses form a minor part of the discussion in this book, it is worth a consideration of the status of the dreams, fantasies and desires which are brought into play in the subjectivation (and the resistance) of the self.

Foucault's own opposition to psychoanalysis is legendary.[14] In line with his argument against normalizing and disciplinary processes, he attacked the 'confessional' mode of psychoanalysis, arguing that it is through this mode that the subject is subjected to knowledge which must form a regulatory schema. And certainly, for contemporary Euroamericans, psychoanalysis has, to a greater or lesser degree, 'passed into the language'. So, in seeking to explain the world, psychoanalytic theories have changed the (Euroamerican) world; they have generated schemata of understanding from which few of us are immune (Ricoeur, 1979). One particularly significant aspect of this is the part played by the psychoanalytic account in the generation of narrative. Psychoanalysis connects disparate events, fantasies,[15] images and so on, into a meaningful whole. According to Ricoeur (1991a), it is one means by which individual lives become 'emplotted': through psychoanalysis, stories which are yet to be told – 'potential stories' – become intelligible narratives:

> The patient who addresses the psychoanalyst brings him [*sic*] the scattered fragments of lived stories, dreams, 'primal scenes', conflictual episodes. One can legitimately say with respect to analytic sessions that their aim and their effect is to allow the analysand to draw out of these story-fragments a narrative which would be at once more bearable and more intelligible.
>
> (Ricoeur, 1991a: 30)

Psychoanalysis, in all its different forms, provides us with a means of structuring our personal narratives, so that, for instance, unhappy relationships or failure to achieve may be routed, via psychoanalysis, within our childhood relationships with our parents.[16] Psychoanalysis is also implicated in the cultural project of the construction of a particular form of 'self' (Rose, 1991). It is not necessary that all individuals undergo analysis or therapy in order to adopt these psychoanalytically based understandings (although most therapeutic models certainly reinforce this view) since this view of the world is found in popular culture, in everyday speech, and so on.

However, there are two issues here, which are often collapsed but which need to be separated: firstly, the issue of how psychoanalysis as a clinical practice and as a frame of reference subjects social actors to its regulatory mechanisms; and secondly, the issue of whether psychoanalytic theory offers a useful explanation in terms of analysing subjectivity. In Britain, psychoanalytic clinical practice has never had the institutional authority that it has enjoyed in France or the USA (Tambling, 1990). Further, the type of theory used in clinical practice is at odds with much psychoanalytic theory which is used for analytic purposes within the academy. To give one example, Judith Butler, whose work has been extremely important (albeit not universally acclaimed) uses a synthesis of Foucauldian and Lacanian perspectives to underwrite her theories of 'performativity'. Yet one would be unlikely to find such a Lacanian perspective in clinical use in Britain or the USA. The British psychoanalyst, Susie Orbach, characterizes Butler's work in terms of its marginality to clinicians: 'The psychoanalysis she's using is the psychoanalysis that nobody [in clinical practice] today uses' (Orbach, with Hollway, 1997: 103).

In Britain, the influence of clinicians such as Klein, Bowlby and Winnicott has meant that object-relations theories, which focus on the early mother–infant dyad, have been more prominent than other schools of thought. Object-relations theory has also been taken up within feminism, probably because its placing of the mother at centre stage makes it seem particularly amenable to feminist theorizing. Yet this school of thought can, as the next chapter shows, place the mother in a more vulnerable position than other forms of psychoanalysis. While some forms of psychoanalysis stress 'adaptation' to social rules, others underline the ways in which adaptation is impossible – the ways in which, for example, normal femininity (and normal masculinity) is something forced, something only achieved with difficulty and never wholly achieved (Rose, 1987). This is where some feminists and other theorists have found Freudian and Lacanian[17] psychoanalysis more useful than object-relations approaches.

Most importantly for my purposes here are the differing ways in which desire is conceptualized in different psychoanalytic perspectives. For non-Kleinian object-relations theories,[18] the desires of the child are realistic in that they are capable of satisfaction, through 'good-enough mothering'. For Freud, as for Lacan, the child's desires are wild and unrealizable: they cannot be (wholly) met. Freud's famous question, 'what does the little girl require of her mother?', contained in his 1931 essay, remains ultimately unanswered by Freud, except in

so far as he specifies that the girl's aims are both active and passive. Jacqueline
Rose's Lacanian reading leads her to conclude that, in the light of Freud's assertion that infantile sexuality has no aim and is incapable of satisfaction:

> it emerges that what specifies the little girl's aim, and her demand, is that she
> does not have one. The question persists, or is repeated, therefore, as the
> impossibility of satisfaction.
>
> (Rose, 1985: 144)

Or, as Juliet Mitchell argues, there is no answer to the question, 'What does the
little girl want?': 'All answers to the question, including "the mother" are false:
she simply *wants*' (Mitchell, 1982: 24; emphasis in original). The girl's desire
cannot be satisfied; her mother is not capable (nor is anyone) of fulfilling her
desires.

Jacqueline Rose sees Freud's work on femininity as opening up the issue of
desire itself – desire as the impossibility of the girl's demands on her mother – an
issue which is foregrounded by Lacan, even more than by Freud. For Lacan,
desire is a basic ontological lack, which is incapable of satisfaction. What the girl
requires of her mother, according to this explanatory framework, is an impossible plenitude, a return to the pre-Oedipal mother – a demand which expresses
an unfulfillable desire. At the same time, it is desire which, together with the
subject's inscription into language, makes the subject human (Lacan, 1977a and
b, 1988).

What is useful, and even subversive, about the Freudian and Lacanian
accounts is the designation of infantile desires as insatiable, as incapable of fulfilment. The mother *cannot* provide the love which the infant desires. Discourses
surrounding mothering so frequently begin from an assumption that mothers
can (and should) provide for children's desires, and, in the process, as Chodorow
and Contratto (1982) argue, 'needs' become conflated with 'wants'. Further, they
frequently conflate infantile fantasy around the mother with social reality, so that
mothers are configured as immensely powerful characters (Dally, 1976;
Dinnerstein, 1976; Friday, 1979, 1991). On the other hand, these infantile
fantasies are made 'real' by their inscription into social policy, into child-rearing
advice, and so on (Bradley, 1989; Walkerdine and Lucey, 1989). Yet this is the
very reason I am arguing that these fantasies have to be recognized as just that –
as fantasies, incapable of fulfilment. In this way, the commonplace distinction
between the social and the psychic can be seen to be undermined: psychic states
can have material consequences, not only in individual lives, but in social
arrangements (Walkerdine, 1985e; Walkerdine and Lucey, 1989; Butler, 1997).
Conversely, material life impacts on and shapes both psychic life and our interpretations of that psychic life (Steedman, 1986).

The Freudian and Lacanian accounts are accounts which tell of the
inevitability of psychic processes, even if these processes are partial and incomplete.
Hence, these accounts of the mother–daughter relationships tell of the inevitability
of some loss of the mother to the daughter: they are fatalistic narratives in which

there is an inevitable cost to the process of becoming social. This is at odds with analyses which *prescribe* separation between mother and daughter as necessary for the daughter's psychic health (e.g. Friday, 1979, 1991) or which blame the mother for the separation from the daughter (Eichenbaum and Orbach, 1982, 1988).

Yet the inevitability of psychic processes is not the whole story: if the distinction between social and psychic reality is a rhetorical one, which does not stand up to scrutiny, then the psyche must be forged within social relations, not only of gender, but of class, 'race', sexuality. Steedman argues that Freud's conceptualization of the loss of the parent to the child within the Oedipal crisis has to be seen in light of the social circumstances through which the adult will interpret the 'first loss':

> [W]e live in time and politics, and exclusion is the promoter of envy, the social and subjective sense of the impossible unfairness of things. The first loss, the first exclusion, will be differently interpreted by the adult who used to be the child, according to the social circumstances she finds herself in, and the story she needs to relate.
>
> (Steedman, 1986: 111)

As Steedman argues, the type of landscape against which one interprets the past *matters*:

> It matters ... whether one reshapes past time, re-uses the ordinary exigencies and crises of all childhoods whilst looking down from the curtainless windows of a terraced house like my mother did, or sees at that moment the long view stretching away from the big house in some richer and more detailed landscape.
>
> (Steedman, 1986: 5)

Later chapters of the book (particularly Chapter 5) take up this theme in considering the ways in which fantasies are formed around and within landscapes of class, as well as gender. The next chapter considers the ways in which both 'child' and 'mother' are classed, as well as gendered and raced categories, and the ways in which some forms of psychoanalysis position mothers as guarantors, not only of the daughter's self, but of the social order.

2 Guaranteeing the social order

Good-enough daughters, good-enough mothers

> For perhaps a century and a half, social and political concerns have linked the rearing and well-being of children with the welfare of society at large. Social ills from crime and juvenile delinquency to military defeat and industrial decline have been connected with incorrect or ignorant practices of child-care within the family. Around the child, lines of force have been established between the objectives of government and the minute details of conjugal, domestic and parental behaviour.
>
> (Nikolas Rose, *Governing the Soul*, p. xi)

The last chapter introduced a discussion of the ways in which Euroamerican selves are forged within relations of knowledge which inevitably involve the workings of power. It is within these relations of power and knowledge that the categories 'mother' and 'daughter' are produced. However, mothers and daughters are not equivalently positioned in relation to these knowledges. I argued earlier that 'child' has (at least) two meanings: it is both an age category and a kin category. Hence, although not all daughters belong to the age category 'child', all belong to the kin category 'child'. If 'mother' is constituted on the basis of the category 'child', and if daughters *as daughters* occupy this category in its familial sense, then motherhood is constituted in terms of its *responsiveness* to daughterhood. This chapter explores the constitution of the category 'child' and considers its implications for the constitution of the good (enough) mother. It brings together the three categories, self, mother and daughter, as it considers the ways in which mothers are produced and reproduced in terms of their responsibility for nurturing the self of the daughter (and, indeed, the son). It does this in order to ground and to contextualize the women's accounts of the relationship, which are analysed in later chapters.

Good-enough children

> I do not think it is correct simply to insist that it is only exploitation and oppression which gets in the way of having a proper childhood, which should be the right of all oppressed peoples in the world. I believe, rather, the other way round, that what counts as childhood today is the culturally specific practices of a few

advanced industrial countries and that there are huge problems with their views of what childhood is when foisted on to Others.

(Walkerdine, 1997: 188)

Most analyses of motherhood, especially feminist analyses, now assume a level of social construction within the category 'mother'; it is assumed that current social relations could be changed, that existing understandings of motherhood are neither natural nor inevitable. However, a radical questioning of the constitution of childhood is rarely incorporated into such analyses, and the effect of this is that a bedrock of naturalism remains. Since motherhood is a response to the child and her/his needs, a lack of attention to childhood means that a radical analysis of motherhood, or of the mother–child relation, becomes impossible. Instead, existing 'truths' about the nature and the needs of the child simply become incorporated into critiques of motherhood, and much of the radical force of such critiques is therefore in danger of becoming lost.

This section will consider how the figure of the child is discursively constituted in contemporary Euroamerican cultures; and it will consider some of the implications of this constitution, for children themselves, and for the families (and especially the mothers) whose task it has become to nurture the selves of children.

For contemporary Euroamericans, the figure of the child is significant, on a number of counts: firstly, childhood is held to be the cradle of the self, the temporal period in which the self is formed; it is understood as a decisive period in narratives of lives. Indeed, childhood is made coherent through the emplotment and narrativization of lives. It is placed on a trajectory of a life in which humans are emplotted as the same entity, from foetus to old age (Ricoeur, 1991b). Within this narrativization, later events are understood as a culmination and actualization of prior events. Hence childhood is the grounds and the foundation of adulthood, and adulthood is made coherent through invocations of childhood. The autonomy which selves are supposed to evince is held to be laid down in childhood

Secondly, 'the good society' is held to result from 'good citizens' who are 'reasonable', whose demands on the system are within 'reason' (Walkerdine and Lucey, 1989). And good citizens grow from good children. As Rose (1991) argues, childhood (in the context of family life) has been the focus of scrutiny from governments throughout the post-war period, in order to ensure that families (and especially mothers) fulfil their obligations to produce such 'good citizens'.

Thirdly, and as Steedman has argued, the child has come to embody the concept of 'interiority', the internalized self:

> The search is for the self and the past that is lost and gone; and some of the ways in which, since the end of the eighteenth century, the lost object has come to embody the shape and form of the child.

(Steedman, 1995: 174)

When selves are to be sought out, understood and actualized, when the 'true' self is both constantly in danger of being lost, and always able to be refound, childhood takes on a special significance. Explicitly in texts which promote the search for 'the child within', more implicitly in a range of sites which promote self-inspection and self-actualization, the wellspring of selfhood is held to be found in our own pasts, our own childhoods.

There is a close association between childhood and 'nature', so that children are usually conceptualized in terms of 'natural' dispositions, and the childhood of adults is conceptualized as having a greater 'naturalness' than their adult subjectivity. As a result, the categories 'child' and 'childhood' have convention-ally remained unexamined and untheorized within sociological accounts.[1] As Chris Jenks puts it:

> It is as if the basic ontological questions, 'What is a child?' and 'How is the child possible as such?' were, so to speak, answered in advance of the theo-rizing and then summarily dismissed.
>
> (Jenks, 1996: 4)

Yet a growing literature on sociological analyses of childhood alerts us to child-hood as socially constituted. As Stainton Rogers and Stainton Rogers note, childhood is 'knowledged into being' (1992: 15): thus, they draw attention to the ways in which this category of human subject is produced within relations of power/knowledge. Further, and as James *et al.* argue, 'social theories of child-hood are grounded in the visions of social order of adult theorists' (James *et al.*, 1998: 57). Children embody the fantasies, hopes, desires and fears of adults (Stainton Rogers and Stainton Rogers, 1992; Jenks, 1996). It is in adults' social and political preoccupations around the self, the social world, and the relation-ship between the two, that theories of childhood are forged.[2]

Childhood, then can be seen as a social *production*. As such, it is produced across a range of sites: it is produced textually, through the texts of develop-mental psychology, pedagogy, statutes of law, in fiction, in biography and autobiography; and it is produced through social practices – the educational system, medicine, the legal system, social work – the practices of those institu-tions whose task it is to monitor 'real' children and their parents. These institutions, in turn, are, at least in part, constituted through, and on the basis of, specific understandings of childhood. There is a set of knowledges around child-hood which claims to speak the truth about the real child and which inform the practices of those whose concern is with children and childhood. And, as with constructions of the self, the primary source of these sets of knowledges is the 'psy professions', whose discourses circulate as broader cultural truths about, and understandings of, childhood, and indeed of personhood.

Because of the very close association between childhood and 'nature', the idea of childhood as socially constructed can be counter-intuitive. Equally, it can be seen as a denial of there being real, embodied children. It is worth, then, exploring this issue. My argument here is not that children do not exist, or that they only exist in terms of the textual and other representations which are made of them. However, neither am I arguing that 'some part of' childhood is natural, and that 'on top of' this nature social roles, expectations, and so on are overlaid (as conventional socialization theories would have it). Indeed, this constitution of childhood into parts, some of which are 'natural' and some of which are 'social' is itself part of the way in which childhood gets constructed. To paraphrase Judith Butler's observations on categories of 'sex', we might ask both where lines should be drawn between what is and what is not constructed, and also, how it is that 'childhood' comes in parts 'whose differentiation is not a matter of construction' (Butler, 1993: 11).[3]

To bracket off this specific temporal period and to name it 'childhood', to afford to the inhabitants of this temporal period specific characteristics, to segregate them spatially and to define them on different terms psychologically, is neither a natural nor an inevitable process. Children are certainly 'real', but their reality as children is an effect, not of 'nature' (however defined) but of social relations, social meanings, social understandings, and social practices, all of which combine to produce the figure of the child.

Childhood: individuality and sameness

Characteristics of 'normal' children are an effect of what is considered, within specific socio-historical formations, to constitute 'normal' personhood: the qualities which are to be nurtured in the child are the qualities which will produce the normal adult. In contemporary Euroamerican societies, it is individuality which is to be nurtured. This individuality is held to be both innate, and as needing to be nurtured through the mother's sensitive care. Individuality is to be nurtured through specific modalities of regulation; through, for example, the use of 'reason'; through appeals to the child's own wishes and desires. As Walkerdine and Lucey (1989) note, 'sensitivity' (the normative accolade given to some mothers, and the type of mothering which is held to produce individuality)[4] demands that the mother make her power invisible. The sensitive mother regulates her children without appearing to do so (Newson and Newson, 1976; NSPCC, 1989). Indeed, her goal is to teach her children to regulate themselves. In this way, the story goes, children will believe themselves 'autonomous' – free from the impositions of (m)others, capable of achieving anything.

Paradoxically, children's uniqueness is achieved through their approximation to the norms of a common childhood. It is through the nurturing of the child's unique, authentic and real self, in other words, that the child is to come to properly represent what children should be like; through these means that child*ren* are to come to more closely represent child*hood* (cf. Holland, 1996). Further, it is through the nurturing of this individuality that children properly become social beings – the good citizens of the good society.

It is here that another paradox occurs: not only is the uniqueness of children achieved through their proximity to a collectivity of children, but also, their very individuality, with its promise of autonomy, self-actualization and self-development, is achieved through forms of self-surveillance. They are bound up in regimes of government at the same time that appeals are made to forms of self-actualization which imply the shrugging off of power (Lury, 1998). Through productive forms of power, the individual is both produced and tethered to her/his own individuality – which must be sought out, realized and achieved. Yet – and perhaps because of an association with self-actualization – this form of regulation is rendered invisible: it is usually read, not as regulation at all, but as proof of autonomy and self-directedness. As Lois McNay observes, 'The normalizing tendencies of modem technologies of power are obscured behind the screen of individualization' (McNay, 1992: 86). Hence, when mothers regulate their children by appealing to self-regulation and self-surveillance, this is regarded as evidence of a state of mutuality and equality between mother and child (Walkerdine and Lucey, 1989). The child's achievement of 'autonomy', in turn, is read as a freedom from the imposition of others' powers.

The model of the child brought into play here is the child as naturally good, and as needing the right environment in which its goodness can be realized. Part of its 'goodness' is a 'natural' autonomy and individuality which must, nevertheless, be nurtured. This environment (potentially) can accord with the child's 'nature' to produce a social world in which nature is realized in a harmonious fusion of nature and nurture. Jenks (1996) has coined the term 'the Apollonian child' as a shorthand for this model of childhood.

The Apollonian child is inherently good and unflawed. In contrast to its 'other', the Dionysian child – a being which is inherently flawed and tainted with evil – the Apollonian child is born good. If s/he becomes 'bad', this is not through any fault in her/his nature, but through the strictures of a society (or a family) which fails to recognize the child's essential goodness and to treat her/him accordingly: 'children in this image are not curbed or beaten into submission, they are encouraged, enabled and facilitated' (Jenks, 1996: 73).

As Jenks notes, it is the image of the Apollonian child which has informed child-centred pedagogy in the last three decades. It is this child, too, which walks the pages of developmental psychology texts, of child-care advice, and so on, in much of the post-war period. The Apollonian child embodies belief in, or desire for, the 'good self' which only has to be actualized to realize its full goodness. It is because the nature of the child is 'good' that the mother is to simply allow that 'nature' to develop. And it *is* the mother who is primarily charged with the sensitive nurturing of this self (Woollett and Phoenix, 1991a).

Certainly, this model of childhood does not go uncontested. Both the 'old' and the 'new' political Right usually stress parental control rather than democratic parenting (Abbott and Wallace, 1992). But significantly, this stress on parental control is bound up with the need for the presence of the father. Hence the mother's 'sensitive' role is not so much displaced as augmented by paternal authority. In recent years, and especially in Britain and the US, pronouncements from both the Left and the Right have particularly targeted poor single mothers (Dennis, 1993; Dennis and Erdos, 1993; Murray, 1994a).[5] These women are seen as producing delinquent children (particularly boys, who lack a male 'role model'). It is here that the nuclear family as the embodiment of both the natural and the moral orders (Barrett and McIntosh, 1982) most clearly appears, as in John Redwood's rather strange statement that 'The *natural* state *should be* the two-adult family caring for their children' (Redwood, quoted in Bates, 1993; emphasis mine).[6] Since women are positioned as causing family breakdown, or as choosing lone parenthood (Smart, 1984; Abbott and Wallace, 1992), the blame for contravening both nature and morality is placed on the mother.

Despite their differences, what both 'progressive' and 'conservative' discourses share is an emphasis on the family as the guarantor of social order. Within this, mothers – most of whom do nearly all the child-care, whether or not they live with their children's fathers – bear the ultimate responsibility for the production of not only the 'good citizen' but also the 'good society'.

Part of Jenks' argument around these oppositional figures of childhood – the Apollonian and Dionysian children – is that, while neither figure ever absolutely dominates definitions of childhood or of individual children, the Apollonian child is more prominent in times and places characterized by disciplinary forms of power, rather than by sovereign power (see Foucault, 1979). Hence, although calls for 'discipline' rest on the Dionysian model of childhood, it is the Apollonian child who largely informs at least 'expert' models of childhood for contemporary Euroamericans.

Indeed, the figures of the Apollonian and the Dionysian child may be two sides of the same coin. The British psychoanalyst Donald Winnicott argued that it is when children have not been enabled to regulate themselves that they have to be subject to a more visible and coercive form of regulation (Winnicott, 1950b). And this concept underwrites much public discussion of childhood. For example, in 1991, Kenneth Baker (then British Home Secretary) identified what he saw as six common characteristics of criminals. These included 'erratic and inconsistent parenting', 'parental neglect' and 'breakdown within the family' (Baker, cited in Carvel, 1991).[7] It is when the 'true' (autonomous) self is not actualized – when the Apollonian child has failed to develop – that the child or young person is conceptualized as Dionysian.

The dream of childhood autonomy embodied in the Apollonian child is the smooth running of society as a whole – an entity which, in its ideal state, is usually conceptualized as a harmonious amalgam of autonomous citizens, regulated by 'reason'. And the person who can produce this state is the mother, who is supposed to engender autonomy within the child. Hence, as Walkerdine and Lucey point out, mothers become the guarantors, not only of the 'good self' of the child, but also of the 'good society'. They are to regulate their children by teaching them to regulate themselves.[8] There is little consideration of the ways in which certain parents and their children are pathologized through the very categories of what counts as 'good-enough parenting'. What we have here is a fantasy of order which masks its own participation in the often violent categories of inclusion and exclusion.

Childhood: normalizing, individualizing, scrutinizing

> In a sense, the power of normalization imposes homogeneity; but it individualizes by making it possible to measure gaps, to determine levels, to fix specialities and to render the differences useful by fitting them one to another. It is easy to understand how the power of the norm functions within a system of formal equality, since within a homogeneity that is the rule, the norm introduces, as a useful imperative and as a result of measurement, all the shading of individual differences.
>
> (Foucault, *Discipline and Punish*, p. 184)

Euroamerican understandings of children are dominated by a fundamental contradiction: all children are the same – they pass through the same developmental 'milestones', they exhibit the same fundamental characteristics, they have the same 'needs'. At the same time, all children are held to be unique. The 'uniqueness' of children is a manifestation of the uniqueness and individuality which Western selves are supposed to exhibit. As Jenks (1996: 122) notes, heterogeneous 'children' are brought together – 'enmeshed in [a] forced commonality' into a homogeneous category 'the child'.

But what must be noted is that this forced commonality rests upon a violence – the exclusion of those who stand outside of its charmed circle. Difference or deviation from this supposedly universal figure, 'the child', is lived out as pathology (Walkerdine and Lucey, 1989). In other words, the existence of such a category creates its own schema of regulation and normalization. If 'normal' children are like X, then any children exhibiting Y are not 'normal' children. While all children are conceptualized as equal (if different), some are more equal than others. The identity 'normal child' gains meaning only through its exclusion of those 'others' who fail to exhibit the characteristics of 'normal children', who are forcibly excluded from the category. As Hall (1996) argues, all identities rest on an exclusion of an 'outside':

> Throughout their careers, identities can function as points of identification and attachment only because of their capacity to exclude, to leave out, to render 'outside', abjected. Every identity has its 'margin', an excess, something more. The unity, the internal homogeneity, which the term identity treats as foundational is not a natural, but a constructed form of closure, every identity naming as its necessary, even if silenced and unspoken other, that which it 'lacks'.
>
> (Hall, 1996: 5)

The apparently open and capacious identity 'child' may not be equally available to all children. Most obviously, this occurs when children exhibit characteristics or commit acts which are held to be 'un-childlike'. One recent example of this in the British context occurred around media coverage of what has come to be known as 'the Bulger case'. In 1993, Robert Thompson and Jon Venables, two

10-year-old boys, abducted the 2-year-old James Bulger from a shopping centre in Bootle, and later murdered him.[9] In media reports of this case, the Apollonian and Dionysian children apparently jostled for space, as Robert Thompson and Jon Venables were characterized variously, as 'evil monsters' (Dionysian) and as damaged (Apollonian) (Jenks, 1996). While the representation of these children as Dionysian is clearly problematic, liberal commentaries, which conceptualize these children as Apollonian, are not without problems of their own.

Within such commentaries, the boys are characterized as (potentially) 'real' children whose 'environment' has failed them. The 'evil' of their act is split off onto their geographical and social environment – their neighbourhood, their class. The environment, in other words, has failed to nurture the child's true nature, and the child has therefore become something *against* nature. And since the mother (and to a lesser extent, the father) is often collapsed into the child's 'environment', it is mothers (and to a lesser extent, fathers) who bear this failure. They become the environment which is itself 'with' or 'against' nature: hence any 'unnatural-ness' found in the child can be simply relocated within the parents.

To pursue this argument, I want to briefly examine Blake Morrison's (1997) apparently liberal and humane commentary on 'the Bulger case'. As Alison Young argues, there is something about the event which demands interpretation – a compulsion to understand, to frame the boys' actions within a coherent narrative. But, as she also argues, there is, equally, something about the event which prohibits interpretation. This prohibition, she argues, inheres in what she describes as:

> a confusion of two orders of being, which the canons of interpretation have prescribed as orders which should be kept distinct. These are the orders of semblance and substance; the confusion of these results in a misidentification of appearance and reality.
>
> (Young, 1996: 112)

This gap between semblance and substance, Young argues, is played out through a series of oppositions: between real and non-real children, real and non-real (or good and bad) mothers, feminine and masculine characteristics. For example, as she says:

> Venables and Thompson *appear* to be children but are not: they are more like evil adults or monsters in disguise. Evil is the lack of correspondence between appearance and being: Thompson and Venables *appear* to be children but *are not*. James Bulger, on the other hand, *appears* child-*like* and is the quintessence of childhood. His innocence consists in the absolute correspondence between his image and his substance.
>
> (Young, 1996: 115; emphasis in original)

Morrison (1997) wants to claim Thompson and Venables as 'real' children, but he is only able to do this through characterizing them as children who *could be* 'real', given the right environment. Their environment – their geographical location, their class, their families – can only be characterized as 'other', as pathological. Their 'badness' is split off from the boys themselves, and on to their environment.[10]

Morrison's attempts to suture the gap between semblance and substance in the case of the two boys only works by reiterating the gap between semblance and substance in the case of their mothers: Ann Thompson and Susan Venables look like mothers, but are not. In contrast to Denise Bulger, who is constituted as both *appearing* and *being* a mother, these two women are represented as the twin 'others' of mothering – excess and lack. Sue Venables loves too much, Ann Thompson not enough. The narrative of Morrison's text impels their exclusion from the inclusionary 'we' who fear our children might meet James Bulger's fate, but not Thompson's and Venables' fate.

The distinction between these three women is clearly played out in the following passages:

> having lost her first baby (stillborn), [Denise Bulger] needed to have [James] with her at all times, and he would go to bed when she and Ralph did, round midnight.
>
> (Morrison, 1997: 46)

> [as James threw babysuits and took sweets and a drink] Denise, flustered, seeing everyone thinking, 'Bad mother – no control of her child', gave James a slap.
>
> (ibid.: 47)

> Neighbours said Ann … hit the kids.
>
> (ibid.: 165)

> There are suspicions about Susan [Venables] who's known to have difficulties settling her children at night and isn't averse to 'discipline' or 'chastisement', meaning a good slap or belting as required.
>
> (ibid.: 167)

Denise Bulger is here the 'real' mother: her actions in letting her child go to bed late, and slapping him, are made coherent through a narrative of maternal care and devotion. Her difference is also marked through the fact that she (at the time) was married and lived with her child's father. This also marks James Bulger's status as 'normal' child, in contrast to Thompson and Venables. The absence of fathers was taken to be a key factor in many representations of the case, including Morrison's. Although it is impossible to represent Jon Venables as father*less* (since his parents spent weekends together), his father is represented as inadequate because he is not 'really' a man. Here is another gap between semblance and substance – Neil Venables looks like a man, but is not; Susan Venables looks like a woman, but her womanliness is a masquerade behind which she hides a 'real' masculinity:

> Mr. and Mrs. Venables. Mr. and Mrs. Average. Your typical couple, no less typical for having separated years ago and for her looking the stronger of the two. They seem well-matched, or complementary: Vamp, Wimp. Neil cries at times, whereas Susan toughs it out: beneath the make-up which she renews each tea-break, only a suppressed anger shows its face.
>
> (ibid.: 38)

This gender disruption is marked in terms of its negative effect on Jon:

> Jon's grudge against his father, if he has one, can't have been his leaving, but his not being a dad to admire. Jon's into movie strong men, heroes and Stallones; whereas Neil's a softie, henpecked, less manly than Jon's mum. Maybe the attack on James was a desperate attempt at machismo, Jon's bid to show he needn't be a mouse like Neil.
>
> (ibid.: 113)

So, Thompson and Venables are recouped as (potentially) 'real' children only through a conceptualization of their parents as monstrous, as damaging.[11] There are, potentially, other narratives here, other stories to be told. I am not claiming that any of these narratives would contain the 'truth' of the event, any more than Morrison's does. The point is that the 'dominant' narratives in this case debar all the (potential) others. Gayatri Spivak (Spivak and Gunew, 1993: 194) argues that the question, 'Who can speak?', is less crucial than the question, 'Who will listen?' Many people might potentially speak about this case – Ralph and Denise Bulger, Robert Thompson and Jon Venables, their parents, the expert witnesses called by the court – but only some will be listened to. Only some of these voices can be seen as making 'sense'. This is where we get back to the 'truths' produced about childhood, and indeed about the self. Only some 'truths' are true, and only some narratives count as coherent.

'Liberal' responses to the Bulger case establish a fictive community – a 'we' – into which all children can potentially be incorporated: but this community is already founded on the expulsion of some children; hence, attempts at recuperation are bound to fail. Within this schema of understanding, the 'otherness' of excluded children can only be displaced; it cannot be undone. These children are inscribed as those who could be real if they had the right upbringing, the right background. In this process, middle-class childhoods are inscribed and re-inscribed as the 'real' ones. All would be well if everyone had such childhoods. There is no room here for a radical questioning of the ways in which middle-class childhood silently occupies the ground marked as 'normal' and 'natural', no room for a critique of knowledges around childhood.

Gendering childhood

It is not only those who are not immediately defined as 'children' who constitute the exterior of 'normal' childhood, however: it is also those who do not display the characteristics ascribed to 'normal' children; those who might *look like* children but *are not* (substantively) children (Young, 1996). Implicitly or explicitly, the categories normal/abnormal children are mapped across categories of class, race and gender, revealing the normal child as white, male and middle class. Walkerdine (1985c), for example, has argued that, despite a formal commitment to 'equality' within the classroom, boys and girls are not positioned in the same way within this space. Boys, she argues, are constructed as 'active', as clever; girls as less challenging, as passive. Yet, Walkerdine argues, these very qualities are induced in girls by their positioning as 'nice, kind and helpful'. Through this positioning, girls become guardians of the covert rules of the classroom (for order, obedience, etc. – rules which ostensibly have no place in a 'progressive' classroom). Through this positioning, too, it becomes almost impossible for them to challenge the teacher's authority: it is this authority they are 'guarding'. This is significant, Walkerdine argues, because these challenges are held to be the foundations of rationality, and thus of 'cleverness'. Within the classroom, she argues:

> Power is apparently invested in equality, in which the teacher, like the child, can be 'won over' by an argument. The pedagogy aims to produce such 'rational powers of the mind'. However, girls who are nice, kind and helpful are guardians of the moral order, keepers of the rules. … A girl so positioned could hardly break rules for which she is responsible as guardian. Yet breaking rules is read as a precursor of 'breaking set', the very basis of rational argument.
>
> (Walkerdine, 1985c: 77)

It is not, Walkerdine argues, that individual girls and boys do not ever resist their respective positionings; nor is it the case that children are unified, with girls displaying only helpfulness and nurturance, and boys displaying only activity and rationality. Her argument, rather, is that the category '(normal) child' is one which is founded on qualities of 'reason', of challenge, and so on, which are constructed as 'masculine' characteristics. Hence girls displaying these characteristics are not 'feminine'; their behaviour is problematic, if not pathological (see Walkerdine, 1985c: 78; also Walden and Walkerdine, 1983).[12]

The main point I want to take from Walkerdine's argument is that 'childhood' is not constructed equivalently for male and female children. This differential construction is found, not only in the classroom, but in accounts of 'development'. For example, one training pack for social workers provides a clear example of some of the ways in which development is gendered:

> (The six year old): Boys take things apart, girls dress and undress dolls. … Boys expose genitals to girls, take off younger children's pants.

(The seven year old): Boys tend to gorge, girls tend to have low appetite.

(The eight year old): Girls and boys separate and deride each other. … Boys and girls separate in play. …

[About sex] Girls more inquisitive for facts than boys. … Boys learn best by watching animals mate. … Some girls are easily stimulated by touch.

(The nine year old): Boys interested in clothes. Dresses himself with untidy results. Tends to throw clothes around the room. Can comb own hair. Girls into trendy clothes – sophisticated and choosy. …

Boys like football, weight-lifting, rough-housing. Girls like dolls and complicated games.

(The ten year old): Girls are very aware of interpersonal relationships – they have best friends and confide family secrets and relate family dramas to their close friends. … Boys are generally more interested in camps.

(Sefton Social Services, 1994/95)

The child here clearly progresses through a series of 'milestones' towards increasing maturity; but boys and girls do not take the same route to this goal. My point here is not that these guidelines are using 'stereotypes'; it is, rather, that 'development' is constructed differently for girls and boys. Since 'development' is itself constructed as a 'natural' process, this gendering is naturalized. Within this account, girls seem 'naturally' to be more relational than boys, more preoccupied with their appearance, and so on. Although it is not overtly stated, the picture which emerges of the 'normal' boy is one of activity and independence. Boys of six are constructed here as actively, aggressively sexual ('Boys expose genitals to girls, take off younger children's pants'); girls' sexuality is passive ('some … are easily stimulated by touch').[13] The boy is active to the girl's passive, independent to her relational. Since 'normal' childhood consists in activity and growing independence, the girl is 'other' to this norm (Walkerdine, 1985c). It is not difficult to see how difference here could be lived out as pathology.

Classing childhood

If girls are constituted as 'other' to the male child, working-class children of both genders are constituted as 'other' to the middle-class child. Recent 'underclass' debates in Britain and the USA, for example, have defined poverty (and, more broadly, class relations) in terms of cultural relations which are transmitted from bad parents (and especially bad mothers) on to their bad and abnormal children.[14] And recent coverage in the British press around a supposed 'crisis in childhood' has, similarly, centred on class. A working-class threat to the smooth running of society is reiterated here, as working-class children are represented as 'not children'. Though class is rarely directly invoked in these debates, it is a structuring absence which informs the debates at the same time that the relations which make a classed society are obscured. It is no longer the ascriptive ties of birth which are represented as holding us back; it is coming from 'chaotic' or 'deprived' families, which just happen to also be working class. The journalist, Melanie Phillips, expresses this view:

> We are going to have two sorts of nations, one of adults from emotionally stable backgrounds who will be successful in every sphere of life – personal relationships, jobs, the lot. The other nation will be from emotionally deprived and arid backgrounds, backgrounds of instability, emotional chaos, parental strife, of moral vacuum. It frightens me.
>
> (Phillips, quoted in Coward, 1994)

As Coward comments, in reifying a notion of childhood innocence, Phillips is also inscribing 'middle class-ness' as normal, against which 'Other groups and their values come to be seen as almost sub-human'.[15] Such a configuration of class and childhood also informs recent government interventions in Britain, for example around children's education. Here, 'failure' in the education system is constituted as the result of bad or inadequate parenting. Hence, government proposals include training programmes in 'parenting skills' (Carvel, 1998). Since it is mainly middle-class children who 'succeed' in education, working-class families become constituted as the source of their children's failure.

It is not social systems of inequality which are being problematized within such interventions: rather, the focus is almost entirely on the family. For example, David Blunkett, the British Secretary of State for Education, recently announced:

> Where there is a problem [in children's education], it is all too often because parents claim not to have the time, because they have disengaged from their children's education, or because, quite simply, they lack even the basics of parenting skills. ... With such a lack of commitment, too often there is also a lack of expectation, [reinforcing] generations of disadvantage.
>
> (Blunkett, in Carvel, 1998)

The term, 'generations of disadvantage' invokes resonances of older 'cycles of deprivation' rhetoric: the 'problem' of working-class existence is explained through a generational transmission of 'faulty' parenting skills, attitudes, habits and practices. Further, poverty is not held to be 'an excuse'. According to Blunkett, 'It is the poverty of expectation and dedication which is the deciding factor' (Blunkett, in Carvel, 1998).

Interventions like this are one important way through which class is made 'real', and through which middle-class family life is validated, silently occupying the ground marked as 'normal'. Against this, those other(ed) families need to be brought up to scratch. In his comments cited above, Blunkett seems to be talking a Bourdieuean turn in his use of an economistic metaphor: it is not economic poverty which is the issue, but another kind of poverty: one which invokes the lack of cultural and symbolic capital. In his elision of lack of school achievement, parental disregard and lack of 'skills', and cycles of disadvantage, Blunkett is giving a new spin to the same old message: working-class people are getting it wrong. To get it right, they should be more like the middle classes. As Valerie Walkerdine argues:

> In a number of domains, middle classness has become synonymous with normality and working classness has been viewed as a deviant pathology, to be corrected if possible by correctional strategies that will make working-class subjects more like their middle-class counterparts.
>
> (Walkerdine, 1997: 29)

But these are just recent manifestations of a long-running mapping of 'normality' on to middle-classness (Walkerdine, 1997) which is configured through the child. As Skeggs (1997) shows, educational provision for working-class children was given initial impetus by a view of working-class people as dangerous and morally deficient; education was 'to act as a stabilizing force and to impose upon children a middle-class view of family life' (Skeggs, 1997: 43). Together with legislation designed to scrutinize mothers' child-rearing practices, it is part of a historical legacy which informs a contemporary figuring of class and conflict in terms of ignorance and (im)morality, rather than in terms of structural inequality. As Ian Roberts puts it, writing on the ways in which working-class people have been represented in community studies, 'One is tempted to throw one's hands in the air and exclaim, "Who are these people?" ... are they stupid?' (Roberts, 1999: 148).

The constitution of the 'real child' as white, male, Euroamerican, and so on, is reiterated across both 'expert' and 'lay' discourses. And it is this constitution of the child which articulates with 'equal opportunities rhetoric'. With the abolition of formal barriers to equality, this rhetoric goes, we can all achieve anything. The 'old' ascriptive ties of class, race and gender need no longer hold us back. This is a story in which anyone can be autonomous.

But in fact we find that not everyone is 'achieving' the same things. So what is going on here? If there is no room within this story for structural mechanisms of inclusion and exclusion, if it is psychological mechanisms which 'hold us back', and if families, and especially mothers are held to be able to nurture the child's 'natural' autonomy, then families, and especially mothers, must be responsible. An emphasis on individual psychology reduces social relations to familial relations. The sting in this particular tale is that social relations which militate against the 'success' or autonomy of many persons become obscured in this focus on individual psychology – a psychology of which the mother, more then any other figure, becomes the guarantor.

Good-enough mothers: dreams of social harmony ...

> Once what is 'in the best interests of the child' has been defined, what parents should be and should do is implicitly and explicitly constructed. Whatever notions of childhood predominate will thus shape the form that parenting should

take. This linkage between what we conceive to be the nature of childhood and that of parenting is based less on the natural unavoidability of parents for children's survival and well-being as on society's structures and socioeconomic requisites, which not only place children in the context of the family but 'parentalize' and, I will add, 'maternalize' them. Thus, when one sees children, one 'sees' parents. When one sees children who have problems, one looks for parents, especially mothers. When one seeks solutions to children's problems ... one immediately turns to parents who are then scrutinized by a variety of establishments.

(Ambert, 'An international perspective on parenting', p. 530; references omitted)

If mothering, in its very definition, is constituted in relation to the prior category 'child', then all normative evaluations of adequate mothering must rest on conceptualizations of what childhood is, and what children need. Further, if the articulation between the self and the social world is such that selves are held in some sense to produce the social world, then such evaluations also rest on specific views of what the social world should be like. This section will examine the relationship between the child, the self, and the social world which are configured through the concept of the 'good-enough mother'. It will show how formulations of the good-enough mother have at their heart both specific conceptualizations of the child, and specific dreams of social harmony.

The phrase, 'the good-enough mother' originated with the British psychoanalyst, Donald Winnicott,[16] who developed the concept as a means of explaining the mother's part in the development of the child's self. In contrast to Freud and Klein, Winnicott concentrated on the 'real' or 'environment' mother, rather than on the fantasized mother of the child's psychic world. In the process, the wild, unrealizable demands of both the Freudian and the Kleinian infants all but disappear, as the child is formulated in terms of a set of needs and demands which are inherently (and naturally) legitimate, which are capable of being met, and which the mother is uniquely equipped to meet.

Because of Winnicott's enormous (and enduring) influence, it is worth exploring his perspective in some detail. For Winnicott, good-enough mothering brings the child from a state of infantile chaos or 'unintegration' to the formation of a coherent ego, with a secure sense of self and other. Through three main (sequential) functions: holding, handling and object-presentation (physical management of the baby, 'holding' its emotions and introducing the world to the baby), the mother paves the way for a state in which the infant can develop a sense of self and can come to distinguish between 'me' and 'not-me'.

However, this transformation of the infantile psyche cannot occur by means of the work of mothering alone – this work must be an expression of the mother's love (Winnicott, 1964). And also, the mother must enjoy herself: 'The mother's pleasure has to be there, or the whole procedure is dead, useless and mechanical' (1964: 27). If the mother fails in any of these processes, the child will not develop its 'real self', but will, instead, construct for itself a compliant 'false self'. Children with 'false selves' are likely, argues Winnicott, to become either overly conformist or delinquent. Lacking the psychic means to properly regulate themselves, they will have to be regulated by more overt and draconian methods. Hence, the dream of social order is twinned with the spectre of social unrest as the child's (emergent) self, the mother's care and social order are linked in a triadic structure. Winnicott's ideal social world is made up of autonomous, self-regulated individuals who are constituted through good-enough mothering.

The phrase, 'good-enough mother' suggests a rather minimal level of adequacy, a standard which almost everyone could attain. Perhaps these 'feel-good' connotations have diverted attention from the exacting standards set by Winnicott himself – an absorption with the child to an extent which approaches insanity, an enabling of the child's 'domination' of the mother, and so on. Carolyn Steedman, while noting how the good-enough mother has 'come to be used as prescription', argues that, 'far from making prescription, Winnicott was in fact describing a historical reality' (Steedman, 1986: 91). In other words, Steedman suggests, the vast majority of mothers must have been good enough, since most children seem to survive reasonably well. But Winnicott himself is ambiguous here: as well as arguing (in the quotation Steedman draws on) in favour of the assumption that 'the babies of the world, past and present have been and are born into a human environment that is good enough' (Winnicott, in Steedman, 1986: 91), he also argued that many of 'those who care for children' (presumably he means mothers) are 'neurotic or near-insane' (1950a: 24). Neurosis and near-insanity are emphatically not in the psychic make-up of the good-enough mother. Winnicott's contention, however, was that these mothers cannot be taught: 'Our hope lies in those who are more or less normal' (1950a: 24). It seems, then, that Winnicott addressed the 'more or less normal' in his radio talks because this is the only group he felt he could work with. The inclusive 'you' of his broadcasts is in fact given meaning by the exclusion of mothers who are not bound up with their babies to the degree that Winnicott regards as 'natural'; the exclusion of mothers who are 'masculine', or who are 'preoccupied' with themselves. The 'good-enough' mother is consistently set in relief by her 'other', the mother who brings failure to her child's development.

The Winnicottian child and mother are bound together in a functionalist relationship in which the child needs to get what the mother needs to give. If the constitution of the mother rests on a specific constitution of the child, then, equally, the constitution of the child relies on the assumption that there is someone there who is both able and willing to meet her/his needs.

Certainly, Winnicott makes the process of being a good-enough mother, or an 'ordinary devoted mother', sound easy: 'If a child can play with a doll, you can be an ordinary devoted mother' (1964: 16). A closer examination of the good-enough mother, however, reveals that to be good enough is a considerable achievement; it reveals a woman whose whole life is bound up with the needs of her child. But for Winnicott, this is *not* an achievement, since it is 'natural'; it is wholly congruent with being a woman. There is a perfect match between what women who are good-enough mothers 'naturally' want, and what infants need.

The pleasures and desires of the Winnicottian good-enough mother coincide exactly with the needs of the infant:

> The mother's bond with the baby is very powerful at the beginning and we must do all we can to enable her to be preoccupied with her baby at this, the natural time. Now it so happens that it is not only the mother that this experience is good for; the baby undoubtedly needs exactly this kind of thing too.
>
> (1964: 26)

While eschewing the role of 'expert', Winnicott engages in the construction of those processes of self-regulation which Foucault (1980, 1983, 1992) identifies as characteristic of the contemporary world. By naming certain (highly delimited) mothering practices as 'good enough', by identifying these practices as normal, by locating good-enough mothering within the 'self' of the mother, and by suggesting forms of pleasure which inhere in these mothering practices, he generates schemata of self-management. As Doane and Hodges argue, 'while creating mothers as agents, Winnicott simultaneously creates them as objects for the regulatory discourse of experts' (1992: 21).

For Winnicott, social order is produced through good selves: the dream is one of social harmony, in which all selves realize their 'natural' potential through having received good-enough mothering. The goal here is self-regulation and autonomy – products of the realization of the 'true' self. This is the formulation which underwrites much of the take-up of the concept of the good-enough mother (or, in more recent formulations, the good-enough parent) (Adcock and White, 1990), all of which rely on a set of truths about the child and the social world. In this formulation, children are all basically the same, and good-enough mothering/parenting is therefore a universal function (or pair of functions) to meet the child's needs. If not all cultures recognize the child in the same ways, then these cultures need to be brought up to the pinnacle of knowledge reached by contemporary Euroamerican societies (Woodhead, 1990).

My point here is not to single out Winnicott's work for special criticism, but to open up a discussion of its embedded assumptions which are often missed through the implication of minimal levels of adequacy attached to the phrase 'good-enough mother/parent'. Winnicott was writing after the Second World War, in a period in which the threat of fascism was a very real memory. Against the collective or 'mob' ethic of fascism, an emphasis on autonomy, on individuality, on questioning, seems coherent (and perhaps even necessary). However, to take Winnicott's theory as timeless and universal dogma (which he himself, it has to be said, promoted) is to cast it as pure knowledge and truth, devoid of political content and divorced from political and historical preoccupations. Further, the years since Winnicott himself was writing have alerted us to the ways in which an appeal to the sovereignty of the autonomous individual can be another (though differently inflected) manifestation of the operation of power. While these issues are ignored, Winnicott's formulations can be brought into other theories without any radical questioning of their content.

... and dreams of post-patriarchy

If 'mainstream' formulations of the 'good-enough' mother have at their heart a dream of democracy, in which all citizens believe themselves to be autonomous, in which all demands on the social system are 'reasonable', feminist appropriations have a somewhat different vision. Here, the dream is one of a society in which gender inequalities are overturned. However, the underlying propositions remain the same: that mothers produce (gendered) selves; that the social world could be transformed through the transformation of these selves; and, therefore, that it is mothering which can (and should) transform the social world. Certainly, most feminist theorists have moved away from Winnicott's almost exclusive emphasis on the mother to incorporate discussion of fathers' roles in producing the selves of daughters and sons, but a radical questioning of 'childhood' itself is rarely present in such discussion, so that 'mainstream' definitions of children's selves and children's needs become incorporated, more or less wholesale, into the analysis.

Nancy Chodorow attempts to rescue Winnicott's theoretical perspective from its more conservative aspects, and to use this perspective to inscribe a central place for the mother within psychoanalytic theory. Where Winnicott was emphatic that only women could mother, Chodorow sees fathers' participation in child-care as an escape from the oppressiveness of mothering and, ultimately, from gendered social arrangements. Chodorow's major work, *The Reproduction of Mothering* (1978) has had an enormous impact on feminist theorizing.[17] The appeal of this work seems to stem from three main factors: firstly, from the fact that her theory offers a way of conceptualizing mothering, and also of women's reluctant participation in their own oppression, without invoking Freudian penis-envy and without positioning women as 'other' to the masculine norm. At the same time, Chodorow moves away from a 'socialization' theory, which would suggest that children start out as gender neutral but (are encouraged to) learn 'gender appropriate' behaviour.[18] Secondly, her analysis may be appealing because her solution (equal parenting by women and men) seems attainable (even if not everyone has seen it as desirable); and thirdly, her analysis seems convincing because of her observation that women in heterosexual relationships seem to get little gratification from men.

Because of Chodorow's wide-ranging influence, it is, again, worth examining her work in detail. Chodorow reworks the story of the girl's early psychic development and of her Oedipal drama, in her discussion of why it is that women (and not men) mother, and, more broadly, of what is at the heart of gendered social relations. In doing so, she draws on the work of non-Kleinian object-relations theory to argue that the original merger with the mother identified by Freud and Klein, as well as by Winnicott, is both blissful and terrifying. The mother seems all-powerful and the child's lack of ego-boundaries are experienced with fear. When the father enters the child's psychic world (the Oedipal crisis) he represents an escape from the mother's all-embracing power. The father, argues Chodorow, has always been perceived as a separate being, and cannot threaten a dangerous merger with the child. The daughter, then, takes the father as a love-object; but she does not entirely revoke her original attachment to her mother. Her attachment to the father is characterized by frustration, since her emotionally distant father either cannot or will not provide her with the love she wants.

According to Chodorow, mothers tend to see their sons as separate from themselves, and to unconsciously sexualize the relationship. By contrast, mothers identify with their daughters; they see them as at one with themselves and may project onto their daughters their dislike of themselves (or parts of themselves). The mother's differential reaction to male and female children sets in motion a train of events which results in their developing gendered personalities. Because women sexualize their relationships with sons, issues of attraction and jealousy become merged, in the boy's psyche, with issues of unity and symbiosis. During the boy's Oedipus complex, therefore, when he represses his erotic attachment to his mother, he also represses his desire for connection. This results in a male personality structure which prizes autonomy and individuality, desires dominance, and fears connection and unity with the 'other': 'The very fact of being mothered by a woman generates conflicts over masculinity, a psychology of male dominance, and a need to be superior to women' (Chodorow, 1978: 291).

Girls, however, do not resolve their Oedipus complex so thoroughly as boys:[19] their Oedipal love for their fathers is not as threatening as the boy's pre-Oedipal love for his mother. Girls, then, do not repress their desire for merger, connection and affection; they develop a relational sense of self. When children reach adulthood, heterosexual relations are fraught with difficulties; men want autonomy, while women want connection. Further, all people who have been mothered seek to recreate the relationship with the mother. Men can achieve this through heterosexual relations, but for women, it is only with their children that they can experience the kind of unity they experienced with their own mother, in their infancy and early childhood. This, for Chodorow, is 'the reproduction of mothering'; women mother daughters who in turn want to mother, and so on. In mothering, women are identifying both with their own mothers and with their children, especially with their daughters, whom they perceive as the same kind of being as themselves. Because they identify with their own mothers, women have a sense of responsibility which is necessary for bringing up children. They also want to either repair their relationships with their mothers, or to retaliate against their mothers. Men fear and despise women's need for connection and are therefore unable to provide what women want. On the other hand, men are everywhere overvalued, so that girls and women idealize them, forgiving them for their failure to adequately provide emotional nurturance.

As Iris Young (1983) remarks, it is not clear what explanatory status Chodorow attaches to her theory; in a sense, it only seems to explain how women and men accommodate to gendered social arrangements. However, (as

Young also notes) Chodorow suggests that women's mothering – and the types of personality structure it produces – are the basis for gender inequality generally. Chodorow argues that women's mothering is one of the key features of the sexual division of labour; consequently, it is at the heart of what she calls the 'sex-gender system'. Chodorow sees social structures as perpetuated through psychic traits, and, ultimately, therefore, through women's mothering (see also Chodorow, 1974).

Chodorow's solution to the impasse she describes is not to seek to educate mothers to do it differently; she does look beyond the individual mother to the social forces acting upon her. Her own proposal is equal parenting by women and men. If this were achieved, she argues, not only would the social world have to change (jobs would have to be restructured, child-care made accessible and affordable, for instance), but also, our psychic patterns would change:

> Children could be dependent from the outset on people of both genders and establish an individuated sense of self in relation to both. In this way, masculinity would not become tied to denial of dependence and devaluation of women. Feminine personality would be less preoccupied with individuation, and children would not develop fears of *maternal* omnipotence and expectations of *women's* unique self-sacrificing qualities. This would reduce men's need to guard their masculinity and their control of social and cultural spheres which treat and define women as secondary and powerless, and would help women to develop the autonomy which too much embeddedness in relationship has taken away from them.
>
> (Chodorow, 1978: 218; emphasis in original)

Equal parenting with men, of course, presupposes that women are able or willing to call on men to share these tasks (Bart, 1983; Sayers, 1986). Recommendations for equal parenting by men and women, in order to make children psychically healthy, might also be seen as a political non-starter for feminism at a time when lone mothers are being singled out for what looks like special demon status. However, more fundamentally, Chodorow's conception of 'parenting' relies heavily on Winnicott's notion of the 'good-enough mother': she says, 'I do not ... mean to raise questions about what constitutes "good-enough parenting" ' (1978: 16). Hence, Chodorow does not address the question of how mothering itself is constituted, nor does she question existing definitions of children's needs, except insofar as she adds a need to be parented by both women and men. As Parveen Adams (1983) argues:

> By conferring the status of unquestionable truth on some aspects of the parent's relation to the infant, [Chodorow] narrows the domain within which the social can have effects. ... She misses the point that the role of parent is itself a construction which needs to be understood in historical terms. Her rough and ready justice rules that the man should do what the woman has done hitherto and she appears to think that this principle of

equality is in itself a critical alteration of social relations. It would seem at least as important to recognise that the characteristics of present day 'mothering' are not universals, that 'mothering' is constituted through a diverse set of practices, not unified in its origins or in its effects.

(Adams, 1983: 51)

Chodorow seems to share Winnicott's view that the needs of children are unchanging and inalienable, and seeks to move the father in to provide for these needs, alongside the mother. For Winnicott, 'it so happens' that what the infant needs to have, the mother wants to give. The concept of children's needs relies on the understanding that there is (or should be) a mother who can meet them. In Chodorow's version, the needs fundamentally stay the same, but it happens that what the infant needs to have, mothers and fathers should be giving. While she acknowledges that infantile desire is incapable of complete satisfaction, and argues, in an article written with Susan Contratto (Chodorow and Contratto, 1982) that 'needs' are not the same as 'wants', there remains a basic bedrock of 'needs'. This is problematic not only because the 'needs' of children are necessarily constructed within particular historic and social circumstances (Walkerdine and Lucey, 1989; Woodhead, 1990): it is also problematic because children's socially constructed needs and the expectations of women's mothering cannot be separated in the manner Chodorow suggests (cf. Urwin, 1985).

This kind of approach to children's needs is also found in work which does not directly follow Chodorow's, but uses similar Winnicottian formulations. For example, Eichenbaum and Orbach argue that the mother, recognizing that her own needs for nurturance are unmet, unconsciously transmits to the daughter a sense that her needs, too, will not be met; that she must not expect to be looked after. She transmits this message to her daughter along with injunctions about gender-appropriate behaviour:

> Unconsciously, mother gives the message to the daughter: 'Don't be emotionally dependent; don't expect the emotional care and attention you want; learn to stand on your own two feet emotionally. Don't expect too much independence; don't expect too much from a man; don't be too wild; don't expect a life too different from mine; learn to accommodate'.
>
> (Eichenbaum and Orbach, 1982: 33)

Since, according to Eichenbaum and Orbach, adequate nurturing in infancy is the basis on which children are able to achieve a sense of themselves as separate from their mothers, daughters seem doomed to go through adult life without a clear sense of 'self', and repeating in relations with adult women, with adult men, and with their own daughters, the conflicts and ambivalences of their infantile relationships with their mothers. These perspectives suggest that there is a more or less fixed set of childhood 'needs'; that these needs are capable of being met; that mothers fail to meet daughters' needs; that if only daughters were better mothered, gender inequality would disappear. Although there is an emphasis here on 'relationality', it is autonomy which is the final goal (Rose, 1991). And this is an autonomy which is especially difficult to achieve, because of the ways in which women mother daughters.

Although Orbach (1997) holds that a stable gender identity is necessary for psychic health, she also argues that gender as currently played out is something 'given' by the mother. She says, 'Your daughter was given a gender. *All of your unconscious went into it*' (Orbach, with Hollway, 1997: 103; emphasis mine). The emphasis on gendered personality structures within accounts like this reduces gender and gender inequality to personality. As Lynne Segal comments of this work, 'Somehow the fact that we grow up in societies where women are under-paid, men are in control of technology, and so on, slips from focus, as a secondary phenomenon' (Segal, 1987: 144–5).

Above all, formulations such as this position mothers, not so much as the guardians and the guarantors of liberal democracy (as in 'mainstream' formulations) as the guardians and guarantors of gender equality. A picture of the feminist 'good-enough mother' emerges, whose mothering is supposed to transform the social world. Since mothers *produce* the gendered self, this argument goes, they can also *undo* the gendering of selves. But this assumes that the shaping of the self is indeed within the mother's gift. It reduces gender inequality to individual, psychic traits, which are engendered by the mother, reinscribing the mother as the producer, not only of the daughter's self, but ultimately of the social world also; and it fails to problematize categories of 'self', 'child' and 'mother'. Further, although feminist prescriptions for good mother-hood undoubtedly have different goals in mind to those of 'mainstream' prescriptions, they are largely built on the same white, middle-class model of both mother and child. It is difficult to avoid the conclusion that, with few exceptions, the 'good mother' of most feminist theorizing is simply a more politicized version of the 'good mother' of conventional analyses.

The next chapter turns to the empirical study to consider precisely this issue of the self, and examines the ways in which the women represented the self in relation to the kin network, the social world, and, indeed, to itself.

3   (Re)producing the self

What are we today?

(Michel Foucault, 'The political technology of individuals', p. 145)

As the last chapter showed, issues of selfhood and subjectivity remain fundamental to Euroamerican understandings of the mother–daughter relationship. The mother is positioned as the guarantor of the self of the daughter (and of the son), and, through this positioning, she becomes the guarantor of a desired social order (Walkerdine and Lucey, 1989). The task of the 'good-enough mother' is to facilitate the self of the child who will become the 'good-enough citizen'. The thrust of post-war psy discourses has been to define the self as something produced through the mother's mothering, and social order as the amalgam of 'well-adjusted' selves.

To achieve this, the mother's own self must be adequate to the task: and so the production of 'good-enough selves' can be traced back generation after generation, as, indeed, can their obverse, the inadequate selves which produce inadequate children in psychological 'cycles of deprivation' theories[1]. This takes on a specific significance between mother and daughter. Insofar as gender is considered within psy discourses (usually within feminist or quasi-feminist appropriations), the daughter's gender is considered as something produced (consciously or unconsciously) by the mother, and femininity as a damaging combination of characteristics which overlies the daughter's 'true self'.[2]

This chapter will discuss some of the complexities of contemporary Euroamerican understandings of selves, particularly as they are mediated through the mother and her mothering. It will do this primarily though looking at the ways in which the women in the study conceptualized the self. Their representations of the self within the interviews highlight some of the difficulties, dilemmas and double jeopardies faced by mothers in different conceptualizations of the self; they also highlight the ways in which contradictions between different models of the self may be contained within the figure of the mother.

Normal selves

The Cartesian self prominent in Euroamerican philosophy and culture is a rational, bounded, autonomous and unique individual (Pateman, 1988; Walkerdine, 1985b; Rose, 1991, 1992a; Strathern 1992a and b). Free from the impositions of others, this individual is both self-contained and in possession of the 'self'. As Donna Haraway argues:

> The proper state for a Western person is to have ownership of the self, to have and hold a core identity as if it were a possession. That possession may be made from various raw materials over time, or one may be born with it. … Not to have property in the self is not to be a subject, and so not to have agency.
>
> (Haraway, 1987: 135)

As several commentators have noted, this model of the self, so apparently universal, developed on the basis of a (male-) gendered subject, and hence on the exclusion of women (Riley, 1983; Pateman, 1988). Nevertheless, this model of the self functions as what Haraway terms a 'regulatory fiction' (Haraway, 1987; cf. Butler, 1993). That is, it regulates lives through the production of schemata of understanding through which the self relates to itself, producing narratives of the self which are congruent with its terms. In this way, selves (or aspects of selves) become normalized/abnormalized through comparison with the production of this bounded, rational and autonomous self.

However, as Moore points out, this conceptualization of the self, though enshrined in Euroamerican law, philosophy and politics, cannot contain the multivalent ways in which selves are understood and lived out. Although theories of the self inform the kinds of narrative of the self through which the self is produced as coherent and stable, and through which the self acts on itself, there is something which escapes this coherence and stability. Moore comments:

> [P]eople have local views of the person, of the sort of people women and men are meant to be, of the nature of the biological make-up of the physical being, of the relations between the human and non-human worlds and many other local theories, and are able to use these ideas to reflect on the nature of their experience and on the kind of person/self they believe themselves to be.
>
> (Moore, 1994: 48)

Disparate and contradictory models of the self can be seen as providing a space for negotiation and refusal of the 'regulatory fiction' of the Cartesian self: in the space between different self-understandings lies the potential for critique and resistance. But the extent to which this happens is an empirical question. The rest of this chapter will explore the women's use of 'local views of the person', and the extent to which they instantiate or loosen mothers' responsibility for 'mothering the self' of the daughter.

The women in this study, probably like most Euroamericans, incorporate various forms of understanding of the self into an overall schema of self-understanding. They produce narratives of lives which are formed through the various discursive raw materials they have to hand. There are three principal models of the self which emerge from their accounts; namely, the self as inherited; the self as socially produced; and the self as unique, intrinsic and autonomous.[3]

The rest of the chapter will consider the models of selfhood and subjectivity used by the women to represent the selves of mother and daughter: it will consider the implications of these models for conceptualizations of motherhood, daughterhood and womanhood; and it will highlight the significance of the figure of the mother in contradictions between, and contestations around, different models of the self.

'Bits of her that are bits of me': the inherited self

> The reproductive model plays off heredity and development through a contrast between the relationships implied in parenting and ancestry and the individuality that must be claimed by and for the child as the outcome of these relationships.
>
> (Strathern, *Reproducing the Future*, p. 165)

In Euroamerican understandings of kinship, familial relations – the relations of persons 'connected by blood or by marriage' – form an important system for classifying the relationship between the self and others (Schneider, 1968: 21; Finch, 1989). Relations of 'blood' are seen as especially significant. As David Schneider suggests, these relationships are deemed 'real' or 'true', and, unlike legal ties, cannot be dissolved. The 'blood relationship', he argues, 'is culturally defined as being an objective fact of nature, of fundamental significance and capable of having profound effects, and its nature cannot be terminated or changed' (1968: 24).

No doubt there are changes here: in increasingly litigious societies, law stands as that which can (potentially) break the ties of 'blood', as in cases of children 'divorcing' their parents (Reed, 1993; Strathern, 1996a), and in respect of the new reproductive technologies discussed by Strathern (1992b) and Stanworth (1987). Yet 'blood' ties remain significant, and may indeed be gaining in significance, as they are reworked in terms of 'genetics'. With an increasing emphasis, in academic and popular discussion, on genetic determinism, the inheritance of some substance from forebears informs people's sense of self (and of other selves) in new, and perhaps unexpected, ways.[4]

Certainly, for the women in this study, the 'passing down' of inherited material was, to at least some degree, held to be constitutive of the self. That is, their own and their daughters' selfhood was explained, at least in part, through reference to kin relations of descent. My questions, 'Who do you take after?' and, 'Who does your daughter take after?' were meaningful to all of the women precisely because both they and I inhabit a social world in which the self can be explained in terms of inherited characteristics. Hence, all of the women explained some characteristics of the self in terms of some substance[5] which is 'passed down' the generations from mothers and fathers to their children. This substance, which some, though not all, of the women specified as genetic material, manifests itself in the person's appearance, in their talents, and in their character traits and temperaments – in 'bits' of the self. As Anna says:

> Sometimes I see bits of her [daughter] that are bits of me that I don't particularly like, but then you're bound to do that with your children. And when you see bits that are you that you do quite like, it's nice, so it balances out.

The process by which this substance is transmitted was not, however, straightforward; it was always considered to be passed *down*, through time, but parents were not seen as simply reproducing themselves in their children. Rather, the combination of inherited material from parents and (to a lesser degree) grandparents produced a combination of characteristics in the child that were unique to that child (cf. Strathern, 1992b). Nevertheless, these features or characteristics could be identified within the self of the person, and might be identified as parts of the self or selves of other persons. All of the women identified characteristics which had 'passed down' from their mothers to themselves, and/or from themselves to their daughters.[6] For many, this inherited substance could be traced back through more than one generation, passing from their own precursors, through them, to their children:

S.L.: Who does your daughter take after?

KATE: I think she's very like me. Everyone says she looks like me, and, erm, she behaves like me I think. She's got some of her father's gifts. He's very gifted with languages and … he's intelligent. … She's acquired those two characteristics. … And I think in some ways she's like my mother. She's got the same determination.

FRANCES: The Chloe [daughter] that's got this job, got herself out of a lousy relationship and got onto a new footing, found herself somewhere else to live, refuses help … that is me, absolutely, and I'm loving it. Mind you, this fighting spirit that bashes on, that's my mother.

Through the notion of an inherited self, the women conceptualized themselves and their daughters as firmly tied within the kin system. The existence of this inherited material within the self suggests a fixity to that self through a tie with the past which *seems* unalterable. In many ways, this is the antithesis of the contemporary 'ideal type' – the individual who is 'free' to 'choose' (Rose, 1991, 1992b; Strathern, 1992a and b). The links with other kin undermine the status of the 'individual', enclosed and bounded self, while the ties to the past constrain the person through self-characteristics which are inborn, rather than made. However, an important feature of this understanding of the inherited self is that of *recognition*. That is, certain characteristics must be recognized as being shared with forebears to enable the self to be understood in this way. Hence, the apparent fixity of the self can be subverted by the element of choice involved in recognizing/not recognizing inherited characteristics within the self.

Despite the apparent fixity of the inherited self, the fact that material is seen to be inherited from a *range* of forebears, and the perceived *randomness* of the inheritance of this material mean that the conclusion cannot be wholly antici-pated. There is a range of ancestors against which selfhood can be appraised[7] and, to an extent, therefore, the recognition of shared characteristics can be chosen. Hence some activity – some consideration both of other kin and of the self – is required in order to fit the self into this system of inheritance. This recognition of the self as part of the kin system was important within all of the women's accounts, and leads to a situation in which certain characteristics can be valued, and 'chosen', or they can be feared, and avoided:

LYNNE: I'm actually quite proud of my maternal grandmother as a relative and I like to think that I take after her.

ELIZABETH: There must be something wrong with the female side [of the family] – I'll have to be careful [laughs]. ... My grandmother and one of my mother's sisters are similar in the sense of being self-centred and being hypochondriacs. ... I tell my mother not to become like that as well. So I'm conscious that it could come to me as well [laughs].

Recognition, then, stands between absolute fixity and absolute choice: it medi-ates the apparent fixity of kin relations on the one hand, and the possibility of 'choice' on the other. Marilyn Strathern points to the wider significance of these processes in Euroamerican understandings of kinship, and of the place of the self within the kin system:

> The child's physical origins lie in the bodies of others, a link as indissoluble as its own genetic formation is normally deemed irreversible. Yet parents only reproduce parts of themselves. Like the fortune one may or may not be born into, the conjunction of genetic traits is assumed to be fortuitous. While the child claims its origins in its parents' make-up, it itself evinces a unique combination of characteristics, and the combination is a matter of chance. This lays the basis of its individuality. Individuality is expected to assist the child to develop that independence which is one manifestation of it (hence the lesser expectation of duty). At the same time, 'individuals' must also be seen as making themselves. Although the basis for the link between parent and child lies in the child's past, what that link means in the future is contingent on how the individual person acts. The nature of interaction, the degree of obligation felt ... all depend on what the child will *make* of its past.
> (Strathern, 1992b: 166; references omitted; emphasis in original)

Paradoxically, it is the tie to the kin system which produces individuality and uniqueness; but uniqueness also has to be *made*, through being acted upon. As

Strathern points out, these understandings of what I have called the 'inherited self' evoke both continuity and change: continuity derives from the 'passing on' of heredity, from the 'taking after' one's forebears; change derives from the perceptions of randomness in the transmission of heredity. But, more importantly for my argument here, both continuity and change are found in what persons 'make of [their] past'. In constructing the narrative of a life, Euroamericans draw on characteristics seen in their forebears, but are able to put these characteristics together in ways which speak both their uniqueness and their likeness with kin members. The assemblage of these characteristics hinges on recognition.

But the system of inheritance may constantly threaten to draw kin members back in to a recognition which may be unwelcome, undermining 'freedom of choice'. This takes on a specific significance for daughters. The fear of becoming one's own mother, which Adrienne Rich (1977), following Lynne Sukenick (1974) has termed 'matrophobia', and which is widely represented in popular culture, may spring from a recognition of (parts of) the mother in the self.[8] For most of these women, the dual processes of ageing and of becoming a mother oneself heightened a 'recognition' of the mother 'in' the self – even of the mother's self overwhelming one's own: as, for example, in the following two extracts, both of which are taken from the group discussion:

CAROLINE: I think as I get older, I do more and more things like her. Which I might not want to do.

HAZEL: I think an awful lot of that's just genetic, though, isn't it? I mean we are half of –

CAROLINE: No, I don't agree with that.

HAZEL: Oh I do, I do. ...... Don't you think there are inherited traits, then, that we get from our mothers or our fathers? I mean I hear my mother's voice sometimes. It's not particularly what she would say, but I think, gosh, that's really like my mum – the tone of voice is. And observing as well.

CAROLINE: Yes. I can even sometimes feel my face looking like – although I don't look anything like my mother – I can feel an expression that's like hers.

HAZEL: D' you think it's acquired rather than –

CAROLINE: I think so.

S.L.: D'you ever feel that thing, 'Oh, I sound like my mother?'

LYNNE: Yeah, but it's something not to do [laughs]. I mean I do it with the children. You know, you come up with the sayings that – and it trips off your tongue. And you think, 'Oh no, I must stop saying that', because they're controlling sayings which you use when, you know, the children are getting too much for you. ... And it's at that point I think, 'You've not thought this through and you're just reacting'. And I sort of pedal back.

HAZEL: You know that it's your mother's tape and not yours.

LYNNE: That's right, yeah.

(GD)

Hazel characterizes the passing on of characteristics as genetic, while, for Caroline it is an acquired, social inheritance. But in either case, the self of the mother threatens to intrude upon that of the daughter. Even when this maternal influence is characterized as social, rather than genetic, it may still be marked on the body, forcing a recognition of the reproduction of (parts of) the mother in (parts of) the self. This reproduction can threaten the daughter's uniqueness. For Lynne, speaking in ways which remind her of her mother belongs to a kind of 'default' position which comes into play through an absence of 'thinking', of rationality. Her uniqueness (figured here through a distance from her mother) must be *produced*: otherwise, characteristics of her mother will simply be *reproduced* in her self.

The dual processes of ageing and becoming a mother oneself involve bearing more apparent similarities to one's own mother as one is growing up. An identification with the daughter may force an identification with the mother. Once again, however, the work of recognition mediates the apparent fixity of the system of inheritance. It is through *recognizing* characteristics which are shared with the mother that these women were able to check those characteristics within themselves – to 'pedal back', and thus to resist the drawing-in of the kin system.

To see parts of the mother reproduced in the self can be difficult for women, since this reproduction suggests an inheritance which bypasses consciousness. Hence, it suggests a potential lack of recognition and so distances the possibility of choice. There is always the danger that the daughter might fail to see 'bits of' the mother reproduced in the self, or that she might not be *able* to change, to 'pedal back'.

However, to see parts of the self reproduced in the daughter can be even more difficult, especially if the recognized characteristics are perceived negatively, since this recognition also suggests an element of maternal culpability. Again, the recognition of these features seems to signify the fixity of the system of inheritance, apparently prioritizing what the mother *is* over what she *does*:

BARBARA: It's always so frustrating, isn't it, when you're a mum? You can see this trait, you know you have it in yourself, you can't stop it, but you somehow wish that you could do something to stop it in your child. ... It's one of the humiliating things about being a mother, I think.

S.L.: Humiliating? That's very strong.

BARBARA: Well you see these traits, these bad faults, and you know there's nothing you can do to control them. I mean there's other things you can do to try and improve your daughter's ... personality. You want to make your child as perfect as possible, don't you? – to try to be as happy as possible, and just to be rounded and perfect and so on. And when you see these traits come out willy-nilly, it is terribly frustrating [laughs] and you think, 'Oh golly, she's got that from me'. And there's nothing you can do about it. Like her lack of self-confidence. Again, there's nothing you can do, and you can talk till you're blue in the face, and you can see it looking from the outside, but of course you know that when you're in that situation you're exactly the same, or perhaps ten times worse. Yes, it really is terribly frustrating [laughs].

Barbara's expression of a lack of confidence passed on 'willy-nilly' from herself to her daughter was typical of the women's accounts: self-confidence was a trait which most women saw as lacking in both themselves and their daughters.[9] This lack of confidence was often seen as characteristically 'feminine': 'like a lot of women'. This is one way in which gender assumed a significance in understandings of inheritance. The women did not see inherited substance as being passed more from mothers than from fathers, but traits which were perceived as 'negative' were more often understood as passing from the mother to the self, or from the self to the daughter.[10]

Femininity can be seen, in this context, as being a 'bit' of the self; a manifestation of certain, usually negative, behaviours and characteristics, rather than something which pervades the whole of the self. In this sense, the women's characterizations of femininity here do not entirely support Moore's argument that, in popular understandings, 'gender identity is manifestly the essence at the core of personal identity' (Moore, 1994: 37). It is certainly the case that all of the women spoke at times as if gender were indeed an essence, but most *also* saw it as something non-essential – crystallized in 'roles' or (as here) in personal characteristics which do not necessarily pervade the whole of the self.

When women deplored these 'feminine' character traits (such as lack of self-confidence, or lack of 'drive'), this was because these traits worked to impede the daughter's full potential. As in some feminist narratives of the mother–daughter relationship, femininity, in many of these women's accounts, can be conceptualized as a (usually dangerous) combination of characteristics which pass from mother to daughter. Since femininity was seen by some women as being passed down in this way, mothers would seem to have to bear some responsibility for the daughter's failure to achieve what she otherwise might. Perhaps this is why Barbara finds this process 'humiliating'.

Through the system of inheritance, the mother can become positioned as producing a particular type of (feminine) self within the daughter, not through what she *does*, but through what she *is*: as Barbara says, 'there's nothing you can do'. In this way, she may be positioned as responsible, not only for her daughter's femininity, but for the results of that femininity – for the lack of confidence or 'drive' which impedes the daughter's progress.

The social self: the relationship with the mother

The women did not consider the self to be *reducible* to a combination of inherited characteristics. They also characterized it as being produced within familial and extra-familial *social* settings. The family, however, and, in particular, the relationship with the mother, was seen as a primary and highly significant setting within which the self is shaped.

The narrativization of the self produced within the realm of psychotherapeutics gives substance to an understanding of the self as constituted in early mother–child (and, to a lesser extent, father–child) interaction. All of the women I spoke to explicitly drew, to some extent, on this narrative: adulthood was seen overwhelmingly as an effect of childhood, and adult emotional states were seen to have their roots in childhood. Hence an understanding of familial interaction in childhood was held to be crucial to an understanding of the adult psyche. However, and as later chapters will show, it is important to note that different women made different investments in this kind of discourse. Those women who had been trained in the 'caring professions', and especially those who had also had some contact with psychotherapeutics, were those whose accounts were most marked by this schema of self- (and other-) understanding. These women had the highest levels of direct access to these knowledges, which then formed an important part of their cultural capital (Bourdieu, 1984).

However, this narrativization of self, in which adult states have their aetiology in the 'deep self' formed in childhood is a compelling one, and not only for those who have been trained in professions which draw on it. Its frequent repetition across a range of sites – not only the formal arenas of psy such as the thera-peutic encounter, but also in women's magazines, TV and radio programmes, child-care advice, and so on (Rose, 1991) is one guarantee of its status as a 'truth'. It is a discourse which may indeed feel empowering for the daughter, who may be able to establish a coherent narrative of a life by reference to her relationship with the mother, and in the process, establish a counter-narrative in which she is able to resist her mother's influence, as both Lynne and Kate do in the following extracts:

LYNNE: My mother established this idea that she ...... established who I was – my iden-tity or my behaviour or my thinking, and I had to internalize that, I had to be that. Er, ... that when it came to interacting with other people, I shift – I use that as a way of interacting with other people ... so that anybody had the right to ...... establish my identity and I lived within their opinion of me, I mean that has been the cause of so many problems in my life, and I think that is basically why both my marriages failed – or why I chose those men – because they established an identity for me, into which I fitted myself. And then eventually I resented ...... them doing that, and the fact that I didn't fit that identity.

Lynne's expression of her mother's forceful self is linked with an expression of her own self as almost entirely shaped by her mother's will, a shaping which Lynne represents as having structured her adult life. Similarly, in the following extract, Kate has been talking about her sense of her mother's 'detachment' during Kate's childhood, and her feeling that her mother had rejected her:

KATE: I think I would have had more, erm, self-confidence and belief in myself if I had felt more, erm, valued by her.
S.L.: Do you think that's put you at a disadvantage?
KATE: It's put me at a disadvantage to the extent, erm, that I expect, probably more than most people, to be rejected, and find it very hard to cope with. ... I mean it doesn't bother me any more, but there was a long time when I felt I had all sorts of prob-lems, and I didn't know why they were. I just assumed that they were my problems.

And then at some stage it occurred to me that this was probably the root of it – I was feeling rejected because I looked for rejection – and I came to realize what this was about.

By linking their own adult problems with their mothers' behaviour during their childhoods, both Lynne and Kate are able to resolve the 'why' of their problems: in other words, they feel themselves better able to understand themselves through understanding their childhood relationships with their mothers. But neither Kate nor Lynne presents her mother's mothering as entirely *determining* of her adult self; Kate considers that she has largely overcome the problem of feeling rejected: Lynne expresses a self which exceeds the identity imposed by others; she does not fit the identity assigned to her. Indeed, and despite the tremendous power often attributed to mothers to shape the daughter's self, it was extremely rare for any woman to present herself as determined by her mother's mothering. Rather, a recognition, an understanding, of the ways in which the mother's mothering shapes the self was the means by which women considered themselves able to 'escape' the patterns apparently set up in childhood.

This is in stark contrast to the women's representations of their own mothers, who, most frequently, were presented as determined by *their* mothers' mothering. The following extract from Hazel's account is one example of this:

HAZEL: I think she [mother] couldn't – possibly because she didn't know what [uncon-ditional love] was herself, she'd never experienced being loved in that way, so she couldn't relate to me that way either.

S.L.: But you [said you] haven't experienced unconditional love from your mother, but you can do it for your children.

HAZEL: But that's been something – I think – I mean a lot of it over the last few years has been conscious. ... I don't think it's possible to love anybody else until you love yourself. Till you really love yourself. And I've never understood what that meant before, because I've never had that model to show me that. My mother didn't love herself, and she didn't love me ...... in the way that I wanted to be loved. ... And I've had to, erm, learn how to love really, I think.

Here, as elsewhere in many of the women's accounts, the mother's story is narrated as one in which the mother herself is largely constituted through the (lack of) maternal care given by *her* mother; but the women's own stories are narrated as ones in which the mother's mothering is an obstacle that can be overcome. Hazel uses the 'therapeutic' understanding of the adult self as consti-tuted in early childhood both to position her mother as a subject constituted through familial interaction, and to position herself as a subject who has moved from a similar place of determination to a place in which she has 'escaped' the psychic patterns which she sees as having been formed through her relationship with her mother. This 'escape' is only achieved through a compensatory self-love and through an *understanding* of the self as produced through childhood experiences. Only through a conscious understanding of these (presumably unconscious) processes can change be effected. Hence it is Hazel's access to this conscious understanding, and her mother's lack of access to it, which marks out the difference between herself and her mother here.

However empowering this schema of understanding may feel, it implicates the daughter within relations of knowledge in which her self is subject to her own therapeutically informed gaze, in which she must constantly scrutinize her self. Moreover, it effectively silences the mother, who can be positioned as wholly responsible for problems in the daughter's life within a narrative which privileges the daughter's perspective. It unifies the mother and occludes the complexities of her own subjectivity. Further, if daughters become mothers themselves, it provides a framework with which they must scrutinize themselves in relation to their own daughters, who are potentially the 'damaged selves' addressed by these discourses (Simonds, 1992, 1996).

The social self: the world outside

The relationship with the mother, though extremely significant, was not, however, considered to be the only social arena important in the shaping of the self. When they spoke as daughters, most women spoke of the extra-familial setting as an arena in which they were able to undo their mothers' influence. Hence friends, lovers, husbands, or the women's own children[11] were able to transmit some of the lessons which they felt they might have received from their mothers. Most often, however, this extra-familial setting was used by the women specifically to mark out the limits of their own ability to produce the selves of their children, or to indicate an arena in which maternal shortcomings might be overcome. Lynne, for example, looks forward to compensatory 'mothering' in her children's lives:

LYNNE: I just have to hope that they have nice, er, early sexual partners who are going to redress that [i.e. her own inadequacies as a mother] [laughs].

S.L.: And do you think they can?

LYNNE: Well, yes, because I think that relationships are about mutual mothering and mutual fathering. And that – that if their partners are going to ...... provide that kind of relationship with them, then they are given the kind of mothering they need better than I'm able to.

Janet, in some ways, goes further in resisting the kinds of post-hoc judgements of mothers that are commonplace. Janet's youngest daughter frequently truanted from school and ran away from home. This behaviour could very easily be made coherent through a positioning of Janet herself, or at least of the familial setting, as responsible for the behaviour: indeed, such a reading of childhood and adolescent 'deviance' has become almost inevitable for Euroamericans. But Janet has alternative definitions of the behaviour. These definitions are, in part, rooted in an understanding of 'bad' behaviour as rooted in the child's familial setting, but they also encompass a refusal of such an understanding through a critique of the broader conditions of adolescent life, and through the developmental model of childhood, in which adolescence is a problem time:

JANET: Clare got expelled from school. Just ...... you know, normal teenage problems. ... She was found in London when she was thirteen. Euston Station She was so unhappy she kept doing mad things all the time. She hated school. Absolutely hated it. A lot of kids do, don't they? It was a lot of competition and she just hated it. Couldn't handle it. I mean school is very competitive, isn't it? So that caused a lot of problems ...... 'cause I wanted her to go to school, of course, and, you know, she was just playing truant all the time. And I'd get in trouble with the school.

Janet presumably knows, through her contact with the school, and through her being 'in trouble' there, that she can easily be positioned as responsible for her daughter's behaviour.[12] Yet Janet seems to be having none of this. Although her questions ('A lot of kids do, don't they?'; 'School is very competitive isn't it?') seem to indicate a lack of complete confidence in her position, she is nevertheless able to refuse a position of blame and responsibility which might attach to her. She does this through the use of alternative understandings of the social world, and of the development of children. Janet's implicit critique of the education system normalizes Clare's behaviour. There is a social world outside of the mother's mothering, and outside of the home, which can be both cause and remedy for problems in the daughter's life. There are also stages through which children pass which means their behaviour may be problematic. Thus, although the model of the 'developing child' functions as a form of regulation for mothers, it can also be used to ameliorate the terms of this regulation. That is, it can be used to loosen maternal responsibilities.

All of the women acknowledged the existence of 'other factors' which might determine the child's self, and the outcome of her/his life, but this did not mean that they necessarily saw their obligations to mother 'properly' as in any way diminished by these other factors. The following two extracts from Rachel's account sum up the very contradictory position in which mothers seem inevitably to find themselves. Rachel made heavy investments in 'expert' discourses of good mothering, and indeed her whole life was narrated in terms of what her children wanted from her. Yet her account here only sums up what most of the women expressed, in one form or another:

RACHEL: When Martin [her son] was a baby, I remember going out ... to dinner. ... And as we drove up ... to where they lived ... I saw this teenager sitting there, injecting himself. ... I just looked at him and it looked so dreadful – his face, you know – lost. And when we got there, I said, 'I just saw this kid mainlining in Piccadilly'. And the woman said, 'Ah well, you don't need to worry; your kids'll be all right, because if you bring them up ...... with lots of love and care and things, they won't do that'. And her husband said, 'Nonsense'. He said, 'It's just luck'. And I think it might be. I mean there are just too many factors, aren't there?

This story – a teenager injecting heroin in a London street – is framed and contextualized by another story – the story of how children develop and of the role of mothering within this development. The young man in Rachel's story seems to embody fears about the success or failure of motherhood; the subtext is the question, 'Will my children become like that?' Rachel presents two perspectives on this question: that mothering can determine the self of the child, and that it cannot – that there are 'too many [other] factors'. Although she apparently resolves the question in favour of the second answer, she is unable to sustain this position and, like the other women in the study, acts as if mothering were in fact decisive. It is in this 'as if' that maternal responsibility and potential culpability are reinstated:

S.L.: Is there anything that would make you feel you'd failed [in terms of mothering]?
RACHEL: If they completely dropped out of …… school and that kind of life, I think I would feel I'd failed. Because although I think it doesn't matter, you know, what you do, I think it does in the end.

Rachel expresses here what was a common theme in most of the women's accounts: a marking out of the boundaries of their own maternal influence coexists with an assumption of almost total responsibility and culpability. The existence of other factors in the shaping of the child's self, then, can offer little comfort to women actually engaged in the task of mothering. Although mothers may *analytically* define mothering as not decisive, it is impossible to actually *do* mothering as if it did not matter.

Since only a post-hoc judgement can be made, when the child has turned out 'good or bad', 'right or wrong', and since there is no way of quantifying, or even of knowing, which factors will be decisive, these women, as mothers, *must* act as if their mothering is crucial. Further, if there is any blame to be meted out, mothers can hardly fail to know that they will be scrutinized (Caplan and Hall-McCorquodale, 1985; Bradley, 1989). Theories of child development work on the assumption that individual or social deviance is rooted in parent–child interaction. Mothers are interpellated within these discourses through government scrutiny of their early mothering in child health clinics, in relations with the school, and so on. These discourses are also a feature of representations of motherhood, for example in child-care advice (Urwin, 1985; Marshall, 1991), in film (Kaplan, 1992; Walters, 1992) and in the mass media.[13] In this way, mothers become subject to these knowledges and must learn to regulate their behaviour in accordance with them. If they fail in this, more coercive measures can be used, the removal of the child being the ultimate sanction (Phoenix and Woollett, 1991).

As with the 'inherited self', then, the 'social self' can be seen as the responsibility of the mother – in this case, less through what she *is* than through what she *does*.[14] Although daughters can overcome 'inadequate' mothering, this is something which both takes effort on their part and involves an understanding that the mother *is* (at least partly) responsible for the way the daughter has 'turned out'.

The intrinsic self

> [I felt] that I needed this distance from them [mother and aunts] in order to become what I then called my 'self'.
>   'Become your SELF?' my mother would shout over the telephone. 'Why should you need to become what you already are?'
>
>   (Kim Chernin, *In My Mother's House*, p. 111)

The third 'model' of the self which I want to consider here is one in which the self is bounded, unique and idiosyncratic; it belongs to the person and to no-one else:

RACHEL: I think you are who you are because of ...... you're born the way you are.

DAWN: You have to have enough faith in them [children] as individuals who've arrived already with some packages of strength and their own positive contributions. ... I remind myself that they are special and complete in themselves, really.

As Marilyn Strathern (1992a and b) argues, the perceived uniqueness of the self is an effect of the random distribution of genetic material: 'A unique combination of characteristics' (1992b: 166). This genetic uniqueness extends beyond the child's bodily or physical characteristics to embrace psychological and emotional uniqueness. The uniqueness conferred by nature is augmented by the uniqueness conferred by 'environmental' factors, including the mother's own response to the child, the world which s/he inhabits, and so on, to produce an idiosyncratic self, a unique combination of nature and culture.

But, in one sense, this 'idiosyncratic' self escapes from the circuits of both the biological/genetic and the social. While it may be an effect of inheritance, the uniqueness of the self means that it becomes dislocated from the kin system. And while the social world may impact on it and shape it, this world does not *create* the self. Rather, as in these women's accounts, it is a core identity which is unique and intrinsic to the self, itself.[15]

In some ways, the existence of this model of self and subjectivity can loosen some of the obligations of mothers to produce the self of the daughter. If the social world outside the family and the influence of other kin members can mark out the limitations of the mother's mothering, so too can the intrinsic self. The 'personality' or 'character' of the child can stand for what is unalterable – outside of the social world into which the mother inculcates the child. In this way, and like a recognition of the wider social world, it can subvert the over-determination of women's mothering in producing the daughter's self. For example:

BARBARA: I don't think you can change a person's character. I think you can give them – you can help to guide them in certain directions. ... Your influence tends to get diluted quite quickly, I think.

SL: So what do you think of these theories that tend to put everything down to mothering?

BARBARA: Well obviously I can't agree with it, can I?

PAULINE: All children are different, of course, I realized the second time. 'Cause the second one was so completely different. So I realized that it wasn't really anything to do with me – well, largely nothing to do with me. It was partly the personality of the child ... just the nature of the child, really.

ELIZABETH: When I've thought about it, I've realized that you can't make a person what they're not. And whatever you do – I really wonder, actually, how much we [mothers] can influence, to be perfectly honest, at times. 'Cause I feel that both my children have been treated the same, they've certainly had the same opportunities, and they've turned out quite different really. So what does that prove? [laughs].

However, the subversion is double-edged. The focus on the daughter's 'nature' and/or the influence of the social world outside the home can mean that mothers can take no credit for a 'good' outcome in their daughters' development. Like Rachel, Barbara uses the concept of 'luck' to mark out the limits of her own control:

BARBARA: I'm not putting anything on, saying, 'Oh well, this is the way I've brought my daughter up, she's all this because it's down to me', because if she had a different character, nature, she might have said, 'No, I don't want to do that. That's not me and that's it.' So I'm just very lucky. It's worked out well for me.

If mothers cannot be credited for what goes right, we might conclude that at least they cannot be blamed for what goes wrong. However (and as earlier extracts also suggest), 'rightness' and 'wrongness' of the outcome do not function equivalently. Few of these women felt that they had failed as mothers in any significant sense, so in that sense, the extract below from Pauline's account is not typical. It is interesting, though, that Pauline, despite emphasizing the 'nature of the child' also attributes some of her daughters' characteristics to her own perceived failure as a mother when her marriage was going through difficulties. For example, she feels that these marital difficulties contributed to what she see as her daughter's fear of commitment, as well as contributing to other difficulties:

PAULINE: I mean it got put right, but you can't eradicate it 'cause it was there. Erm, and I wasn't a very good mother at the time 'cause I was very involved with my own problems, at a time when they both needed somebody stable to be there. And, er [sighs] my younger daughter did badly in her A Levels, I think because of it.

Further, when I asked the women what *would* make them feel they had failed, most recounted an exhaustive list of potential failures. This acceptance of culpability co-existed, for most women, with a critique of the mother-blaming endemic in Euroamerican culture (Rich, 1977; Arcana, 1981; Caplan and Hall-McCorquodale, 1985). This is explicit in these extracts from Kate's account:

KATE: If your children go wrong, it's possibly because it's not your fault at all, it's other influences and characteristics of their own. And I think mothers tend to be so prone to guilt that they tend to take the blame for everything that goes wrong, and not enough of the credit for what goes right. ... There are all sorts of influences, and you can't be blamed for everything.

but at the same time ...

S.L.: What would make you feel you'd failed?
KATE: If they were obviously unhappy. If they had to resort to something like drugs because of their unhappiness. If they were sort of frenetically seeking pleasure by going to discos and pubs the whole time, which they don't. If they felt the need to be unkind to people. If they had unhappy relationships. ... If they had a succession of unhappy [relationships] where they'd been treated badly, or treated the other person badly. ... Or if they – I suppose if they had some sort of illness or accident and I thought it was my fault – if I didn't take sufficient care of them to – to take care of their welfare. ...... And I suppose all the obvious ones like turning to crime, which I hadn't even considered, but some children do become delinquent. I would feel I'd failed if that happened. Or if they were dishonest or deceitful.

Elizabeth and Barbara, too, despite rejecting an understanding of mothering as determining, express a culpability in their lists of potential failures:

ELIZABETH: I suppose if the children basically didn't want to know me, or, you know, wanted to withdraw and keep away and weren't too interested. I suppose that .... would be hurtful and I suppose I would assume there was a reason for it, which one puts down to failure.

BARBARA: If I felt we didn't have a relationship, if I felt she couldn't turn to me, if she didn't find that we were a support ... I think I would have felt I'd failed. ... If she'd gone off the rails and was a delinquent, I *obviously* would have felt I'd failed her (emphasis added).

How is it that mothers can be marked out as both responsible and not responsible? That selves can be marked as both innate and produced through mothering? This apparent contradiction is contained within the mother's constitution in terms of her responsibility to nurture the 'true', autonomous self of the child. This responsibility remains mothers' primary psychological task. It is a responsibility which rests on specific constitutions of both 'nature' and 'culture', as the child's self is discursively produced as natural and intrinsic, but also as only capable of realization through the mother's sensitive care.[16] Nature and culture are curiously amalgamated here.

Good-enough selves

There is a coalition of naturalism and social constructionism in most under-standings of childhood selves, and this coalition is frequently figured through the mother. Children are held to be natural beings – sometimes having a greater natural-ness since they are less attuned to the demands of culture (a state held to be antithetical to 'nature'). At the same time, it is mothers who *produce* children.[17]

Although the two terms appear oppositional, 'nature' and 'culture' go hand-in-hand in this context. The child's 'natural' self emerges through the cultural intervention of good-enough mothering within a model of a culture which is therapeutically attuned to the demands of 'the natural', and thus constitutes itself as an enabling culture – enabling the demands of nature to be fulfilled.

Indeed, this enabling culture may be seen to be therapeutically defined in terms of the maternal. Adam Phillips, for example, argues that, where Freud had conceptualized culture as paternal – a prohibiting and denying context – Winnicott marked culture as maternal – a context which (at least potentially) facilitates and enables the 'True Self' (Phillips, 1988): 'culture' is marked here as that which enables 'nature' to be realized.

This marking of culture as maternal has continued as a major trajectory within psy discourses since Winnicott. He conceptualized culture as maternal largely on the basis of his prior formulation that 'dependency needs' were the primary human needs, and that these needs were capable of being met, given the right (familial and extra-familial) environment,[18] and this characterization continues.[19]

'Culture' and 'nature' become attuned in the same way that the selves of mother and child are often held to be attuned. Psy discourses have conceptual-ized 'culture' as that which can (ideally) enable and facilitate the self, in much the same way that the good-enough mother does so. Just as 'good-enough' mothers, by definition, facilitate the 'real self', so too do 'good-enough' (therapeutically informed) cultures. And just as the therapist can stand in for the good-enough mother (Winnicott, 1963; Eichenbaum and Orbach, 1993), so too can a thera-peutically attuned culture. We are back to the 'good society' which is an amalgam of 'good selves', produced by 'good (enough) mothers'. But the 'good-ness' of good selves is assumed to stem from their nature being realized. Not only does nature require some assistance from 'culture', the very dividing line between the two is being shaken. The shaking of this dividing line may have taken on a new, or heightened, meaning within the 'enterprise culture' (Keat and Abercrombie, 1991).

'Enterprise culture' is, as Keat (1991) notes, an 'elastic term', which embraces a range of meanings. However, it is usually taken to refer to an economic, social and cultural system characterized by a non-interventionist state, economic liber-alism, and an appeal to market mechanisms, augmented by 'cultural' forms of enterprise, 'as concerned with the attitudes, values and forms of self-understanding embedded in both individual and institutional activities' (Keat, 1991: 1).[20] While the appeal to 'traditional' forms of authority and to moral conservatism implied by the enterprise culture seem fundamentally at odds with the project of self-actualization and freedom from 'external' authority promised by psy, the two come together in a conceptualization of the self as something to be worked on, something 'striving for fulfilment, excellence and achievement' (Rose, 1992b: 146). As Keat argues, the 'ethic of the self' found in humanistic psychology (and, by extension, in contemporary psy discourses)[21] is:

> in many ways congruent with the political rhetoric of enterprise: an active, self-motivated individual, accepting responsibility for its own fate, keen to identify clearly its aims and desires, to remove barriers to its fulfilment, to monitor its success in realizing them and so on.
>
> (Keat, 1991: 11)

Enterprise, then, comes to inflect the ways in which both the self and the social world are understood. Further, the relationship *between* the self and the social world is being changed within discourses of enterprise. Strathern, for example, argues that the nature/culture binarism which has held sway in the social sciences (and arguably in popular narratives as well) is being eroded by a culture which is 'enterprised up': in which human enterprise does not work 'against or out of nature' (Strathern, 1992a: 40) but in which 'nature' and 'culture' work hand-in-hand, such that they are no longer separable. Strathern's example of 'quality' provides an indication of this kind of process.

To speak of the 'quality' of something is, as Strathern points out, to use an ambiguous term: 'quality' refers to something innate; something which makes an entity what it is. At the same time, it refers to something 'superadded'. But, in the enterprise culture, everything is there to be marketed, chosen and consumed. In these circumstances, the two meanings of quality collapse: '[t]he natural, innate property and the artificial, cultural enhancement become one' (Strathern, 1992b: 39). Strathern adds:

> This is not a new essentialism but a collapse of the distinction between the essential and the superadded. ... What is collapsed is the difference between what is taken for granted in the nature of the product and what is perceived to be the result of extra human effort.
>
> (Strathern, 1992b: 39)

For Strathern, this kind of development is eroding the binarism between 'nature' and 'culture' in a multiplicity of areas, including in conceptualizations of the self. To modify Strathern's phrase, we might say that the self is being 'enterprised up'. Through processes of incitement to enhance the self, itself, contemporary Euroamericans are incited, through psy, to 'superadd' a quality *to* the self by means of a dis-covering of the true quality *of* the self. Although the rhetoric of 'enterprise', with its connotations of ruthlessness and ambition, might seem a long way from the apparently gentler discourses of psy, the two come together in the constitution of the self as that which must be sought out, realized and achieved (Keat, 1991; Selden, 1991) – a self which is made perfect through the exercise of choice in self-enhancement in a context in which the enhanced self becomes a product to be consumed (Rose, 1992b; Simonds, 1996). As Simonds argues in her analysis of self-help literature, it is through the consumption of the perfected self that the production of the 'true self' occurs: 'We are *all* consuming selves and we are *all-consuming* selves' (Simonds, 1996: 15; emphasis hers).

The 'enterprising self', then, is a self which *makes* itself: and it does so largely through the lens of psy knowledges which posit an integral *true* self. These knowledges are themselves 'marketed', 'enterprised-up' (Strathern, 1992b: 38) in self-help literature, in child-care advice literature, in age-related scales on children's toys (Urwin, 1985), in advertising which tells us, 'It's good to talk',[22] in assertiveness-training programmes, and so on. Enterprising selves are held to be enterprising by nature (Selden, 1991)[23] and created by (as well as helping to create) enterprising culture. In this way, the distinction between what is essential and what is produced is destabilized.[24]

But it is important to be clear about the specific ways in which mothers are positioned in this 'enterprising-up'. Mothers *potentially* can facilitate the quality-as-essence of the (child's) self, and so produce a quality-as-enhancement to the self. In effect, it is the mother's nurture which will enable the realization of the child's 'natural' self. Mothers' adherence to the knowledges of psy, which involves their nurturing of the child's 'true self', is what will guarantee their being able to do this. In practice, however, mothers seem rarely to be considered to be able to nurture this self, especially so far as daughters are concerned. Female selves are constituted as especially problematic – always in danger of being 'lost' or damaged (Simonds, 1992). The problematic, damaged or malfunctioning female self addressed within self-help literature, for example, is one which is produced by the mother:

> Quite simply, the message being spread is that our parents screw us up. And since women are the ones who do the bulk of parenting in this culture, mothers reap most of the blame for screwing up children in self-help books.
>
> (Simonds, 1992: 176)

But self-help is only one, relatively explicit, manifestation of the ways in which mothers are positioned as the obstacles to the daughter's achievement of the 'true self'. Mothers are situated in this way across a whole range of sites – in child-care advice, in theoretical texts, in popular culture, and so on. In some cases, this is more explicit than others, but, inevitably, the sensitive, 'good-enough mother' finds her 'other' in the bad, insensitive mother who fails to allow the real self to flourish. It is this figure of the bad mother (and her offspring, the bad child) which marks out the boundaries of the 'normal'.

This is the basis on which mothers are subjected to the gaze of the psy professionals: through which they are both regulated and (ideally) regulate themselves. It is also the basis on which children are scrutinized, and through which daughters can regulate themselves with reference to the 'true self' of psy. The regulatory fiction of the self, then, does not simply revolve around a model of the self which is unique, autonomous and rational, but also around a model of the self in which culture and nature become combined within an enabling, enterprising culture, in which the self is incited to engage in processes of realizing the true self. These processes promise freedom but they are the means by which Euroamericans subject themselves, and are subjected to, ever more complex processes of government and regulation. And, as Nikolas Rose argues:

> The irony is that we believe, in making our subjectivity the principle of our personal lives, our ethical systems, and our political evaluations, that we are, freely, choosing our freedom.
>
> (Rose, 1991: 11)

Concluding remarks

I began this chapter with Foucault's characterization of the issue which has exercised European philosophers since Kant – the question, 'What are we today?'. This question matters, not because we should be searching for the truth *about* the self, but because Euroamericans are addressed, interpellated and constituted as specific kinds of self. This goes beyond the individual self to the government of populations. The democracy which is deemed to be forged 'in the kitchen'[25] relies on assumptions about the self, its development and its regulation. The 'autonomous' subjects of liberal democracy are constituted both as making themselves and as being made by the mother.

To be sure, the women's conceptualizations of the self discussed here cannot be reduced to a single, or to a unidimensional model. In this sense, Moore is right to observe that people have local views of the person, which may or may not accord with the ways in which they are addressed *as* persons. But it is noteworthy that each of the models of the self considered here is double-edged so far as the mother–daughter relationship is concerned: they can tighten the obligations and responsibilities of mothers for nurturing their daughters' selves, at the same time that they potentially can loosen these obligations and responsibilities. Hence, the space for resistance, at least on the part of mothers, is very limited indeed. Whichever way they turn, their obligation to nurture the daughter's self is reiterated.

The next chapter will consider more fully this obligation, especially insofar as the daughter's self is understood in terms of its (potential or actual) autonomy.

4 Girls growing up
Regulation and autonomy

The last chapter discussed mothers' responsibility for nurturing the self of the daughter – a responsibility which is configured through different 'models' of the self. It introduced the ways in which the notion of an intrinsic and unique self leads to a situation in which mothers become responsible for nurturing that self. This chapter continues that theme, focusing more fully on women's conceptualizations of the daughter's intrinsic self as it considers maternal stories about this self. It considers the conceptualization of the daughter's self as 'autonomous' and considers, too, some of the problems and tensions inherent in conceptualizing the self in terms of autonomy.

'Letting her be herself': nurturing autonomy

> The desire is that the child become itself, and that by becoming itself its connection to the watching adult become plain.
>
> (Steedman, *Strange Dislocations*, p. 129)

For most of the women in this study, definitions of 'good mothering' practice were overwhelmingly tied up with the motif of 'letting her be herself'. This was seen as a crucial element (for some women, it was *the* most crucial element) in being a 'good mother'. 'Letting her be herself' was a phrase which arose again and again in these women's accounts. For example:

HAZEL: I've tried to teach her how to be ...... herself.

FRANCES: I let her be herself.

RACHEL: I think you are who you are because of ...... you're born the way you are. What your mother does is to allow that to continue .... undamaged, I suppose. I mean I can't see a mother making more out of somebody than they had the potential [for] to begin with. All you can do is allow that potential to develop. ...... You can thwart the potential, I think, by being a bad mother.

What these women express here is a self (in the daughter) which is essential, inherent and intrinsic. But mothers have a responsibility to *nurture* this self. As Rachel's account expresses, children are born with differing amounts of 'potential', but good mothers bring out whatever potential is there. It is this formulation which underwrites most contemporary definitions of good mothering practice. The autonomous self, although it is deemed to be 'natural', must be nurtured by the mother. The 'good-enough' mother will 'naturally' care for her child in such a way that the child's 'real self' (autonomous, self-directed) develops (Winnicott, 1965a). In turn, what underwrites the concept of 'letting her be herself' is the contemporary equation of self-directedness with freedom and autonomy (Foucault, 1979).

Not all women used this formulation, however. Two working-class women, Janet and Margaret, and two middle-class women, Pauline and Elizabeth, did not speak about letting their daughters 'be themselves' at all. For these women, their daughters just *were* 'themselves'. In contrast, those women who *did* use this expression saw 'being oneself' as something daughters (and sons) had to struggle towards, and in which they had to be assisted by mothers. I want to emphasize that I am not suggesting that women who did not use this expression are evincing greater authenticity in their family lives or that their children's selves are 'really' more authentic. Rather, I am drawing attention to the ways in which women's knowledges of, and investments in, specific forms of regulation and specific models of the self are likely to inflect both the ways in which they understand their own and their daughters' selves, and the ways in which they mother. Those women who *did* make heavy investments in the discourse of 'letting her be herself' had all been trained in the 'caring professions' and/or had had contact with some form of psychotherapy or counselling. Hence, they 'knew' psy discourses of self-development, and of the significance of actualizing the authenticity of the self. Interestingly, Pauline, who had trained as a teacher, also 'knew' these things, but as we will see in Chapter 6, she had an unusually critical stance on the discourses of self-actualization engendered by psy.

The phrase, 'letting her be herself' may be commonplace to contemporary Euroamericans, but it is important to examine the implications contained within the phrase. Its use implies, firstly, that the daughter has an innate self which is hers alone; secondly, that it is possible to 'be' or 'not be' this authentic self; thirdly, that 'being oneself' is preferable to not being oneself; and, fourth, that the mother has the ability to 'let' or 'not let' this authentic self develop.

This, in turn, is underwritten by the 'Apollonian' model of childhood (Jenks, 1996) introduced in Chapter 2 . The Apollonian child embodies belief in, or desire for, the 'good self' which only has to be actualized to realize its full goodness. This is why 'being oneself' is held to be preferable to 'not being oneself'. In this sense, mothers' heavy investments in discourses of self-actualization for their daughters – expressed in 'letting her be herself' – would be marked as wholly normal and desirable within psy. Against this are those other(ed) mothers whose mothering is not based on sensitive interaction and with the nurturing of the child's autonomy, but on authoritarianism.

In the rest of this chapter, I want to offer an alternative reading to this normality and desirability – not to reverse the dichotomy so as to pathologize mothers (or mothering) who invest heavily in 'letting her be herself', but, rather, to show the tensions and contradictions inherent in this formulation, and to show how regulation is at work through apparently enabling and liberating discourses.

Getting it right, getting it wrong: autonomy, class and mothering

The notion of the unique essential self, naturally autonomous yet struggling towards the *achievement of* autonomy, although rooted in Enlightenment philosophy, has assumed a new significance over the course of the twentieth century, and this significance has, at least in part, been congruent with the development of the psy professions. Ellen Ross's (1993) work on Victorian East London, for example, suggests a clash of models of selfhood between early-twentieth-century educationalists and the working-class mothers whose children they were educating. Ross suggests that, while mothers regarded their children in terms of their place in the kin structure and in terms of kinship obligations, educationalists were promoting a view of the child as individual – separate from, and with lessened obligations to, kin. While mothers placed their children within a system of inheritance and obligation, the new educational professionals were placing these same children outside of such systems, both providing (some) children with the means to leave the ascriptive system of class, and positioning them in terms of obligations towards the future (i.e. their own future achievement) rather than in terms of obligations to the past (i.e. the kin system). Thus, in contrast to working-class mothers, who:

> command[ed] most of their children's time and labor until their late teens or even longer, and ... expected teenagers to make great sacrifices of their own pleasures and ambitions to the household's requirements ... [educators] viewed their pupils as individuals rather than as family members and encouraged the children (or at least those whom they had singled out as gifted) to make something of themselves.
>
> (Ross, 1993: 162)

What Ross analyses here is a conceptualization of self which escapes from the circuit of kinship. These working-class children were to be taken out of a class which was seen to be crystallized within the family. By these means, they were deemed to be able to realize a 'natural' talent or giftedness which was seen to inhere within the self.

The other side to this story is the assumed pathology of the class these children were to leave behind. As Skeggs (1997) notes, mass educational provision in Britain was viewed as a compensatory mechanism for working-class children. In contrast to their 'morally deficient' families, it was to transmit a set of values which the children could then transmit to *their* children:

In general, it was hoped that education would form a new generation of parents whose children would not be wild, but dependable and amenable. The concerns about the potentially polluting and dangerous working class were seen to be removable if mothers were educated to civilize, that is, to control and discipline themselves and their husbands and sons who were likely to be the cause of anticipated problems. It is part of a process in which the mother acts as an invisible pedagogue.

(Skeggs, 1997: 43; references omitted)

This historical legacy has informed a situation in which class and class conflict are figured in terms of morality, rather than structural inequality, and in which the solution is seen to lie within the regulation of the family, primarily through the mother. As Skeggs notes, 'Working-class women, especially (potential) mothers are both the problem and the solution to national ills. They can be used and they can be blamed' (Skeggs, 1997: 48).

It is through 'faulty' methods of regulation that working-class mothers, and working-class families, are blamed: the dream is that, through learning 'appropriate' methods of discipline, they will become more like their middle-class counterparts, and in this way, 'used' to guarantee a dream of social harmony. Middle-classness becomes the norm against which others are measured: it is also the norm to which working-class people are supposed to aspire (Blackman, 1996; Walkerdine, 1997). Consider, for example, Kellmer-Pringle's analysis of the different ways in which differently classed parents regulate their children. Kellmer-Pringle elides middle class and 'democratic', and working class and 'authoritarian'. In 'democratic' (middle-class) homes, she argues, there is greater verbal interchange between parents and children, and the child is part of the decision-making process within the family:

This means that there are more frequent, prolonged and reciprocal interactions between parents and children. These foster two other aspects of behaviour: readiness to approach new problems with an open mind and a sense of personal independence.

On the other hand, less conversation is needed in the 'authoritarian' home since mainly non-verbal forms of prohibition and punishment are employed, and words are used more to threaten and enforce obedience rather than to make the child understand the rationale behind social behaviour. It may well be that cuffs and blows are resorted to more often by working-class parents partly because they are less able to put their feelings into words. The use of actual physical violence in socially impoverished or disturbed homes is likely to produce poorly socialized children who will then carry the same behaviour into the next generation.

(Kellmer-Pringle, 1980a: 50; references omitted)

These 'poorly socialized' children of the working classes are controlled by external, rather then internal, regulation. Reason is not inculcated into them;

hence they cannot be independent, rational selves. This account suggests that children like this are not properly *individual*; and that this lack of individuality leads to their not being properly *social*. The spectre of social unrest is raised, and working-class families are made the proper target of the regulatory gaze of state agencies (Phoenix and Woollett, 1991). Hence, although autonomous selfhood is understood as relying on inner regulation and self-directedness, those people who fail to achieve the necessary self-regulation must be subjected to a more visible and overt form of control (cf. Winnicott, 1950b; Murray, 1994a).[1]

Whether it is read as 'democratic', as 'sensitive' or as 'natural', the type of mothering associated with white, middle-class women is marked as 'normal', with any deviation from this 'norm' constructed as pathological (Woollett and Phoenix, 1991a). Walkerdine and Lucey (1989), however, offer a different reading of class differences within mothering to that presented in most developmental psychology texts. They argue, firstly, that middle-class women, many of whom work in the 'caring professions' that draw on 'progressive' theories of child development, have greater access to these knowledges. Because these knowledges are represented as timeless truths, these women receive the accolade of 'knowing' the 'truth' – the 'right' way to do mothering – which is, in turn, represented as something natural. Secondly, and perhaps more crucially, they argue that the notion of 'democratic' mothering, of the priority of 'reason' and so on, may simply have little *meaning* for working-class women. Working-class women, they argue, have little investment in performing mothering work which obscures regulation, since they are very well aware of the very overt workings of power and regulation in their own lives, and it is this knowledge they will pass on to their daughters. Of the white, working-class women in their own study, Walkerdine and Lucey comment:

> They know that you cannot have what you want. They do not believe that they are free or have access to plenty. They are poor, often live in bad housing, they work hard, the world is hard. They must teach this to their daughters and they do so often, by making their power visible. They stop, they say no, they regulate overtly. It is a liberal fantasy to believe that power is removed if regulation is made covert, if the girl believes herself ... to be an agent of free choice, of free will. This autonomy is a sham.
>
> (1989: 138)

In other words, the norms themselves have been founded on the basis of a specific form of (bourgeois) family life, and rest on specific understandings of the social world. But, more than this, however working-class mothers regulate their children, whether or not they adhere to the norm of 'autonomy', the same *meanings* are not put on to either their behaviour or the behaviour of their children. Walkerdine and Lucey comment:

> If working-class children [are] quiet in the waiting-room of a doctor's surgery they [are] repressed. If they [are] noisy they [are] hooligans. If middle-class

children [are] noisy and [run] around they [are] 'independent and autonomous'.

(Walkerdine and Lucey, 1989: 41)

The inflection of subjectivity through psy has meant that the self is deemed to
be able to escape the circuits of both kinship and the social: that is, it is held both
to be able to escape the ascriptive ties of birth and to undo the effects of 'socialization' within the family. In this way, both class and gender are simultaneously
obliterated (as they are seen not to matter) and reinstated (as working-class children, and girls of all classes are seen to deviate from a middle-class, male norm).
It is (psychological) autonomy, rather than social positioning, which has become
the issue.

The concept of autonomy has been criticized in a number of feminist analyses on the grounds that autonomy is a 'masculine' attribute to which neither
women nor men should aspire, a result of men's rigid ego-boundaries (e.g.
Hartsock, 1987), or on the grounds that autonomy always has to be held in
tension with dependency (Benjamin, 1982, 1988). Hartsock, following
Chodorow, conceptualizes women's 'relationality' as engendering a specific (life-
affirming) relationship to the world. This relationality is an effect of being
mothered by someone of the same gender. Benjamin sees mothering as crucial in
maintaining in the child's self the tension between dependence and autonomy
which she posits as a basic human 'need'. If the child is allowed free rein with
her/his fantasies of omnipotence – if the mother (or both parents) indulges
her/him, then the child will be unable to recognize the autonomy of the
(m)other, and will wield overbearing autonomy (and sadism) in her/his adult life.
Conversely, the mother (or parents) who are overly punitive will create a child
with no autonomy, who is only able to recognize the autonomy of the (m)other.
The trick, Benjamin implies, is for the mother to refuse to be psychically
'destroyed' by the child at the same time that she engenders the child's own
autonomy: that she 'feel separate and secure enough to be able to tolerate the
thwarted child's anger without giving in' (Benjamin, 1988: 71). Also, she must
avoid the situation in which the child 'will never take a full swing at the parent
[*sic*] to test if she will survive' (Benjamin, 1988: 72).

However, both of these forms of critique rest on an essentializing of childhood and its 'needs', and essentialize, too, the figure of the (good) mother as the
one who recognizes those needs. Autonomy remains theorized as something
which is in the gift of the mother, and both dependency and autonomy become
reduced to personality traits. Further, and as Lois McNay (1992) notes, although
Benjamin attempts to reappropriate the concept of autonomy in the service of
feminism, she is ultimately unable to do so, since she remains within the terms of
the autonomy/dependency binary that she herself criticizes. In the process,
Benjamin reinstates the figure of the nurturing mother, simply reworking nurturant motherhood so that it encourages relationality in addition to individuation
and autonomy.[2]

Above all, these critiques of autonomy fail to consider the ways in which autonomy itself may be form of regulation: it is theorized as if it *really were* a freedom, or escape, from the workings of power. Yet autonomy, in its current Euroamerican usage, consists in an increasing self-regulation and self-surveillance (Foucault, 1979, 1982, 1990; Rose, 1991). As Rose comments:

> T]he norm of autonomy secretes, as its inevitable accompaniment, a constant and intense self-scrutiny, a constant evaluation of our personal experiences, emotions and feelings in relation to images of satisfaction, the necessity to narrativize our lives in a vocabulary of interiority. The self that is liberated is obliged to live its life tied to a project of its own identity.
>
> (Rose, 1991: 254)

That this self-regulation should be considered 'freedom' is a measure of the normalization of techniques of governmentality by which subjects themselves are normalized.

Mothers who invest in these discourses do so through engaging in practices of self-management and self-regulation. The mother must manage her self, and teach the daughter to engage in practices of managing *her* self – to regulate her*self*. Indeed, it is impossible for mothers to be 'mothers' without regulating their children; not to do so is in itself marked as deviant. No matter how much discourses of motherhood propose that the mother should mother 'sensitively', generating 'freedom' within the child (Neill, 1971; Ainsworth and Bell, 1974; Hetherington and Parke, 1986), nobody is proposing that mothers should let their children do whatever they want. It is mothers' responsibility to ensure that children *are* properly regulated – a fact which is indicated by the blame attached to mothers when children are seen to be in some way 'deviant'. As Holland argues, both 'moral Conservatives and child-centred liberals' panic when children's activities seem to be outside of the control of family and school (Holland, 1996: 158).

However, some forms of regulation are 'read' as control, while others are not. The absence of *overt* control is read as not control at all, but as the mother's sensitive facilitating of the child's 'true self'[3] (Winnicott, 1965a; Newson and Newson, 1976; Adams, 1971; NSPCC, 1989). This 'true self' is held to be intrinsically 'autonomous'. Self-regulation is normalized as the 'right' form of regulation, or indeed as autonomy – the lack of regulation. In this way, the self's relationship *to* itself – and the regulation inherent in this – becomes obscured.

It is within the familial setting that the achievement of this 'real' and 'autonomous' self is held to be primarily and fundamentally produced. The mother's interaction with the child, and her unconscious motivations, are understood as crucially important to the task of nurturing the child's self (Winnicott, 1958, 1960, 1965a; Bowlby, 1953, 1978a; Kellmer-Pringle, 1972b, 1975, 1980a). Clearly, to do this properly, she must understand both her own and her child's self in terms of autonomy and individuality. Yet some mothers cannot be relied upon to do this. Mothers who are black and/or working class are frequently held to favour 'authoritarian' modes of child-rearing; they control and direct their children (Adams, 1971; Triseliotis, 1972; de H. Lobo, 1978; Kellmer-Pringle, 1980a; Shaffer, 1985; Everingham, 1994).[4] In contrast, white middle-class mothers use 'democratic' methods, using reason and guiding the child toward understanding. Authoritarianism is understood by 'progressive' therapeutic discourses as functioning as an inhibitor to the child's acquisition of language, and, more significantly, to her/his sense of autonomy. This in itself is seen to lead to delinquency and other forms of anti-social behaviour; these children will fail as the 'good citizens' of tomorrow.

While it has become impossible to stand outside of such understandings of the self, of individuality and of autonomy (Rose, 1996a), not all persons stand in the same relationship to these understandings. Some of the women in this study could claim an easy familiarity with these psy knowledges by virtue of an education and training which had steeped them in these understandings. Others had a more attenuated relationship with them. Some women were employed to monitor and regulate those mothers who could not be relied upon to 'get it right'; while others are those being watched and monitored.

Doing it differently

If commitment to communication and/or to the discourses of 'letting her be herself' are one means of maternal self-management, investments in mothering unlike one's own mother form another set. Although not all the women in this study were antipathetic to their own mothers, every woman expressed, to some degree, a desire to mother unlike her own mother. For example:

LYNNE: I want to redress ...... er ...... the kind of relationship my mother and I had ...... in my relationship with Naomi. ... And I want to give her the sense of independence and, er, self-respect, which I was not given as a child.

DAWN: I do feel we all had a lot of pressure on us to achieve. To a certain extent, it's something that I've found difficult to come to terms with, any sort of failure. I tend to set rather high standards for myself. And maybe as a reaction to that, my academic expectations of the girls are really ...... I don't ...... I try not to put much pressure on.

BARBARA: I think I knew from the start that I wanted to bring her up in a different way to the way my mother brought me up. ... I felt I wanted to give her every possible chance academically – educationally. Not pushing, but wanting to show her things, give her all the opportunities I hadn't had. That I do know. ... I wanted to be, er, yes, I would give her a lot of love – she would be very much wanted and loved. ... And I think again, because my mother hadn't listened to me, I felt that I wanted to be much more tolerant with her. So all these ideas probably came from my relationship with my mother. All the things that she didn't do, I wanted to do.

FRANCES: I suppose I may have got the early years really wrong, but I mean I don't think I have, 'cause it was straightforward, 'cause I knew …… to do the opposite of what my mother had done.

What kinds of identifications, desires, fears and fantasies are expressed in this desire to 'do it differently'? There is an identification with the daughter expressed, as women speak of a desire to give their daughters what they did not have. But there is also an identification with the mother, as women position themselves as 'the good mother' who will nurture the daughter in ways they believe their mothers did not. They are both the good mother and the nurtured daughter:

GINA: I think I gave them my perfect childhood.
HAZEL: You've tried to do that.
GINA: I tried to give my children what I wanted in my childhood.
HAZEL: I think that's what all mothers do, actually.
GINA: Yeah, my mother did the same with me. She came from such a poor background, really, really poor. And so what she gave me was her idea of – … I had a lot more than she had. And so she gave me that. And I might not [laughs] I might not have liked it. I would probably have liked my mother to be a lot more kind of irresponsible. Not irresponsible, but sort of more alternative, or whatever, and a lot more liberal and free.

(GD)

In her individual interview, Gina expresses some of the desires and fantasies associated with maternity, and the ways in which they can be bound up with giving one's children one's own 'perfect childhood':

GINA: My mother was very much one of those working-class mothers, where you don't play in the house. You know, the house has got to be kept clean. You play outside. Your friends don't come into the house and mess the house up. Er, you don't have people round for tea, unless it's something special, or they're your relations. … She would always get very nervous if visitors came, you know. Everything would have to be just so. … So I had it in my head, when I decided that I wanted children, that … I wanted to have people in and out all the time. Lots of life, lots of different kinds of people, lots of different influences, different ages. You know, *life* in the house. … I wanted to live in a big rambly house. I wanted a big garden, you know. I wanted there to be trees, somewhere the kids could play. I suppose I had middle-class aspirations for my kids. I wanted them to be a bit like the Famous Five[5] [laughs]. I wanted them to have sort of adventures, and dogs, and, you know, erm, sort of paddle in streams. … I wanted the skies always to be blue, and the sun to shine, and I wanted to make jam and cakes and bread and do all those things (original emphasis).

But Gina's account here indicates the ways in which the desire to 'do it differently' can be bound up with fantasies around class. It also indicates the ways in which this desire is mediated through the daughter's ownership of (legitimated) cultural capital. Gina's fantasies of her motherhood and, more broadly, of family life, centre on an idealized childhood which is free from working-class anxieties about cleanliness, about respectability, and so on. This fantasy is informed by what she sees as the easy expansiveness of middle-class life (and remember the Famous Five had servants to clean up after them and had no need to be troubled about issues of respectability, given their clear sense of middle-class – and white – superiority). Gina's fantasy of a perfect (middle-class) childhood informs her fantasy of motherhood – as indeed it must, given the constitution of mother-hood as a function necessary for the 'doing' of childhood.

More generally, it was in their expressions of 'doing it differently' that class differences among the women, although not absolute, became most marked. Quite simply, the type of mothering which women spoke of as receiving from their own mother varied according to their mother's class position. So, women with working-class birth families spoke frequently of their mothers' demands on them, or of their teaching them lessons, for example, of how to get on in the world. In marked contrast, no woman with a middle-class birth family expressed this. The following quotations, from Anna, Caroline and Rachel, all middle-class women with middle-class mothers, are typical in this respect:

ANNA: I've never known her [sighs] – I've never felt that she was …… openly inter-ested enough. You know like offering options or …… discussing possibilities. It never really happened. It was always, you know, 'Oh, whatever you think's for the best, you do it'. But I mean, often, growing up, you didn't really know what was for the best. … I would have liked her to encourage me more to have done – to do more at an earlier age than I actually did.

CAROLINE: It's funny …… it was quite unusual [for my parents] to actually say, you cannot do something.

RACHEL: They just let us grow up and do our own thing really.

Women with middle-class mothers tended to criticize this felt lack of involve-ment and to express a (retrospective) desire that their mothers had been more involved in their lives, and given them more direction. Yet, in their own moth-ering, these women's commitment to nurturing autonomy impelled a policy of non-intervention in their daughters' lives. So, these women were subject to two competing sets of demands – that they mother differently to their own mothers, and that they also adopt a similar style to that which they represent their mothers as adopting. Despite this, the demands of a more 'hands-off' approach to moth-erhood – the discourse of 'letting her be herself' – seemed to win out, as they repeatedly subjected themselves to this kind of demand.

But for other women, it was communication which was the key area of distinction between their own and their mothers' mothering. Janet and Margaret – two working-class women with working-class mothers – singled out communication in this way. Interestingly, both women attributed their mothers' lack of communication with them, not to faults in the mother's character (as other women usually did) so much as to circumstances:

JANET: [My mother] missed out on the important thing – we never talked. ... But it wasn't her fault. She had too much ...... else, you know, on her mind. 'cause we were always very poor, there wasn't a lot of money, so she was constantly worried about money, and my dad's drinking. And just ...... the wear and tear of bringing up six kids – not much time for anything else.

MARGARET: Me and my mum didn't get on. But I think it was just circumstances, and then she was having to work anyway. We never used to see her. So it was, 'Be good, don't do anything, don't move'. We just had to sit there all day.

Neither of these women used the discourse of 'letting her be herself'.[6] For both of them, their self-management centred around communication with their children. This was the feature which they defined as key to 'good mothering'. They set a high value on talk and on open communication between themselves and their children, even if they found it difficult at times:

S.L.:   What qualities d' you think make a good mother?
JANET: A good ear. Listening. Talking to your kids, being concerned – but genuinely, you know. Properly listening. It's hard, sometimes, to do that, listen to people properly.

MARGARET: When she [daughter] was younger, I used to hit her, but now ...... I seem to listen to them more, and I get them to sit down and listen to me, instead of them shouting and running off. So we get on really well as mother and daughter.

But even among those women who *are* steeped in the knowledges about the 'right' way to mother, there are differences in positioning. Some will find their own childhood and childhood family life represented as normal within these knowledges: others will find only pathology. Women who have grown up in working-class families have a specific relationship to these knowledges: they know the 'right' way to mother; *and* they know that the type of family in which they grew up is marked as 'lacking' as 'other'. Like all the women in the study, they were critical of their mothers' mothering practices; but they also stand in a unique position in that they have experienced mothering from a working-class mother *and* they have access to knowledges which construct this mothering as 'bad mothering'; as authoritarian and undemocratic, as inhibiting the development of the daughter's real, autonomous self. Their desire to 'do it differently', then, is shaped by their distinctive position in relation to the class-based construction of 'good mothering'.

The following two extracts, from Lynne's and Frances' accounts, illustrate well the class-based construction of 'good' mothering, and the ways in which this construction can generate specific anxieties around class and mothering. Lynne and Frances were born into working-class birth families and now described themselves as middle class. This shifting of class positions raised particular problems for their own mothering. In common with most other women who had experienced this social mobility, they considered that they had little knowledge of how to mother well because of the lack of an adequate role model in their own mother. Their accounts are unusual, however, in their explicit foregrounding of social class:

LYNNE: I'm not the kind of person who can patiently accept their children's bad behaviour, or their children's constant irritated whining, which gets completely on my nerves. I can never – I used to watch women when I was a young mother; I used to watch more experienced, more middle-class women patiently explaining to their children why it wasn't reasonable to scream blue murder in the middle of Marks and Spencer's. And I thought, 'My god, this woman's a heroine – she's a hero of motherhood! How does she do this?' Because I just walloped mine and got furious with them, and then felt guilty about not being patient.

FRANCES: You know, you weren't worth much because you were from that [working-class] background. And you had to behave – be respectable, which is what Linda [her sister-in-law] is doing to her kids. ... There wasn't this sort of ...... what is it? stiff upper lip bit, which must be terrible. But then there was a great shortage of money, and watching mum worry about money. ...... I do wonder if there aren't some sort of class differences that condition the way women mother. That's my sense of it. I mean, just going into stereotypes, there's your average respectable working-class – their children have got to be clean and neat and well-behaved and get severely punished if they're not. I watch that with my nephew and niece and I see trouble there, I see unhappiness. ...... Then there's your trendy ones like I suppose I became in the way I treated Chloe, and clearly my brother thought that was terrible – and my mother. ... You know, I let her be herself. And then of course they can say, 'Well, look what happened to her later.'

'What happened' to Frances' daughter was that she left her mother's home to live with her father when she was 14. Frances clearly reads this as failure on her own part. Her story of a stormy and conflictual relationship with her daughter might seem to indicate the failure of even 'trendy' mothering. But Frances' response was to blame *herself*; clearly, she must not have done it properly. She says that she sent 'mixed messages' to her daughter, that she *desired* control. In this way, she positioned *herself* as failing.

These two passages foreground two important aspects of 'sensitive' and 'democratic' mothering: that is, 'reason' and 'autonomy' ('letting her be herself'). For Lynne, it is patient explanation which is one important signifier of middle-class motherhood. No anger, no conflict here: just the inculcation of reason. Reason and autonomy are closely linked within discourses of 'democratic' mothering. Reason is deemed to give rise to independence of thought and autonomy in the child. Reason displaces passion, reducing desire to 'feeling'; the presence of reason indicates the absence of conflict (Walkerdine, 1985b; Flax, 1990). For Frances, 'letting her be herself' is the thing which marks out her own motherhood from that of other family members. And it is this, too, which makes her mothering 'trendy', signifying a newer knowledge to replace the older knowledge of authority and control; and signifying, too, an access to that knowledge which only some people have. This knowledge is coded as rightly belonging to, and used by, the middle classes, against whom working-class people can be seen as lacking up-to-date forms of knowledge. This is similar to the situation in the 1960s when child-centred parenting began to be promoted by the psy professions, when, according to Rose:

> [W]orking-class families suffered, at best, from a kind of cultural lag whereby they were fated to play out the child-rearing nostrums of a past age, which progress had made redundant. Thus they stressed obedience, tidiness and habit formation in their children – the values of Truby King but not those for the new age of liberalism. At worst, the physical, intellectual, and emotional constraints upon the family lives of the working class seemed to be positively dangerous to the prospects for their children.
>
> (Rose, 1991: 184)

'Authoritarian' mothering from a working-class mother, powerfully constituted as 'bad' mothering, may induce in women a desire to 'do the opposite' – to be the 'good', middle-class mother. Yet this cannot guarantee the absence of conflict, as Frances' story highlights. But so authoritative is this understanding of mothering that it is difficult to critique it: instead, failure is seen to reside within the mother, who can only have 'got it wrong'.

Dependence and independence

Despite the investments of many women, especially middle-class women, in nurturing autonomy within their daughters, the nurturing of this autonomy did not, in fact, seem to be enough to ensure their daughters' 'independence'. Hence some extra activity was needed: women saw themselves as having to do *more* than let their daughters 'be themselves'; they also had to 'push' them towards independence. This 'push' was a theme in the accounts of all the women, even those who did not invest in discourses of autonomy and self-actualization.

However, independence was not seen as coming easily or automatically. Rather, it was something towards which daughters have to strive. Daughters' position as 'women' (or potential 'women') meant that 'independence' was not a natural state for them: rather, the attainment of independence required some intervention from the mother: what I call here the 'push to independence':

S.L.: What are you trying to teach [your daughter]?
ANNA: Er, just to be – to have enough foresight to do enough to be completely independent if she wants to be; to equip herself with the skills to be her own person. And

to have – hopefully – equal relationships. You know, even if she's in a partnership, she can still keep that part of herself separate that needs to be independent. I think that's really important.

BARBARA: It's better if you have that .... not be too dependent on the husband – have your independence, self-sufficiency. That's something I've always impressed on Julia, that she must try and be self-sufficient and, er, independent.

While dependence on men was frequently specified as a particular trap into which women could fall, dependence on the mother was also something from which the daughter had to be pushed:

JANET: [I've tried to teach them] how to look after themselves ... mentally and physically. Be totally independent of ...... anybody else, and – well that, really. And to, er, survive on their own, because I mean I might not always be here. Well I won't always be here.

The women's accounts suggest that they see 'independence' as an intrinsic part of 'normal' adulthood; hence the mother's pushing the daughter away from dependence, and towards independence, is a feature of her obligation to ensure the smooth running of the child's transition from childhood to maturity. Indeed, contemporary Euroamerican understandings of adulthood posit independence as a *sine qua non* (Fraser and Gordon, 1994).

According to Fraser and Gordon (1994), the meaning of 'dependency' has shifted from its pre-industrial usage as a term which denoted structural relations of inequality to its contemporary usage as a term which denotes individual pathology. In late capitalism, they argue, 'dependence' has come to be seen as a psychological, rather than a political category. They link this shifting meaning with the *formal* abolition of much legal and political dependency: this has resulted in an 'equal opportunities' rhetoric which proposes that *anyone* can now achieve *anything*. Failure to do so can only be a result of individual pathology, of dependent personalities.

In practice, as Fraser and Gordon point out, this rhetoric *obscures* structural relations of inequality:

> [T]here is no longer any self-evidently good adult dependency in post-industrial society. Rather, all dependency is suspect, and independence is enjoined upon everyone. Independence, however, remains identified with wage labor. ... In this context, the worker tends to become the universal social subject: everyone is expected to 'work' and to be 'self-supporting'. Any adult not perceived as a worker shoulders a heavier burden of self-justification. Thus, a norm previously restricted to white workingmen applied increasingly to everyone. Yet this norm still carries a racial and gender subtext, as it

supposes that the worker has access to a job paying a decent wage, and is not also a primary parent.

(Fraser and Gordon, 1994: 324)

Fraser and Gordon's analysis points to the ways in which women, especially if they are mothers, have difficulties in being 'independent', and hence have problems in occupying the category '(normal) individual'. However, it is important to note that the negative and individualistic concept of 'dependence' which Fraser and Gordon identify also *intensifies* the responsibilities of mothers in its identification of dependence/independence as features of the 'self'.

My argument here is that the 'equal opportunities' rhetoric critiqued by Fraser and Gordon, while it appears to sever ties with the past, actually *intensifies* these ties, through the person of the mother. In one sense, the premise that all opportunities are open to all cuts the ties with the kin system; we are no longer to be bound by ascriptive characteristics, and hence we can be truly autonomous. However, the tie with the kin system is simultaneously reinforced through the figure of the mother. If individuals fail to achieve, then what impedes them cannot be structural constraints, which are held to have disappeared through a commitment to equality of opportunity. The answer must lie within themselves: they must lack the *desire* to achieve. In this way, lack of autonomy, or 'dependency' can be located within the self. It is no longer seen as a state arising from hierarchical social relations, but as a pathological feature of the personality (Fraser and Gordon, 1994). It is the attainment of a specific type of 'self', then, rather than political struggle, which becomes the only legitimate means of contesting inequality: we can all, this discourse promises, be 'independent'. As Fraser and Gordon argue, 'Fear of dependency, both implicit and explicit, posits an ideal, independent personality in contrast to … those considered dependent and deviant' (1994: 332).

Those positioned in this 'dependent and deviant' way are, Fraser and Gordon argue, overwhelmingly, poor women, black women, single mothers. The old equation of 'dependence' with 'women', they argue, is giving way, in post-industrial society, to a usage in which:

> [G]rowing numbers of relatively prosperous women claim the same kind of independence that men do while a more stigmatized but still feminized sense of dependency attaches to groups considered deviant and superfluous. Not just gender but also racializing practices play a major role in these shifts, as do changes in the organizing and meaning of labor.
>
> (Fraser and Gordon, 1994: 312)

So *some* women now have access to a valued 'independent' status, while others have their 'dependent' status reiterated. But part of this process involves the psychologizing of dependency, mediated through the figure of the mother. Personal narratives are made intelligible through the location of adult psychological states in early familial interaction. Since the adult's psyche is understood to be rooted in childhood, the unconscious motivations which give rise to a 'dependent' personality must result from parental behaviour which has shaped the child's early development. And since mothers, rather than fathers, usually do this child-care, mothers can be seen as the source of their children's 'failure'. An assumption that there *are* equal opportunities means that there is simply nowhere else to go, other than to the closed, dyadic structure of early mother–child interaction.

Implicitly or explicitly, it is this assumption which underwrites some feminist accounts of gendered subjectivities, where the argument often proceeds on the basis that, not only does the creation of women's (and men's) subjectivities begin and end in the mother–child dyad, but that these subjectivities are the source of women's oppression. Karlein Schreurs (1993), for example, argues that:

> Nowadays, women certainly have more options in deciding how they want to shape their lives. However, this does not mean that more subtle mechanisms have lost their impact.
>
> (1993: 3)

But the 'more subtle mechanisms' to which Schreurs is referring here inhere entirely in women's psyches (primarily in their 'fluid ego boundaries'), which are in turn determined by their relationships with their mothers (cf. Benjamin, 1988).

The underlying assumption is that there really is formal equality between women and men. In this way, inequality and oppression can become personality traits, themselves traceable to the way in which women have been mothered.[7] This leads to the suggestion that what women need is to be mothered differently.[8] At the heart of these accounts is an assumption that there is a straightforward correlation between what the mother is and what the daughter becomes – that is, between the 'selves' of mother and daughter. Since mothers are 'feminine', this story goes, they will impose femininity on their daughters. Conversely, if mothers stop being 'feminine', their daughters will be free from this oppressive obligation. Webb (1992), for example, locates feminism as a property of the self which can be inculcated through the mother's mothering: she asks, 'How can we pass feminism across the generations?' (Webb, 1992: 31) and suggests that feminist mothers' political stances lead to a particular style of mothering in which the positive aspects of being a woman are reinforced. This in turn, she suggests, leads to a particular type of 'self' within the daughter; this 'self' is strong and self-directed, and hence, Webb suggests, 'feminist'. Webb's argument represents the obverse side of analyses which locate gender oppression as a property of the self, also inculcated through mothering. Both types of argument stress equally the need for 'autonomy' and 'independence' in the daughter; and both position the mother as responsible for the *production* of this autonomy and independence.

These arguments individualize feminism and reduce feminism to individuality.[9] They also obscure the multiplicity of ways in which gender is produced in the subject, as well as the many forms of gender inequality which cannot be reduced to personality types; and they unify the figure of the mother, giving her a coherent and relatively straightforward self which, consciously or unconsciously, impacts on the self of the daughter. The proposition which underlies many of these arguments – that the daughter cannot become autonomous because the mother's failure to adequately nurture her makes autonomy difficult – obscures wider political reasons why women have problems in occupying the category 'autonomous individual'.

Tensions: control and independence

The women assumed an almost total responsibility for pushing their daughters towards independence. Despite many women's recognition of structural factors which might impede their daughters' attainment of independence, there was no question that the responsibility for the 'push to independence' properly belonged to the mother. But there is a tension embedded in this responsibility: it was usually in discussions of the 'push to independence' that some of the difficulties and tensions inherent in the rhetoric of 'letting her be herself' became most apparent. The women wanted their daughters both to fulfil their potential and to be independent; yet this seemed to require an intervention which is at odds with 'letting her be herself'. For example:

S.L.: What kinds of things have you tried to teach your daughter?

LYNNE: Erm ...... to be herself ...... erm ...... but within limits [laughs]. I don't want to impose on her the kind of ...... definitions that my mother imposed on me. So I've tried very hard not to define her. But then I have tried to adjust her behaviour away from the kind of silly, soppy, little-girl image that ...... that I see as being quite damaging to ...... to women's, er, ability to get on in the world.

S.L.: What does it mean to let go?

GINA: Ooh .... it means to let go control. ... Allowing her to be an individual, with her own opinions, that are not my opinions, perhaps. Respecting that. ... She was gonna drop out [of university] after the first couple of terms. ... Now when she came home and said to me, 'I think I'm gonna take a year out,' I was thinking, 'Oh no, don't do that!' ... [But] instead ... I kind of guess what I said was, 'Have you thought about this, or have you thought about that? Do you think you could go on a bit longer with this?' or whatever. You know, I tried to think of ways round it, *which might also be control,* but I didn't directly say, 'I think you're really stupid to do that, you'd be mad to do that' (emphasis added).

ANNA: I'm fairly liberal, I suppose. Sometimes I wonder if I should be a bit more – well, place a few more restrictions on her, but she doesn't seem to need it so I don't.

S.L.: So you wouldn't say you try to control her?

ANNA: No, I don't think so. No, I don't think so. Well, only in that I wouldn't be very happy if she didn't have a career for herself, that sort of thing. I would try and control

...... well, no, I couldn't control it, but I wouldn't be happy if she didn't want to ...... train or go into higher education. I mean, I couldn't do anything about it, but I wouldn't be happy about it.

S.L.: What would you do?

ANNA: Well, all I could do is present her with the possibilities of not doing, and the possibilities of doing something. I couldn't force her. ... I would do what I don't think my mother did, and just show her what the possibilities were. But in saying that, perhaps it wouldn't come out as simply showing what the possibilities were. Perhaps it would seem to her as if I was trying to pressure her. I can't know that.

S.L.: If you could start again, what would you do with your adult life?

RACHEL: I would do what I was going to do when I was in the sixth form, which is do medicine, I think. ... At the time ... I was sick of studying and the rest of it and just wanted a degree. You know, three years and that was it. Then I thought I would do it again and got a place and, erm, you know, when you've done a degree for three years and then you think, can you stand four more years of studying? And I didn't. Because you keep thinking, I'll be old by then. But then when you – you realize you're not old. ...... No, I would try and stop Emily from doing that, but then I know you shouldn't try and get your kids to do, you know, what – not to repeat your mistakes, 'cause it just makes them more kind of stroppy. But I think I would have liked somebody to be a bit more strong about it when I was nineteen, and sort me out a bit more, which my parents didn't. They just let us grow up and do our own thing really, without trying to. ... Maybe they didn't know how.

As well, a mother's desire for her daughter to achieve independence may stand in tension with her desire for a close relationship with the daughter:

LYNNE: I suppose the problem with making children independent is they become independent of you. And with Naomi I don't want that to happen, whereas with the boys, I ...... you know, it's not such an emotional bond.

Although not all women described their relationships with their children as gendered in the way Lynne does, for most of them, the intense affection they felt for their daughters existed in tension with their felt obligation to guarantee independence. In other words, they wanted a closeness between their daughters and themselves, but they also felt they *had* to make their daughters independent, creating the situation in which these daughters 'become independent from you'. Yet the women clearly felt they had no choice in this: there was no point, in any of their accounts, in which they refused the obligation to ensure their daughters' independence.

Brannen *et al.* (1994), in their study of family life, found that the white, middle-class mothers in their research were similarly caught in such a tension: they desired an easy intimacy, akin to friendship, with their teenage children, but they also wanted to exercise control over these children. Jamieson (1999), commenting on this research, characterizes these mothers as desiring the 'pure relationship'[10] with these children. Arguing that there is no 'pure relationship' which can stand outside the politics, obligations and exigencies of everyday life, Jamieson points to the 'precarious balancing act' (1999: 489) in which these mothers had to engage, caught between the demands of intimacy and the demands of control.

This is what mothers have to contend with: they are supposed to 'allow' the actualization of the 'true self' at the same time that they control their children. Mothers of daughters face a special difficulty, in that their obligation to adopt a 'hands-off' approach can be fundamentally at odds with their desire to pass on to their daughters the experience and the knowledge they have gained. The promise of the actualization of the autonomous self is that this is a self which transcends the strictures of gender (and, of course, those of class and race). Yet the women here underscore the inadequacy of this formulation: despite making heavy investments in discourses of autonomy, they also want to guide and advise their daughters, and consider that they have the experience with which to do so. The cost to women of trying to contain the demands of the daughter's autonomy against the demands of pushing her towards independence is rarely considered.

Indeed, it was unusual for any woman to express overtly a sense of a cost to themselves in their daughters becoming independent. However, it was in discussions of the daughter's adolescence that an ambivalence sometimes did emerge; but this ambivalence could be contained by the discursive construction of adolescence as a time of rebellion and of individuation.

Adolescence and independence

> During the years from twelve to seventeen, a second weaning takes place from dependence on parents and on authority in general.
>
> (Kellmer-Pringle, 'Deprivation and education', p. 49)

In the 'developmental' account, childhood does not abruptly come to an end, but leads 'naturally' into the period of transition between childhood and adulthood known as adolescence (Stainton Rogers and Stainton Rogers, 1992). Adolescents are not adults: for example, in Britain, they lack the full legal status of adults such as the right to vote or to drink alcohol in pubs. After the age of 16, they can legally marry and consent to heterosex, but this does not necessarily make them 'adults' either, as the censure attached to 'young mothers' indicates (Phoenix, 1991; Phoenix and Woollett, 1991).[11] Further, under current British social security law, young people aged 16 to 18 do not ordinarily receive state benefits, making them dependent on their parents in similar ways to younger children.

But adolescents are not children either; the end of their childhood is signified in a number of ways: legally, through their criminal responsibility[12] and their ability to do a limited amount of paid work; culturally, by their physical maturation.[13] Within the developmental account, the end of childhood is also signified by, for example, an increasing importance being attached to peer relationships, and also by adolescents' rejection of parental values. Although not all developmental accounts represent the relationship with the parents as necessarily difficult (see Phoenix, 1991), the rejection (or partial rejection) of parental values is normalized in many accounts (Erikson, 1950; Freud, 1958; Gallagher and Harris, 1976; Treadwell, 1988).

A normative and normalized rebellion is closely linked with the adolescent's transition to 'independence' and individuation (Ollendorf, 1971; Mahler *et al.*, 1975). Because independence is constructed as an integral feature of 'normal' adulthood, adolescence, as the mediating period between childhood and maturity, is understood largely as the move from (childhood) dependence to (adult) independence. As Stainton Rogers and Stainton Rogers argue:

> Issues of what criterion or mixture of criteria should be employed to mediate the transition from juvenile to adult status are themselves reflections on what is desired and valued in the constitution of the adult.
>
> (1992: 160)

It was during adolescence that individuality and autonomy were held, by the women I spoke to, to 'really' begin. Adolescence was the time when 'you begin to develop into an individual'. It was seen as a crucial time in terms of the achievement of authentic, individual (and independent) selfhood. Equally, however, adolescence was seen by the women as a quintessentially *strange* time. It was described as the time during which daughters rejected the values of their mothers, but this rejection was always seen as temporary. For mothers of postadolescent daughters, these years were described as a time of difficulty and struggle within the relationship; but, at least, these difficulties came to an end. As Barbara said of her 20-year-old daughter, 'We're over the worst now.' Or, as Pauline put it, after adolescence, her daughters 'were like human beings again'.

In this sense, adolescence was often seen as a time when the self is *overlaid* with something else. Usually, this 'something else' was seen as springing out of a desire to be as unlike the mother as possible:

HAZEL: She's just that classic teenager, so there's all that teenage stuff overlaying what I consider to be her personality.

Yet Hazel clearly also believes (or hopes) that the 'teenage stuff' will disappear at some later date, as the following extract indicates:

HAZEL: My daughter is just starting to go through the process of finding out who she is, separate from me. You know, she is – she's stopped being a vegetarian [Hazel is a vegetarian]. She's really starting to look at who she is, separate from me. I mean she'll probably come back to being a vegetarian. You know, it's the little things .... I think she's never learned how to rebel, because I've given her – she's had so much freedom, she's had so much choice that it's like, 'What can I do to be different from her?' So she's having to find her way – find out who she is.

DAWN: How d' you feel? What do you feel?

HAZEL: I feel absolutely fine about it. I think she's beautiful. I think she's absolutely fine the way she is, you know.

(GD)

Hazel consistently related her daughter's adolescence in wholly positive terms, even when she related incidents in which her daughter had been apparently rude or unpleasant to her. In the extract above, Dawn's question suggests that she expects some negative response from Hazel; but Hazel expresses only positive feelings. Her investment in her daughter's 'autonomy' appears to enable her to accept Leah's rejection of her values, and her currently being, as Hazel puts it, 'a stroppy bitch'. These characteristics are contained firmly within the story of adolescence, in which adolescent daughters *have* to rebel in order to become more 'themselves'.

Other women tended to speak more ambivalently about their daughters becoming 'independent' or 'separate', but this ambivalence was again contained by an understanding of adolescence as a difficult and strange period, but one which was nevertheless 'natural' in the daughter's development. Some women expressed a sense of pain at the disagreements and arguments that they said had characterized the period of their daughters' adolescence. For others, the pain they felt during this period centred around a physical estrangement between mother and daughter:

FRANCES: Chloe was – oh, it was marvellous. She was ever so affectionate. And that changed, really, with adolescence. ... Occasionally, through the pains of her teens, I'd say, sometimes, 'Do you want a cuddle?' 'cause, oh God, I missed it. I still do. And she'd come for a cuddle and a cry – oh, once or twice.

DAWN: I go to her and give her a cuddle, but there seems to be a bit of this, 'I'm getting big.' You know, 'Keep your distance,' sort of thing.

It should be noted, though, that not all daughters *wanted* physical separation from their mothers: some mothers themselves ended the intensely physical relationship which most women described as a characteristic of their relationships with their young daughters.

RACHEL: When she [daughter] was little, it was very physical, always biting her and cuddling her. They always came into bed a lot. Erm, and then – maybe because she's started growing breasts. I mean it's a lot more difficult at this stage to know where you can grab people. ... And also she's so much bigger now. ...... But I mean I still kiss her every morning and every evening. But there's not so much of the rough and tumble kind of thing any more. Sometimes she'll say, 'You don't cuddle me as much as you used to.' ...... But it's not because I don't want to, it's because I feel that she's growing up and you can't keep pinching bottoms when they're that big [laughs]. It's not that I don't want to.

Part of the 'strangeness' of adolescence, then, centres around the mother's (or daughter's) perception of the necessity of maintaining the adolescent's bodily boundaries. Part of the 'independence' to which adolescence is seen to be the threshold rests on a physical separation between the mother and the adolescent daughter. Often, the women invoked 'nature' to account for this physical separation. For example:

RACHEL: Olivia used to have worms a lot, up until eight or nine. ... In girls, they crawl out of the anus and into the vagina. And when she was quite little, I said, 'I'll have to have a look'. ... So I'd have to get cotton-wool buds out and dig out these worms. ... And there was nothing, you know – it was quite natural that I went and dug around with these cotton-wool buds and got these worms out. But now it wouldn't be. If she had them now, it would be quite different. And something's happened.

S.L.: Why is that?

RACHEL: It's puberty, isn't it? It must be signs they give out. I mean now I can't imagine doing it ... I mean it would be ... easy to show her physically how to use a tampon, but that would be just incredible. ...... I remember a friend of mine at college saying that she had a friend in school whose mother [laughs] was an army type, she said, and when it came to periods, she just got this tampon and shoved it inside this girl [laughs]. And she said it was like being raped by your mother and really awful. And I can imagine, it would be awful. So there is a change and it's two-way, I think. Bodies become much more ...... private. And you get all the zones that are no longer touchable. ...Possibly even something more than that – something nature does.

Since post-pubertal bodily contact ordinarily connotes sexual activity, and since sexuality is seen to be the 'deepest' and most authentic part of the self (Foucault, 1990; Wood, 1985), the cultural imperative for physical separation might be seen as bound up with the imperative to maintain the integrity and autonomy of the 'self'.

The maintenance of bodily boundaries between mother and daughter is a state which will lead, not to a return to physical closeness between mother and daughter, but to the daughter's establishing of adult sexual relations (Stainton Rogers and Stainton Rogers, 1992). Certainly for the women I spoke to, adolescence seemed to be inextricably linked with both an emerging sexuality and an end to bodily intimacy between mother and daughter: discussions of the daughter's adolescence always involved elements of these two other themes. Again, 'nature' was invoked in discussions of the daughter's sexuality:

GINA: ... I was determined that she wasn't gonna – that if she was gonna have sexual relationships, then ...... she wasn't gonna have to hide them, and that she was gonna be able to be in her own house and feel comfortable about it. I didn't want her to

> have those back of the car experiences and feel like it was something wrong. ... I
> wanted it to be a natural experience.

In this extract from Gina's account, sexual relationships are *potentially* 'unnatural', but the mother's facilitating of the daughter's sexuality also has the potential to make sexual relations 'natural'. The 'push to independence', then, may involve some felt obligation, on the mother's part, to ensure the daughter's enjoyment of a 'natural' sexuality.

But, culturally, some forms of sexuality are configured as more 'natural' than others. Two of these women's daughters had had lesbian relationships, and neither of these mothers expressed any particular concern over this (and one positively welcomed it). But all of them inhabit a set of relations in which heterosexuality is naturalized and normalized;[14] and it is in these relations that the figure of the mother is most readily seen as problematic. It is the mother, very often, who is represented as holding back the daughter from a 'free' expression of (hetero)sexuality.

Nancy Friday (1979) suggests that all the daughter's problems stem from her relationship with her mother. Having denied their own sexuality by *becoming* mothers, mothers go on to attempt to restrict and deny their daughters' sexuality, instilling guilt and shame, and imposing restrictions. It is only through the expression of (hetero)sexuality that women, for Friday, are able to achieve any level of self-fulfilment and self-actualization (see also Friday, 1991). Yet even the heterosexual relationship, so promising of freedom, is not immune from the mother's pernicious influence: 'Above all, we have introjected her anxiety about sex' (Friday, 1979: 436).

For Friday, not only difficulties between individual men and women, but gender inequality itself stem from the mother–daughter relationship. According to Friday, women do not succeed in the world of paid work because they fear success; a fear which stems from the daughter's fear of competition with the mother. It is the mother herself, through her domination of the daughter's childhood, who has engendered this fear.

By making mothers the root of their daughters' problems, she is able to simultaneously acknowledge difficulties for women in hetero-relations and to present these relations in idealized terms.[15] In a manner which is evocative of Philip Wylie's (1942) account of 'Momism', Friday seems to have created two classes of women – mothers, sexually repressed and denying, and the rest – women whose relations with men act as a buttress against their mothers' influence.[16]

Although her book is an extreme (and perhaps notorious) example of its genre,[17] Friday draws on two common cultural constructions of sexuality: that the realization of the true 'self' is only achievable through the 'free' expression of sexuality (Foucault, 1990); and that heterosexual relations are marred by women's 'guilt' – a guilt which is a legacy from their mothers (Smart, 1989). As Carol Smart (1989) comments, contemporary Euroamerican constructions of women's sexuality are such that sexuality is seen as an essence which by-passes consciousness. Hence women's consciousness is constructed, not as an expression of what the woman *really* wants, but as 'an inappropriate moral standard imposed by mothers on daughters'. It is 'the mouthing of a convention which defeats the woman's own potential for sexual satisfaction' (Smart, 1989: 30). This construction of sexuality has far-reaching implications: there is a conflation between what men desire from women and what women themselves desire. As Smart points out, this leads to the conclusion that women cannot really express their authentic desires; hence 'if women say "no" they do not *really* mean it' (Smart, 1989: 30).

The daughter's 'natural' development into a 'naturally' heterosexualized woman can be represented as an increasing 'independence' or 'autonomy'. But as Smart's analysis suggests, the much-valued 'independence' and 'autonomy' into which adolescents are supposed to grow is itself one of the processes through which girls become gendered, and through which they become (self-) disciplined within femininity and compulsory heterosexuality (Rich, 1980). Far from being 'autonomous', they are positioned in terms of their relation to men.[18]

Concluding remarks

Not only in terms of their daughters' sexuality, but in terms of their overall development into adult women, mothers of daughters face a series of contradictions. They are supposed to inculcate a self which is inner-controlled within the daughter, yet they must also be sure that the daughter turns out 'well': thus they are caught in the tension between guiding and advising, and leaving the daughter to her own devices. Further, the obligation to nurture an autonomous self within the daughter places them under an obligation to ensure their daughter's 'achievement' in the face of social inequalities. As a result, the daughter's failure to 'achieve' can be blamed, not on a social system which militates against her 'achievement', but on her mother. Mothers must negotiate these contradictions without any overt consideration of the cost to themselves. They become the guarantors of autonomy, the central condition of normal personhood, but normality for mothers, as for their daughters, is constructed in terms of a heterosexual and feminine identity tied to relationality, rather than autonomy. This is an issue I will return to in Chapter 6: in the next chapter, the focus will turn to daughters' stories about the autonomous self.

5 Daughterly stories

Matrophobia, class and the self

> I was to end up ... believing that my identification was entirely with her, that
> whilst hating her, I was her; and there was no escape.
>
> (Carolyn Steedman, *Landscape for a Good Woman*, p. 55)

The last chapter showed how most of the women's mothering was structured by a felt demand to 'do it differently' to their own mothers. Their identifications with both their mothers and their daughters entailed both a desire to give their daughters what they had lacked and a set of anxieties that they would fail to achieve this. This chapter will consider more broadly the ways in which the women's subjectivities were defined in relation to, and usually against, that of the mother. Where the last chapter focused on maternal stories in relation to daughters' autonomous selves, this chapter examines the women's conceptualizations of their own selves in the context of their relationships with their mothers. It will also look at some of the ways in which some daughters' notions of autonomy and of the autonomous self are tied up with a dread of becoming the mother, and at the mediation of this dread through the classed position of both mother and daughter.

'She couldn't see who I really was': defining and being the self

A very few women spoke of their relationships with their mothers as ones in which their mother seemed wholly accepting of 'who they were'. Anna for example, said of her relationship with her mother:

ANNA: I can always be me, warts and all, which ...... I suppose applies to any member of the close family. But I suppose she's the only one who's seen me develop, warts and all, isn't she? Yes, I mean like your own children have only known you for a certain length of time – and probably anyone else that's around now.

But this expression of a mother's understanding and acceptance of a daughter's self was rare. Most women related their relationships with their mothers as relationships in which their mothers failed to understand 'who they really were'. For example:

GINA: I was really, really upset by – by the fact that she couldn't see who I really was, you know.

CAROLINE: ... she pigeonholes people. And I think this is one of the things I've found hardest to deal with – and still do. People like certain things and are going to be certain things. And there's no changing. ... I don't know what she thinks about me. She obviously thinks I'm a late developer because I had very bad school reports. And I think ...... I think she probably thought I was a bit thick. She wouldn't put it in those terms. But ... I think I suffered from that. And I still do feel very ...... angry about that.

For some women, their mothers' perceived inability to *see* who they were made it difficult, they suggested, to *be* who they were:

LYNNE: My mother established this idea that she ...... established who I was – my identity or my behaviour or my thinking – and I had to internalize that, I had to be that.

HAZEL: I just felt constantly in conflict [with my mother], in order to maintain who I was. .... And I was pushed to extremes – I went to extremes I probably wouldn't have gone to in order to do that, to be me.

The mother here is configured as able to impose an identity on the daughter through her inability or unwillingness to see the daughter as she sees herself – precisely, an inability or unwillingness to 'let her be herself' – the trope used by so many women and discussed in Chapter 4. For Caroline, this is a situation which is general to the mother–daughter relationship:

CAROLINE: Maybe daughters are always tied to some extent to their mothers, maybe they never quite ...... break away. And while you're tied to your mother, you're not just you, but you're the person that your mother thinks you are. And then you can fall into that in some way.

For Caroline, then, daughters have (at least) two identities: one, possibly fictive, or at least 'not you', which is the mother's perception or definition of the daughter; and one which 'is' the daughter. But the latter identity can be overcome by the former, as the daughter 'falls into' an identity which is established by the mother.

But some women are in a distinctive position here. As the last chapter indicated, it was women who had experienced 'upward' class mobility who spoke most consistently of the need to let their daughters 'be themselves'. Similarly, it was this group of women who expressed most anxieties around their mothers' perceived inability to let *them* 'be themselves'. These women 'know' the 'right' way to mother and also 'know' that their own (working-class) mothers do not fit into this construction of 'good motherhood'. Their desire to 'do it differently' in their own mothering is shaped by a class-based construction of 'good mothering'. For these women, their own mothers stand as signifiers of how *not* to mother, and, further, of how not to be adult women. But the accounts of this group of women, more than those of any others, also indicate that they experience tremendous anxieties around an identification between the self and the mother. More than any other group of women, these women suggested that their own authentic, autonomous selves may be overwhelmed by the selves of their mothers: they expressed fears that they would *become* their mothers. I want to suggest that this fear stems from insecurities around their class positioning, and that these women's mothers may come to signify a class position to which they fear returning.

The rest of this chapter will focus primarily on these women who had experienced 'upward' class mobility, since their accounts are the most expressive of their feelings about their own authentic or autonomous selves. In particular, it will examine the ways in which the stories they tell about their class situation and class mobility inflect the stories they tell about their relationships with their mothers, and vice versa – the ways in which their stories about their relationships with their mothers inflect their stories of class mobility.

Matrophobia and class

> [T]here are no stories for [working-class mothers] comparable to the glamour accorded to the dreams of their daughters. ... I want more for them and those stories are nowhere to be found.
>
> (Walkerdine, *Daddy's Girl*, p. 186)

Women who had been born into working-class families but who now defined themselves as middle-class were the women who most frequently expressed this fear of becoming their mothers, and some expressed this very forcefully. For example:

HAZEL: I'm very like my mother. ...... I had an extremely difficult relationship with my mother. ... I had an extremely difficult relationship, and my goal in life for an awful long time was not to be like my mother. And you know there's still – I mean there's bits of me now that see that I'm like her, and that's me and that's fine, you know. But there's still parts of me that – I will not be like my mother. You know, I *will not*. Erm, I guess I am very like her. ... I mean I think I've tried to be not my mother in loads of ways (original emphasis).

FRANCES: One thing she [daughter] did say when she was leaving – because she was terribly upset about hurting me – she said she just didn't know where she was with me because of my mood swings. And that's exactly what I'd said to my mother and that was devastating.

S.L.: So did you feel like you were being identified with your mother?

FRANCES: I thought I'd become my mother.

S.L.: And you didn't want that?

FRANCES: No. That's very painful still.

S.L.: Why don't you want that?

FRANCES: [crying] 'Cause I found my mother too hard to be with and now the same thing's happening to me. ... I'm not only on the receiving end of this, but I know what Chloe – I think I know what she's feeling and I know it's not gonna improve.

Adrienne Rich's (1977) conceptualization of 'matrophobia' introduced in Chapter 3 locates this fear within both the oppression of women and women's attempts to break free of that oppression. The mother, Rich argues, symbolizes 'the unfree woman' whom the daughter dreads becoming (Rich, 1977: 236):

> Thousands of daughters see their mothers as having taught a compromise and self-hatred they are struggling to break free of, the one through whom the restrictions and degradations of a female existence were perforce transmitted. Easier by far to hate and reject a mother outright than to see beyond her to the forces acting upon her.
>
> (Rich, 1977: 235)

At the same time, however, that the daughter dreads becoming the mother, Rich argues, she may feel an overidentification with her:

> [W]here a mother is hated to the point of matrophobia, there may be a deep underlying pull toward her, a dread that if one relaxes one's guard, one will identify with her completely.
>
> (Rich, 1977: 235)

Certainly, there are problems with this conceptualization. Rich unifies the mother here and occludes *her* attempts at resistance, representing her as little more than the transmitter of misogynist lessons and degradations. However, this passage does seem to me to encapsulate the daughter's ambivalence between identification with, and fear of becoming, the mother which emerged repeatedly in the course of the research, particularly among women who had left their mothers' class position. However matrophobia is not just an effect of the 'restrictions and degradations' of female existence. It also takes place around a particular configuration of class.

I have argued throughout this book that black and white working-class mothers are subject to a construction of their mothering as 'inadequate', 'insensitive' or 'authoritarian'. Daughters of these mothers who *also* 'know' this discursive construction of motherhood are in a peculiarly vulnerable position. Women who occupy a different class location to that of their mothers may fear, not just becoming their mothers, but becoming their *working-class* mothers. Their matrophobia may be bound up with a fear of coming to inhabit this position of pathology, constructed as lacking, as 'other'.

It is important to reiterate here my earlier argument that working-class and middle-class cultural competencies and knowledges are not socially constituted as 'equal but different': rather, they are arranged hierarchically, with working-class people's difference from middle-class people being *made into* inequality (Walkerdine and Lucey, 1989). As Lisa Blackman says, 'working-class difference signifies pathology – it is 'Other' to the middle-class orientation' (Blackman, 1996: 362). Beverley Skeggs asks, 'who would want to be seen as working class?' and adds, 'Possibly only academics are left' (Skeggs, 1997: 95).

The 'working classes' have been the source of much disappointment and disgust for the middle-class observers who have studied them, and, in large part, this is marked out through the lack of legitimacy granted to working-class cultural capital. Ian Roberts (1999) notes how sociological accounts of working-class life have historically positioned working-class people as untrustworthy, disgusting, apolitical (or right-wing) and chaotic. The claims to 'objectivity' within many of these accounts, Roberts suggests, work to produce a scientificity which simply obscures the positioning, prejudices and desires of middle-class observers. Similarly, Walkerdine argues that 'the working-class' has come to be the repository of desire and fascination for middle-class people:

> And what of The Working Class? What are the fantasies proved time and again in empiricist social science? There are too many to name, but those of us who have grown up as any of those Others know exactly how we have become subjected. We are the salt of the earth, the bedrock of the revolution; we are working-class women with big hearts, big arms, big breasts; we are stupid, ignorant, deprived, depriving; we are repressed, authoritarian, and above all we voted Thatcher into her third term of office. We are revolting, anti-democratic. We suppress our children and do not allow them autonomy. How many more of these truths will there be?
>
> (Walkerdine, 1989: 206)

Working-class *women* stand in a specific relationship to this pathologization. The work of authors like Skeggs, Steedman and Walkerdine indicates how working-class women are particularly marked as 'other'. Eulogized in the figure of 'Our Mam' (Steedman, 1982, 1986), or pathologized as bad and insensitive mothers (Walkerdine and Lucey, 1989; Walkerdine, 1990), or laden with sexuality and dirt (Skeggs, 1997), or displaying the wrong amount and type of femininity (Walkerdine, 1997), these women are constituted as exotic and repulsive 'others' when observed from a middle-class perspective. They are also positioned as particularly disappointing from the standpoint of Left politics: they are the cultural dupes who want the trappings of capitalism at the expense of the real class struggle. These women become objects in a plot in which the only position for them to occupy is one of pathology.[1]

It is little wonder, then, that women might want to mark an 'escape' from such a position. To grow up a working-class girl is to grow up subject to the knowledge that you are excluded from a range of cultural and material resources which are highly valued. To grow up the daughter of a working-class mother and then to find that your family life is represented in pathological terms is to have this lesson brought home to you very sharply.

Indeed, it was extremely rare for middle-class women from middle-class birth families to express *any* fear of becoming their mothers; and *no* working-class women expressed this fear. So, although many of these women considered that their mothers failed to understand them, their mothers did not signify a threat to their 'authentic selves' to the extent that they expressed a fear of becoming their mothers. For example, Caroline, a middle-class woman from a middle-class birth family, believes, as we saw earlier, that part of the daughter's identity is the mother's definition of that identity: but this does not mean that she fears that she will become her mother:

CAROLINE: I feel so – actually so very deeply different from her. ... I don't feel any worry about an identification with her. Not seriously.

S.L.: So you don't feel you will ever turn into your mother?

CAROLINE: No. That was never something in the past, and it's not now.

(GD)

For the middle-class women who had been born into working-class families, however, their mothers seem to represent what they might have been, if not for their 'escape'.[2]

Distinguishing the self

> [F]or all the eulogies to equal opportunities, comparatively little is written on the trauma of leaving and isolation, the disdain with which one is supposed to treat the place from which one has come and the terrible guilt that we and not they have got out, have made it, and will work in conditions that they will never know.
> (Walkerdine and Lucey, *Democracy in the Kitchen*, p. 12)

The women who had 'moved class' traced their trajectories to a middle-class position through two main routes: education, and marriage to a middle-class man. Five of the women (Dawn, Hazel, Kate, Frances and Pauline) located their 'move' to a middle-class position within their education. All of these women were educated to at least degree level, and their education had led to jobs which would be defined as 'middle class': all of them worked (or had last worked) within education and training. Their education, then, provided them with a set of skills and qualifications which they could trade on the jobs market and which secured their status as 'middle class'.[3] The other two women in this group, Barbara and Lynne, were more equivocal about the source of their class movement. Lynne, at the time of the interviews, had left her former job in the health service to re-enter education, but located 'becoming middle class' at an earlier point – her marriage to a middle-class man. Barbara, similarly, saw her current class status as deriving from her marriage, but also saw this position as being reinforced by the social circles in which she moved.

So, the women did use more or less conventional narratives to trace their movements from one class location to another: the narrative of the working-class girl set on the road to 'equal opportunities' through education; and the narrative of the working-class girl's leaving her class position through heterosexual romance and marriage.

But to leave the analysis there would tell us nothing about the fantasies, desires and insecurities associated with 'moving class'. It would also reveal little about the very personal ways in which class is lived 'on the pulse', as Annette Kuhn puts it (Kuhn, 1995: 101), or about the ways in which class is inscribed into the self. And, indeed, these 'conventional' narratives were not the principal means by which the women marked out their class mobility. Much more frequently, they invoked what might be called cultural artefacts of class: artefacts which they primarily expressed through the tropes of knowledge, intelligence and taste – the very stuff of middle-class cultural capital. It was the possession of this capital which distinguished the women from their working-class mothers. Further, many of the women made clear that the possession of this kind of cultural capital – expressed through the tropes of intelligence, knowledge and taste, for example – was not necessarily linked with the possession of economic capital. Several of the women were less financially well-off than their parents; yet their hold on specific forms of knowledge and taste marks their own position as middle class in a way their mothers' is not. The women, then, used their possession of legitimated cultural capital to draw distinctions between themselves and others, and, most frequently, from their working-class mothers. In the following extract, Hazel is drawing the kind of distinction which was common in the accounts of these women: a distinction based on the possession/lack of knowledge and taste:

HAZEL: You know, it's like her [mother's] advice about food was crap, you know. She thought I was dreadful, giving the kids wholefoods. She thought it was dreadful. That was why they had tummy aches, you know. I should be giving them white flour, white sugar. Fancy not giving them sweets, how awful [laughs]. It was crap [laughs], it was just way off the mark. I mean her taste in furniture and – you know, she liked Capo de Monte figurines and my taste was wrong.

Although class is not mentioned in this extract, it is signified again and again, in the distinction between different kinds of food and in the accompanying value attached to wholefoods, and in the slippage from food (associated with health, lifestyles, and also with 'good' mothering) to furniture and ornaments (associated with aesthetics). Hazel's working-class mother does not 'know' about wholefoods; neither does she know that Capo de Monte figurines are 'wrong'. The cultural capital which Hazel's mother possesses is the 'wrong' kind: it is not legitimated, and so cannot be 'traded' as symbolic capital. Hence, she must occupy, within this account, a place of abjection, as Hazel's daughterly and maternal identities are founded on the expulsion and exclusion of her mother.

This self/(m)other distinction was drawn through various means in the women's accounts – through distinctions between mothering practices, in 'intelligence', as well as through aesthetics. Many of these women used the pairing intelligent/stupid to distinguish themselves from their working-class mothers. For example, Barbara, who says of herself, 'I don't think I'm particularly dim', and who emphasizes her own use of 'reason' and 'rationality' in dealing with problems, describes her mother as 'A bit – a bit stupid really. Not very – certainly not intellectual'. Similarly, Frances describes her mother as 'very stupid in some ways'.

It seems to me that the kinds of 'distinction' made by these women – the ascribing to the self of cultural artefacts such as knowledge, intelligence and taste – are born out of two (related) sets of anxieties: firstly, the anxieties which arise out of being associated with working-class existence, and out of a dread of returning to it; and, secondly, the anxieties which arise out of a sense of being 'impostors' in a bourgeois world.[4] It is a way of constructing the self as possessing legitimate knowledge, in contrast to the mother, who does not. 'Cleverness' or 'intelligence' may be a metaphor for a form of knowledge which is highly class-specific – for a world of knowledge which the daughter has entered and from which the mother is excluded. The designation of this knowledge as 'intelligence', and its lack as 'stupidity', naturalizes both, constructing them as innate characteristics. In this way, not only does the possession of this form of knowledge act as a form of distinction between mother and daughter, it also marks out that distinction as located within the 'selves' of each of them.

So, not only was these women's current middle-class position inscribed through the possession of legitimated cultural capital, but the possession of this capital was represented as an integral component of the self: less about what they owned than about *who they were*. This naturalization is certainly not confined to their accounts, but is part of broader cultural representations about cultural ownership (Bourdieu, 1984; Lury, 1996). As Celia Lury comments:

> Taste [and, we might add, other forms of cultural competency] not only provides a means of defining why some goods are better than others, but also a means of defining the people who use such definitions, and why they are better or worse than others.
>
> (Lury, 1996: 93)

In this way, class becomes configured into the self. This is explicit in the extract below from Barbara's account:

BARBARA: You know, this idea of ketchup on the table. All that sort of thing I did away with immediately. I always wanted – er, I don't know – ......
S.L.: Tablecloths? [laughs]

BARBARA: Tablecloths, yes! [laughs]. And my husband, well he accepted it, but now he's beginning to think, well, you know, why? Like eating fish and chips on the prom sort of thing. I didn't want anything to do with that and he's got a habit of doing that and Julia's got a habit of doing that, and I feel – hmmm. I enjoy being …… middle-class. Yeah, I do. I'd hate to …… to go back. It's not back – there's no back and forward, is there? To not have the …… – I've changed so much. My lifestyle's so different. You know, the sort of house I have, the way I decorate it. The activities I have, my pastimes, are all – I suppose could be classed as middle-class. And I love it, *that's what I am*. As a little girl, everybody else had these plastic eggcups. I always had the one that wasn't broken when we were bombed out [in the War]. It was china, and it was decorated. And it was always Barbara's, and Barbara always had to have the same spoon. But *that was me*, from, you know, knee high. I always wanted to get out. There were fine things in life that I wanted to appreciate [laughs]. Does that sound dreadful?

S.L.: No. I identify with that, actually.

BARBARA: Oh good. 'Cause I just feel dreadful sometimes saying it.[5]

(emphasis added)

Despite evocations of change, Barbara inscribes her 'real self' as middle, rather than working class through the use of taste and knowledge marked as specifically middle class. It is her possession of this taste and knowledge, too, which Barbara uses to distinguish herself from her mother. In a sense, she inscribes herself as always-already middle class through constructing a narrative of class mobility in which becoming middle class is an actualization of the 'real self'. Indeed, all of these women were able to narrativize middle-class cultural capital into the self – and thus to inscribe 'being middle class' as an intrinsic property of the self, and the self as always-already middle class – by claiming intelligence, knowledge and/or taste as features of their childhood selves. Such an inscription is enabled, according to Paul Ricoeur, by the conventions of narrative themselves. He comments on contemporary narrative forms that:

> The quest has been absorbed into the movement by which the hero … becomes *who he [sic] is*. Memory, therefore, is no longer the narrative of external adventures, stretching along episodic time. It is itself the spiral movement that, through anecdotes and episodes, brings us back to the almost motionless constellation of potentialities that narrative retrieves. The end of the story is what equates the present with the past, the actual with the potential. The hero *is* who he [sic] *was*.
>
> (Ricoeur, 1980: 186; emphasis in original)

Narrative, then, configures an identity through a movement towards self-actualization: the hero *becomes* who s/he *always was* (Ricoeur, 1980, 1991b; Somers and Gibson, 1994). In this context, it configures an identity in which the woman realizes her 'true self' through becoming middle class. This narrative takes on a particular inflection in an 'enterprise culture' (Keat, 1991; Strathern, 1992b) in which the self becomes a project to be worked on, and in which the 'true self' is a nascent entity which is brought to birth through this project.

But this movement is loaded with anxieties: 'eating fish and chips on the prom' is something Barbara's husband and daughter can do easily, since they do not have to prove their middle-class status. Barbara herself is in a less privileged position: she may be mis-recognized, so that she is seen, not as a middle-class woman for whom eating fish and chips in public is a temporary casting-off of convention, but as a working-class woman who does not know any better. In a sense, it makes little difference whether others really do see Barbara in this way: the point is, she herself is able to judge and monitor *herself* using these criteria. As she says:

BARBARA: You've got these two aspects of your life, which you try to juggle. I mean I'm sure a lot of people don't think of you or I as anything other than middle-class, and, er, they would be quite surprised. And yet, at the back, you've got this other side of you.

In other words, Barbara (and I) might be able to 'pass', but there remains within the self a continual reminder that the legitimated cultural capital one owns is a relatively recent acquisition – another 'side' which might threaten to exceed containment within a middle-classed self. Although Barbara's 'other side' is 'at the back' – which appears to signify depth and therefore authenticity, she, like the other women under discussion here, represents her 'real self' as middle class. This complex and sometimes contradictory model of the self defies any easy categorization of class position or class consciousness according to 'objective' criteria. Class positions cannot be simply taken up and left, even if one has the (financial) means to do so: class is embedded in people's history.

Indeed, for all of these women, their movement across class categories was accompanied by expressions of anxiety at not knowing *enough* – not quite getting it right. They frequently spoke of a feeling of some lack in themselves – some lack which was linked with a sense of inhabiting two worlds, and of coming to belong more in the new, middle-class world, but of really belonging nowhere. Several of these women spoke with great pain about their own sense of exclusion from the wealth, the confidence, or the knowledge which they saw as residing within, and belonging to, the middle classes. Those women who had been 'educated out of their class' described this process as most marked at school or university, but some women experienced it still. Kate passed the Eleven Plus examination and went to a grammar school, the first person in her family to do so:

S.L: Did it feel strange at school, erm, going to a grammar school as a working-class girl?
KATE: Yes, very much so [sighs]. It was, erm, difficult getting used to being with people who were so self-possessed. I mean there weren't very many working-class kids at our school, and, erm, the acceptance that people were going to achieve highly, that

was not something that was common in working-class circles. ... And I felt quite isolated there.

Frances, similarly, went to a grammar school (at which 'the working-class kids' were sent for elocution lessons!). Frances spoke of her determination to get to university, despite her teachers' suggestion that she was 'teacher training college material'. Yet her time there (during the 1960s) was fraught with anxieties:

FRANCES: I noticed it acutely at university. Especially with a subject like French, 'cause the middle-class ones had been abroad and could speak French – well I hadn't and I couldn't. And I equated a facility with languages with intellectual ability. And I was so scared. And I was too scared to leave 'cause I thought I'd have to pay the money back.

Unlike Frances and Kate, Barbara did not pass the Eleven Plus, and went to a secondary modern school. Her account was filled with her sense of academic failure, heightened by her marriage to a man who had for a time worked as an academic:

BARBARA: I think socially, when you speak to [middle-class] people, they're tapping in to a wealth of knowledge that you haven't got. Because they've had more money, more privilege. They've travelled more, maybe. They've done more. And you haven't had that.

As these extracts indicate, the women's portrayal of their sense of lack centres primarily, not on money, but on *knowledge*. That is, their sense of being excluded from a middle-class world is a sense of being excluded from particular forms of knowledge. This knowledge is portrayed as being the product of a materially privileged life, in which there is enough money to travel, to 'do more', but wealth and knowledge are intimately bound up, as the very phrase, 'a wealth of knowledge' indicates.

These women's entry into a middle-class world has provided them with a measure of cultural capital which gives them, among other things, a privileged vantage from which to judge their mothers' mothering. But their relatively late acquisition of this cultural capital seems to give them only a tenuous hold on knowledge. They may have enough knowledge to enable them to get it right, but they have no prolonged history of knowing this.

Further, there is always the danger that you might *not* pass; that someone might 'see through' you. Indeed, the very desire to pass indicates a failure to pass.[6] Accents are a particular pitfall here, particularly in Britain, where they (are assumed to) clearly mark social location. 'Middle-class' accents are preferable in most social sites,[7] but only when they are (or can pass as) *authentic*. When they are not, or cannot, they become a joke. In being 'revealed' as inauthentic, they are simultaneously marked as a pretension, which Bourdieu (1984: 251) defines as 'the recognition of distinction that is affirmed in the effort to possess it'. 'Pretentious' is a charge levelled at people in whom there is (considered to be) a gap between *being* and *seeming* (Bourdieu, 1984); between who they 'really' are and who they seem to be. Barbara related her anxieties at accompanying her husband to Cambridge University in the early years of their marriage: 'if you felt a failure anyway, you certainly felt it by the time you left there'. Later in the interview, she commented on my lack of a regional accent:

S.L.: Well, I did work at losing my accent, at one stage in my life.

BARBARA: Yes, I think I did too. And when I lived in Cambridge, I picked up very quickly an Oxbridge type accent, and kept it in America, because they loved it over there [laughs]. But my mother, my mother was a snob, and she's a lot like Thora Hird. And if you see Thora Hird on some of these [TV] programmes, that's my mum ... the expression, the voice, that's my mother! ... And in *Last of the Summer Wine*, she's like my mother there, except my mother ... wasn't as houseproud as that. But you know the way she changes her voice – well my mother was like that. When she talked to certain people she would put it on *really*. (original emphasis)

The character Barbara is referring to here is Edie (played, as she says, by Thora Hird): a working-class Yorkshire woman who from time to time changes her 'authentic' Yorkshire accent into a parody of a 'posh' accent. This, coupled with an obsessive cleanliness and a preoccupation with (sexual and other) respectability signifies a specifically feminized form of ambition.[8] This significa- tion is played for laughs. The joke is that Edie *cannot* pass: she cannot get it right. Her attempts at a 'cultured' accent fail; her 'authentic' class identity asserts itself, irrespective of her self-perception.[9] It is funny (if it is) because of the gap between *being* and *seeming*. 'We' (the audience) can see this gap; we can also 'see through' to the woman's 'other side' which *exceeds* containment.

The comedic potential of women who attempt, through the acquisition of 'good' clothes, 'proper' accents, nice houses, and so on, to pass as middle-class is exploited in this character as in others.[10] This is not the parodic distancing suggested by Russo (1994) as being a constituent of the 'female grotesque': these characters are grotesque because they apparently want to be taken *seriously* (see Skeggs, 1997).[11] Parody and excess simply do not have the same meaning if the joke is on you.[12]

In juxtaposing (and counterposing) her own change in accent with her mother's, and in juxtaposing both with the comic figure of Edie, Barbara indi- cates her awareness of the pitfalls lying in wait for anyone who tries to 'pass'. In watching characters like Edie, Barbara is the 'other' before whom (aspiring) working-class women can be shamed. These women's desires can be marked as pretensions, provoking 'calls to order'; 'Who does she think she is?' (Bourdieu, 1984: 380). But the longings and desires embedded within these characters are also *her* longings and desires; the desire to 'own' the markers of distinction.

Barbara's 'real self', like that of the other women in this group, is presented as 'always-already' middle class. Yet she also must contain another 'side'. The contain- ment of this 'side' is especially difficult because the desire to 'better oneself' (the working-class desire for middle-class privilege) is frequently seen as illegitimate

(Steedman, 1986). Indeed, this desire was spoken of, by Barbara and other women, as ridiculous or pathetic when it belonged to the mother. For example:

HAZEL: [She was] very acquisitive. She had to have, you know, the latest in everything, all the gadgets in the kitchen, you know. ... She was a poor old insecure thing who needed a lot that she never got.[13]

Those women in this study who have changed their class location have done so through acquiring the cultural capital which makes this possible. They have narrowed the gap between ambition and possibility through acquiring the knowledge, if not the history, which enables knowing what 'getting it right' means (Skeggs, 1997). But their links with their mothers – continually threatening to re-emerge, in spite of their disavowals – are constant reminders of how easy it is to get it 'wrong', to become a spectacle; while their lack of a middle-class history makes their position a precarious one.

(Not) inhabiting the habitus

With the exception of Dawn, who spoke of her mother as 'pushing' her to achieve through education, women who had changed their class position spoke of their mothers as resenting their education or indeed as 'holding them back'. For these women, mothers seemed to represent ties to domesticity, standing as stumbling-blocks to the world that was rightly their daughters'; this world was the middle-class world of education, of careers, of 'opportunity':

FRANCES: There was no real support from home [when I went to university]. My dad was pleased but my mum was very jealous. She didn't want me to go to university.

S.L.: Did you feel a special bond with your mother?
KATE: No I didn't, no. ...... I wasn't what she wanted. I have a cousin who [laughs] my mother was very close to, and she was very special to my mother. And this cousin is absolutely dotty and empty-headed, and my mother found it very hard to cope with an intelligent daughter, I think. And, er, when I got a place at the grammar school, she was absolutely amazed [laughs]. ...... I think she felt very insecure about it, didn't like it. ...
S.L.: D'you think your mother felt it was outside of her world?
KATE: Yes, I'm sure. And it was a very, erm, difficult thing for working-class people, you know, sort of going beyond yourself and mixing with middle-class kids and that sort of thing. And I think she was worried about the money angle, you know, school uniforms and that kind of thing. It was all quite, erm, tricky, whereas my father enjoyed it. He was very proud of the fact that I was getting education, that I was going to better myself, in inverted commas. He felt it was good.

In most of these women's accounts, as in Frances' and Kate's, working-class fathers offered more support and encouragement to daughters to 'better themselves' than did working-class mothers. The mother seems uniquely to represent these women's ties to working-class life, a relation of dependency from which they have to break free. Valerie Walkerdine writes of a similar phenomenon in her relationship with her own mother:

> [Academic men] wanted to be the protector and I wanted to bask in their protection. It provided an entry into a bourgeois world and an academic elite, so unlike the protection of, and dependency on, my mother. She, in my fantasy, was going to trap me, tie my hands to the sink; while they would liberate me to the possibility of my entry into education.
>
> (Walkerdine, 1985a: 83)

Education, in particular, was seen by the women as providing a way out of this relationship of dependency; a way of moving away from the working class and distancing themselves from their mothers. But their accounts contain many indications that this move, this distancing, is achieved only with pain, and is never achieved completely.

Although these women have acquired a measure of symbolic and cultural capital, they have not inherited these capitals, but 'bought' them within systems of education and training, or through the relationships of their adult lives. They cannot fully occupy what Bourdieu calls the 'habitus' – the 'second sense' or 'feel for the game' – of the middle classes. Bourdieu defines habitus as a 'system of dispositions' within the social actor, which:

> generate and organize practices and representations that can be objectively adapted to their outcomes without presupposing a conscious aiming at ends or an express mastery of the operations necessary to attain them.
>
> (Bourdieu, 1977: 72)

Inculcated from birth, habitus derives from one's position in a particular family form (with its attendant economic, cultural and symbolic capital), as well as within systems of education. It is a 'factor of social difference' (Fiske, 1992: 163). The habitus of different social groupings (such as different classes) are, for Bourdieu, marked unequally and hierarchically.

The notion of habitus is an especially useful one in this context, since, as Diane Reay (1996: 69) comments, it 'conceptualizes the present in terms of the past'. Habitus thus provides a way to see 'class' both spatially and temporally (Fiske, 1992): it enables an analytic focus on the *history* which constitutes (part of) the subject. As Bourdieu puts it, 'The habitus – embodied history, internalized as a second nature and so forgotten as history – is the active presence of the whole past of which it is the product' (Bourdieu, 1992: 56).

But what is relatively underdeveloped in Bourdieu's analysis is the way in which this history is subject to disruption when persons move across categories such as those of class. While habitus is not 'set' at birth (or at any other point), but is continuously subject to adaptation and change (depending on the person's specific social situation), dispositions can become 'sedimented', so that traces of *earlier* 'second sense(s)' remain. This is clear if we consider the ways in which habitus is embodied. It is manifest in accents, styles of speech, in/ability to take up social space, in clothes, in manners, in ways of walking, and so on (Bourdieu, 1984, 1992). This goes beyond the more or less conscious 'representation of self': it incorporates non-cognitive elements of the bodily hexis:

> The process of acquisition [of embodied habitus] – a practical *mimesis* (or mimeticism) which implies an overall relation of identification and has nothing in common with an *imitation* that would presuppose a conscious effort to reproduce a gesture, an utterance or an object explicitly constituted as a model – and the process of reproduction – a practical reactivation that is opposed to both memory and knowledge – tend to take place below the level of consciousness, expression and the reflexive distance which these presuppose. ... [The body] does not represent what it performs, it does not memorize the past, it *enacts* the past, bringing it back to life. What is 'learned by the body' is not something one has, like knowledge that can be brandished, but something that one is.
>
> (Bourdieu, 1992: 73; emphasis in original)

In this sense, then, habitus is naturalized: rather than being conceptualized as an effect of social location (and, therefore, of social inequality) it is constituted as an intrinsic feature of the self.

But this raises questions for movement across categories. If, as work like that of Blackman (1996), Skeggs (1997) and Walkerdine (1990, 1997) suggests, middle-class existence is constituted on the basis of a radical exclusion, pathologizing and othering of working-class existence, what happens when people occupy both a working-class and a middle-class habitus during the same lifetime? What happens, in other words, when the 'something that one is' is dislocated in time and space, and when a later habitus is founded on the pathologizing of an earlier one? Within the accounts of these women who have changed their class location, there are expressions of a *disrupted* habitus. Their 'feel for the (middle-class) game' is relatively weak, and this is manifest in their expressions of lack. All of these women might be able to 'pass' as middle class, but there remains within the self a continual reminder that the habitus claimed is not one which can be fully inhabited; that the dispositions implied (by the habitus) are not fully possessed.

Women who have only a short history of being middle class may have to constantly construct and reconstruct themselves as the possessors of knowledge. One way of achieving this is by affirming a sense of their 'real' selves as in contradistinction to the 'real' selves of their working-class mothers. The story of class mobility, for these women, is a story, not only of departure from the mother, but of difference from her. But because the differences between the self and the mother are naturalized, they become, not something achieved, but differences which were always-already there. In other words, these women's differences from their mothers were differences in the 'authentic self'. Hence, a departure from the mother (for example, through education) can be understood as a realization of this authentic self. These processes construct the mother as 'other' to the daughter's self. However, this construction of the self is often accompanied by an insecurity around not being knowledgeable *enough*: so the distinction between 'self' and 'other' must be constantly reinscribed within the daughter's story. As the next section discusses, this reinscription may be played out around a set of fantasies which enable the kinds of anxieties discussed by these women to be dealt with.

'Somebody else's child': family romances

> [T]he family romance is the story we tell ourselves about the social and psychological reality of the family in which we find ourselves and about the patterns of desire that motivate the interaction among its members. The family romance thus combines and reveals as indistinguishable the psychological subjective experience of family and the process of narrative.
>
> (Hirsch, *The Mother/Daughter Plot*, p. 9)

> [The] fantasies [of the family romance] have certain effects upon the lived relations of the family themselves, but they are also devices which allow certain difficulties to be dealt with.
>
> (Walkerdine, 'Some day my prince will come', p. 91)

Another way of distinguishing the 'real self' from that of the mother is through the construction of a self which is not 'really' a part of the birth family. There are elements of this in Kate's account, above, in her suggestion of intelligence as a rare phenomenon in her family. Other women were more explicit:

LYNNE: I always wanted to be somebody else's child. I thought they'd got mixed up in the nursery. I used to imagine I was some princess. I never felt as though I fitted.

HAZEL: I've always said I felt like a cuckoo in my family. Like, 'This isn't my nest! What am I doing here?'

LYNNE: But I'm still finding reasons why I'm not her child. I watch her now … and I can see my mother getting more like her mother, and behaving the way her mother behaved when she got older, in this kind of petulant, demanding manner. And this kind of matriarchal, 'Do this, do that, do the other,' kind of attitude. And I think, I am never, ever going to do that. You know, this is a reason not to be like her, that I do not want to continue this pattern, of how you get to be when you're sixty. I would do anything to avoid it.

(GD)

This construction of a self which does not fit with the birth family may be a way of further securing the distance between the self and that family. Lynne's account is typical here in that this distancing revolves around the figure of the mother.

This process may be part of an attempt, on the women's parts, to deal with their fear that they will become their mothers. It is a process which is bound up with fantasies around the self. If the daughter does not 'belong' in the birth family – if she is not her mother's daughter – then she cannot become her, no matter how much she may feel an 'underlying pull' towards her. The differences between the self and the mother can be further naturalized through a fantasy of the self as not *really* being inherited from the mother (see Chapter 3).

A story of class mobility, then, is also a story about the self and the selves of others. It may comprise a myth of origins which constructs the self as *never* belonging within the working-class birth family. The move to a middle-class position, then, can be told as a *return* to a place in which one 'really' belongs. The subject of the present interprets the past in the light of her/his social location and evaluation of that location,[14] and this interpretation and reinterpretation can incorporate unconscious fears and desires. These fears and desires can be made 'real' through the myths and stories which people tell about their lives (Steedman, 1986).

The rest of this section will analyse the ways in which the women interpret the past through the present in their narratives of social mobility; it will also analyse the ways in which their fantasies about their selves inform these narratives. To do this, I want to juxtapose their accounts with Freud's narrative of a fantasized reworking of origins in his 1909 essay, 'Family Romances'.

In this essay, Freud describes and analyses the process through which children come to feel that their parents are not, in fact, their parents; that they are really the children of more noble or more glamorous parents. Freud describes two stages in this fantasy reworking of origins: first, children come to feel that their parents do not love them as much as they would like – that they are not the unique focus of their parents' love. At the same time, they come to know other parents and realize that their own are not unique. At this stage, children, in fantasy, replace their parents with more noble parents, imagining themselves to be adopted, or step-children.

In the second stage, according to Freud, children learn something of the process of reproduction and come to realize, as Freud puts it, that 'pater semper incertus est' (the [identity of] the father is always uncertain), while the mother is 'certissima' (most certain, or very certain). So at this stage, the child no longer doubts her/his maternal origins. Instead, it is the father, and only the father, who is replaced by another, more exalted father. At this point, children's fantasies revolve around the replacement of the father – a process which Freud sees as stronger in boys than in girls, because of the underlying conflict over authority between father and son. At the same time that the father's status is increased in this way, the mother's is diminished, as the child imagines her conceiving her/him through an adulterous liaison.

Freud's essay is an account of the psychic mechanisms we use to deal with what he sees as the inevitable realization that our desire for our parents' love cannot be fulfilled. Equally, it is an account of the child's identification with the parent of the same sex. Freud makes it clear that the displacement of the parent is an indication of the overwhelming importance of her/him. However, Freud's emphasis here is on the father and the son, and on the conflict over authority played out between them. As Marianne Hirsch (1989) points out, the mother, for Freud, is ultimately no more than an instrument in the psychic drama played out between father and son. The daughter, too, seems to be abandoned in Freud's account as he shifts his attention from the (sexually undifferentiated) child to the son, who must work out his Oedipal crisis.[15]

Despite these absences, Freud's account here is a useful one: it provides a way of looking at the loss of the mother to the daughter as inevitable – and, therefore, as not something which the mother is able to prevent (see Chapter 1). In Freud's account, the parents *cannot* satisfy the child – cannot love her/him as s/he wants to be loved. The *romance* of the family romance is the child's attempt to bridge the gap between a fantasized, desired, parental love and the love s/he feels her/himself to receive. In this, Freud's account stands in stark contrast to those feminist and non-feminist analyses which present the mother–daughter relationship as one in which the daughter *really was* inadequately loved. This formulation has continued from Bowlby and Winnicott to contemporary writers such as Eichenbaum and Orbach. It proposes that the mother really can satisfy the daughter's (and the son's) demands for love. When she does not, her mothering is deemed inadequate.[16] For Freud, however, the girl is bound to be disappointed with her mother, since she simply wants so much from her – unshared love, undivided attention, and more.

Freud's account of the 'family romance', then, provides a way of conceptualizing the *inevitable* loss of the mother to the daughter, and of the ways in which the daughter may (psychically) deal with this loss. However, there are features of Freud's account which are open to challenge. Firstly, Freud's lack of emphasis on the mother seems to be based, at least in part, on his assertion that the mother is 'certissima'. Since the child cannot manipulate her/his maternal origins, the mother is not the object of fantasy in the same way as the father is. However, Freud's assumption is questionable: to whom is the identity of the mother certain? Although the identity of the mother may be certain to those around her at the time she gives birth, for the child, there can be no such certainty. S/he has to rely on what s/he is told. Most obviously, this lack of certainty occurs when children are adopted at birth or in early infancy, when they may or may not know of their origins, but there is always room for doubt.[17] If the mother is uncertain, then she can, in fantasy, be replaced.

My second challenge to Freud's account centres on its universalism and reductionism. Carolyn Steedman (1986) argues that the exclusion of which Freud wrote in his original essay is not just the child's exclusion from the parents' love, but also mirrors a broader exclusion – an exclusion from material wealth and status. She suggests that it is no accident that the fantasized parents possess more material resources than the 'real' parents. Although Freud mentions this, he does not seem to notice its implications (Steedman, 1986; Chegdzoy, 1992).

Steedman places the child's sense of loss and exclusion within the context of the social and historical circumstances of the child's, and later the adult's, life, suggesting that the sense of exclusion which gives rise to the family romance is likely to be heightened in working-class children, who really are lacking in wealth and other valued resources, and who inhabit a world constructed as lacking, as 'other', and as pathological. And this sense of exclusion is not wholly overcome even when women enter a middle-class world and gain a measure of cultural and symbolic capital. Hence, I think, the tremendous anxieties of these women who must simultaneously inhabit this world and deny the exclusion which preceded that entry.

The specific circumstances of a woman's life, both in childhood and in adulthood, and the historical moment into which she is born, and in which she lives, will crucially mark out the shape of her psychic formations, and, specifically, of her 'family romance'. The 'family romance' may also be a means of distancing the 'real' self from that of the mother in a way which contains the fear of becoming the mother. If women are not their mothers' daughters, then they cannot become them.[18] The question remains, if these women are not their mothers' daughters, whose daughters are they?

'I wished she'd been my mother': replacing the mother

A feature of the 'family romance' is a desire to *replace* the mother with another, more 'suitable' mother. There are elements of this search for replacement mothers in the accounts of all the women who changed class position. For example:

KATE: There are certain people I'd have liked to have had as my mother. Shirley Williams is one of them. ...... I think she'd be an absolutely wonderful mother. ... She seems a very warm person and, erm, a cuddly person. A delightful person – I think she's lovely. ...... She sort of is exuberant and it spills out all around her. She'd make a wonderful mother.

BARBARA: There was a lovely lady who was the mother of one of my friends, who didn't mother me, but who I wished – oh, I wished she'd been my mother.

LYNNE: I think if I'd met an older woman who could have been ...... closer, who could have provided that kind of [mothering] relationship for me, with that closeness and support and total acceptance ... then I might have been quite happy to shift my allegiance, er ...... and just mainly felt my responsibility in the duty that I see my mother as [deserving] because she gave me life. Erm, but because there is no other woman in my life that can provide that, then she's the only one that I've got, in a sense, so I have to keep kind of creating that with her ...... perhaps because I need it.

The search for replacement mothers dislocates the practice of mothering from the person of 'mother' in ways which suggest that mothering is an activity which could be done by persons other than the women's own mother.[19] This theme is also found in some feminist accounts which link mothering (as an activity not necessarily linked with kin relations) with political activism, or which posit the mother–daughter relationship as the model for bonding between women.

Patricia Hill Collins (1991), for example, writes of the significance, in African-American communities, of 'othermothers' – 'women who assist bloodmothers by sharing mothering responsibilities' (1991: 119). Collins argues that the practice of othermothering relieves biological mothers of the burden of shouldering child-care alone and, further, that it subverts the notion, embedded within capitalism, of children as 'private property':[20]

> By seeing the larger community as responsible for children and by giving othermothers and other nonparents 'rights' in child rearing, African-Americans challenge prevailing property relations. It is in this sense that traditional bloodmother/othermother relationships in woman-centred networks are 'revolutionary'.
>
> (Collins, 1991: 123)

Collins also suggests that othermothering can be the basis for a community activism, in which a communitarian nurturing ethic is established, and in which black women can form relationships of 'shared sisterhood' through othermothering. In a similar vein, Adrienne Rich, in her depiction of a 'woman-centered university' (Rich, 1973/4), proposes a similar form of 'mothering the mind' in relationships between *all* women teachers and their women students:

> A woman-centered university would be a place in which the much-distorted mother–daughter relationship could find a new model: where women of maturer attainments in every field would provide intellectual guidance along with concern for the wholeness of their young women students, an older woman's sympathy and unique knowledge of the processes younger women were going through, along with the power to give concrete assistance and support.
>
> (Rich, 1973/4: 139–40)

All these analyses propose that women can (and should) 'mother' each other, irrespective of kin relations (see also Simons, 1984). However, there can be real dangers in such a quest for mothering outside of kin relations. Collins' analysis locates mothering within a specific set of social relations, in which biological and othermothers have shared interests in dislocating mothering from kinship. In her account, othermothers take on responsibility for children, exercising an authority over those children, as well as nurturing them. In analyses like Rich's and Simons', however, 'real' mothers are not considered; mothering is represented as consisting entirely of nurturant activities; and an identification is assumed between the 'daughter' and the (feminist) 'othermother'.

While on the one hand, these latter analyses would appear to value and validate the work which women do in mothering, on the other hand, they remove mothering, not only from kin relations, but from the regulation which, I have argued, forms a necessary and intrinsic part of mothering. The positive and negative features of motherhood become 'split' (Sayers, 1984), with its nurturing, caring aspects displaced onto replacement mothers, and its regulative aspects remaining with the birth mother.

Indeed, this apparent celebration of motherhood may only be achieved at the expense of 'real' mothers. These mothers may be discarded to be replaced by more 'suitable' role models (Davis, 1992). 'Real' mothers can be seen as the embodiment of gender oppression, passing on this oppression to the daughter, while the replacement mother provides an 'escape'; a mother who embodies freedom and liberation. As Deanna Davis comments:

> Usually the gritty and demanding world of the care of infants and children disappears in such formulations; 'mothering' becomes a metaphor for a nurturing attitude toward other people that is not dependent on biological motherhood or even female sex. As a metaphor, mothering can be seen as a radical reshaping of society, a revolutionary act. ... It is my contention that such uses of mothering provide simultaneously an acceptance of mothers and motherhood and a distancing of the daughter from the too-close identi- fication with mothering as the bearing and nurture of children.
>
> (Davis, 1992: 513)

Moreover, the search for replacement mothers can be the search for the mother of fantasy – for the mother who will love and accept the daughter, and demand nothing in return (Chodorow and Contratto, 1982). It can also be the search for a fantasized middle-class mother – for the mother who 'gets it right', both in terms of her mothering, and in terms of her lifestyle. It is no accident, I think, that when the women in this study actually identified women whom they wanted as replacement mothers, these women were middle class. Substituting a fanta- sized, middle-class mother for your own working-class mother may be another way of inscribing the self as 'always-already' middle class; a way of constructing a new birth family which 'fits' with the self, precisely because the self does not 'fit' with the 'real' birth family.

Such a substitution may also be an attempt, on the daughter's part, to provide herself with the 'sensitive' mothering that she both 'knows' is 'right' and also 'knows' is not associated with her mother's (working-class) mothering. In either case, the daughterly 'self' can be emplotted as following a trajectory in which she becomes what she always was (Ricocur, 1980) – the middle-class daughter of a middle-class mother.

Disreputable desires

> I want books on the shelves ... I want paintings on the wall and red wine on the
> table and lots of different cheeses. I want   I want – I want
>
> ('Sandra' in Willy Russell's *Breezeblock Park*)

> I did envy, and I did want.
>
> (Walkerdine, 'Notes written after an interview for a job', p. 83)

To want and to envy the markers of a middle-class existence is to be in a peculiarly vulnerable position, especially for women, who already stand in a difficult
relationship to those desires. As Carolyn Steedman comments, in Britain at least:

> there is no language of desire that can present what my mother wanted as
> anything but supremely trivial; indeed, there is no language that does not let
> the literal accents of class show, nor promote the tolerant yet edgy smile.
>
> (Steedman, 1986: 113)

What Steedman's mother wanted was 'fine clothes, glamour, money, to be what
she wasn't ... things she materially lacked, things that a culture and a social
system withheld from her' (Steedman, 1986: 6) – desires, in other words, for
specific forms of femininity which were not available to working-class women
like her.[21]

Yet there are few narratives into which women could inscribe this kind of
desire:[22] there is, for example, no female equivalent of the heroic tale of the
'working-class boy made good' (Steedman, 1986). Instead, women's desires for,
and envy of, respectability and material goods are marked as apolitical, trivial,
pretentious (Steedman, 1986; Fox, 1994). Yet, as both Carolyn Steedman and
Pamela Fox point out, these desires, this envy, should be situated within *political*
struggles around dispossession and exclusion. Why should people not envy what
'a culture and a social system' withholds from them? Indeed, how could they not,
when what is withheld is constituted as *inherently* desirable, and *inherently* normal?
And why are desires like this trivialized? Is it because they are represented as
peculiarly 'feminine' affectations? Is it because they stake a claim on an existence
which is not rightly yours?

It is largely the cultural configuration of class, and the inscription of class into
a 'self' which can enable middle-class observers to despise and to ridicule the
aspirations of working-class people. Virginia Woolf, commenting on the collec-
tion of working-class women's autobiographical writings in *Life As We Have
Known It* (1931), laments the women's obsessions with 'baths and money', and
characterizes the women's concerns as 'the narrow plot of acquisitiveness and
desire' (in Fox, 1994: 25). As Pamela Fox points out, the implication that this
'narrow plot' is unworthy of, or outside of, loftier and more worthwhile political

concerns, obscures the politics which surround the desires that the plot articulates. Fox comments:

> Sixty odd years later … we are still troubled by that 'narrow plot', threatened by its implications. … The 'desire' which it names enacts a refusal of the boundaries circumscribing working-class existence and cultural production. Posed against more explicitly oppositional narrative formulas, it impels the writing of a secondary plot that tells another, equally pressing, class story.
>
> (Fox, 1994: 25–6; references omitted)

In a supposedly 'classless' society, 'posh' accents in the mouths of working-class people still have comic potential. And the desire for acquisitions – foreign holidays, kitchen gadgets, new furniture – can be seen as despicable when they are working-class desires. Working-class women's desire for 'words and things' – for 'proper' accents and for 'nice things' is constructed as petty, as pathetic, as laughable. How difficult it can be, then, to acknowledge those desires within yourself, especially when you have seen similar desires within your mother – the woman who is 'other' to the self. There is no language which could make working-class women's desires for class privilege 'respectable'; but there *is* a language in which the mother can be castigated for her failure to ensure the daughter 'achieves'.

As Valerie Walkerdine (1985d) suggests, women may engage in fantasies of escape; 'from drudgery, the pain of being a woman, a mother, the pain of being working-class' (1985d: 124). But the 'other side' of the self remains to induce shame and a sense of exclusion. This, together with the silencing of the expression of working-class desires, and a relative absence of cultural narratives around women's class mobility, means the resolutions in which the women I spoke to engaged are not easily or wholly achieved.

Concluding remarks

For women who have left their mothers' class position, the mother may represent the place they have left behind, but to which they fear returning. The construction of a self wholly dislocated from that of the mother represents one solution to the daughter's anxieties around these issues: daughters may tell their stories of class mobility as stories in which they were *always* middle class, and so were *never* their mothers' daughters. In this way, their stories about their class location inflect their stories about their relationships with their mothers: their mothers represent the (class) position from which they have 'escaped'. But also, the stories the women tell about their relationships with their mothers inflect their stories about class: their 'othering' of the mother – their stories of their mothers' selves as wholly other to their own – inscribes their own class position more decisively.

As Sennett and Cobb (1977) famously observed, class inflicts 'hidden injuries'. Being in the 'wrong' class can involve, not only material lack, but the pathologizing of selves which are seen to be diminished or lacking. And 'moving class' does not necessarily involve walking the happy road from 'wrong' to 'right', from lack to plenitude. As these women's accounts show, the buffers against a world one wants to leave behind can be very precarious indeed. And the question – the call to order – 'Who does she think she is?' may be constantly lurking in the background – not only in the minds of others, but in a self which is obliged to scrutinize itself:

> You can so easily internalize the judgements of a different culture and believe – no *know* – that there is something shameful and wrong about you, that you are inarticulate and stupid, have nothing to say of any value or importance, that no one will listen to you in any case, that you are undeserving, unentitled, cannot think properly, are incapable of 'getting it right'. You know that if you pretend to be something else, if you try to act as if you were one of the entitled, you risk exposure and humiliation. And you learn that these feelings may return to haunt you for the rest of your life.
>
> (Kuhn, 1995: 97–8; original emphasis)

The women discussed here are enmeshed in a set of social and political relations in which they are very vulnerable indeed. Their class stories, and the stories of their mother–daughter relationships, are not happy stories; neither do they fit easily with many of the 'ennobling' narratives of resistance. Yet these narratives would silence the pain, the desires and the fears of these women, as of many others. As Pamela Fox (1994) notes, resistance narratives tend to approve only certain forms of behaviour – those already deemed 'progressive'. And Mariam Fraser (1999) shows the ways in which a 'performative' politics of resistance, based on forms of aestheticization, will inevitably fail when it comes to class politics, since the aesthetic used is *itself* classed.

These women's accounts of class are located in social relations in which there is a constant risk that they will be rendered laughable and pretentious. As such, they risk exposure to the judgements of others. But they also move us toward a radical questioning of the political circumstances which surround their desires and their fantasies – towards an exposure of the ways in which women like this have been shamed, silenced and pathologized.

More than this, their stories expose both the ways in which class is part of the self, and the ways in which class movement brings its own fragmentation. They also show the tremendous significance of the maternal figure in the daughter's own sense of herself. But what about the mother's sense of *her* self in the mother–daughter relationship? This will be the focus of the next chapter.

6   Maternal stories, maternal selves

[W]hen the model of 'mothering' itself escapes questioning we, as feminists, have abdicated the infinitely complicated task of seeking the means towards the institution of new norms.

(Parveen Adams, 'Mothering', p. 51)

The previous three chapters have focused primarily on the 'selves' of daughters – of the women themselves as daughters, and of their own daughters. This chapter will turn to a consideration of the ways in which maternal 'selfhood' is defined and understood. In particular, it will explore the relationship between constructions of children's needs and the meanings attached to mothering.

Most analyses of the mother–child relationship tend to focus on either the mother in isolation from the child, for example, in terms of women's change in 'role' or 'status' in the transition to motherhood (Oakley, 1980; Baker, 1989) or on the child in isolation from the mother (an especially prominent feature of developmental psychology). However, the meanings attached to motherhood cannot be adequately or fully understood without an investigation of the ways in which children's needs are defined. These meanings are centrally important in terms of the ways in which mothers understand themselves, and are understood by others.

The good (enough) mother

To explore this issue, I want to begin by considering the definitions of mothering given by the women I spoke to. I asked them, 'What do you think it means to mother someone?': these are some examples of their answers:

LYNNE. Erm to care for, to nurture. ...... I suppose to be available for them as well in the sense that ...... you're there to fulfil their needs.

RACHEL: Well, I suppose just to provide them with an environment in which they can grow up, really. Physically keep them healthy, and emotionally ...... secure. So they can grow up as sort of un- ...... undamaged as possible, and then live their own lives.

KATE: To take care of them, to look after them …… both in terms of their physical and emotional needs, I guess. Being able to provide support when it's required.

Although all the women defined mothering in roughly these terms – that is, in terms of meeting the child's physical and emotional 'needs' – it is the meeting of emotional needs which forms the major preoccupation of their accounts, so that physical care hardly seems to count as 'mothering' at all:

S.L.: What does it mean to mother someone?
PAULINE: I think to care for them, erm, to care about their welfare, what happens to them, and to help them to …… make the best of their life, really. Look after them materially as well, but I don't – I wouldn't put that as – [laughs] – I wouldn't neglect them, but I don't think it's about dressing them and washing them and things like that, that's incidental. I think it's more a relationship thing, really.

S.L.: What about a bad mother?
JANET: Just feeds and clothes the kids. Takes no notice of them.
S.L.: Doesn't talk to them?
JANET: Yeah. That's the most important thing.

Mothering, then, *means* meeting children's needs. Children's needs, and especially their emotional needs, are the *point* of motherhood. What mothers are there for is to 'fulfil [children's] needs'. The extent to which they do this successfully is the measure of good (or bad) mothering. So, according to the women's accounts, good mothers give children what they need (principally, attention, unconditional love, communication, freedom), while bad mothers either fail to give their children these things, or give them too much of them.[1]

Mothering is not static, however: there was a sense in which all of the women saw children as being most 'needy' during infancy and early childhood. At the same time, however, the needs of children were seen to change, so that mothers themselves had to be adaptable. As Pauline says: 'Being the mother of a little baby – I think a lot of it is physical care. Being the mother of an adolescent is a lot more about understanding.'

However, it seems that mothers do not so much mother *less* as mother *differently* as their children grow older. Certainly, women are likely to have more time for activities and identities other than mothering as their children become less dependent, but, as far as mothering itself is concerned, these women, at least, remained attuned to the (changing) needs of their children. Their present lives (with children ranging in age from 10 to 28) continued to be tuned to the needs of their daughters and sons. Pauline, for example, related a story of how her daughter had telephoned her repeatedly throughout an evening and a night, eventually waking her at one o'clock in the morning; this daughter (aged 26) wanted advice on dealing with her boyfriend's grief at the death of his dog. Other women financially supported their daughters well into their twenties, cared for grandchildren, and spent a great deal of time helping daughters with emotional crises. Indeed, their accounts are suffused with a sense of their children's neediness. It is not that the women necessarily resented this; clearly, there is pleasure to be gained from delivering this kind of support. Yet this support seems to be very rarely reciprocal. The 'relationship thing' between mother and daughter is profoundly unequal.[2]

Of course, this relationship between mothering and children's needs seems obvious. Children have needs; mothering involves caring for children; therefore, mothering means meeting needs. However, to take this formulation at face value is to obscure, not only the way 'needs' become socially constituted, but also the ways in which power works through meanings attached to, and definitions of, children's needs.

Children's needs are assumed to derive from some intrinsic quality of children themselves, rather than from the social and cultural context in which adults formulate statements about children's 'nature'.[3] Indeed, in general, 'need' is often supposed to constitute a more or less fixed, knowable and objective part of 'human nature'. Yet, as Linda Alcoff argues:

> The reality is ... that needs are terribly difficult to identify, since most if not all theories of need rely on some naturalist conception of the human agent, an agent who either can consciously identify and state all of her or his needs or whose 'real' needs can be ascertained by some external process or analysis. Either method produces problems: it seems unrealistic to say that only if the agent can identify and articulate specific needs do the needs exist, and yet there are obvious dangers to relying on 'experts' or others to identify the needs of an individual. Further, it is problematic to conceptualize the human agent as having needs in the same way that a table has properties, since the human agent is an entity in flux in a way that a table is not and is subject to forces of social construction that affect her subjectivity and thus her needs.
>
> (Alcoff, 1997: 344)

So far as children are concerned, their very 'nature' can be seen as being constituted *in terms of* its 'neediness'. Children's 'needs' are discursively constructed as more or less fixed, as objectively knowable, and as *capable* of being met (Walkerdine and Lucey, 1989; Woodhead, 1990). Further, it is only by having these 'needs' met that the child will grow up psychically 'healthy'. These constructions of 'need' have the status of a scientific 'truth', but they are rooted in specific political preoccupations. They reflect specific social concerns and social beliefs about the nature of, not only children, but also the adults that they will grow into, and the society in which they live. For example, and as Woodhead (1990) points out, 'autonomy' is a characteristic highly valued in Euroamerican cultures, but one which may have little meaning or value in other cultures.[4] Making autonomy into an inherent 'need' of the child obscures this social and historical specificity through processes of naturalization.

Yet 'needs talk' carries tremendous authority. This authority inheres in three principal features of needs statements. First, statements and knowledges about children's needs originate, in the main, from the authoritative 'psy professions'. 'Needs talk' therefore carries the authority conferred by the disciplinary bases within which it is formulated. It assumes the status of 'truth' through its apparent basis in scientific discovery.[5]

Secondly, the very formulation 'needs' invokes a moral/ethical compulsion; 'needs' has an authority which alternative formulations (such as 'wants' or 'desires') would lack. 'Wants' can be met, or not. 'Needs' *must* be met, or (the implication is) dire consequences will result. Who can argue against a *need?* Hence, once children are defined in terms of 'needs', then, by extension, something must be done to meet those needs. Thirdly, the term, 'needs' invokes implications of a more objective reality than alternative formulations. As Woodhead puts it:

> Framing professional judgements in terms of 'children's needs' serves to direct attention away from the particular adult value-position from which they are made. Projected on to children themselves, they acquire spurious objectivity. In this way, cultural prescriptions for childhood are presented as if they were intrinsic qualities of children's own psychological make-up.
>
> (Woodhead, 1990: 72)

The constitution of childhood in terms of an inherent and universal set of 'needs' is a deeply embedded feature of Euroamerican 'psy' knowledges in the post-war period and underwrites most popular and academic discussion of concerns around children and their parents. In an explicit form, it can be found in work as apparently diverse as that of the British psychoanalyst Donald Winnicott (writing in the 1950s and 1960s) and the North American philosopher Sara Ruddick (writing in the 1980s). For example, Winnicott argues that:

> The essential needs of the under-fives belong to the individuals concerned, and the basic principles do not change. This truth is applicable to human beings of the past, present and future, anywhere in the world and in any culture.
>
> (Winnicott, 1964: 184)

Ruddick, in her work on 'maternal thinking' (Ruddick, 1983a, 1983b, 1990) outlines a basic, universal category of maternal work which exists in relation to a fixed and universal set of children's 'needs'. She supports her argument in favour of universalism of children's needs by arguing that not to universalize childhood (and what she sees as its 'complexity') is racist. But such a move is only racist if we envisage Euroamerican cultures as having 'got it right' about childhood, against which other cultures have got it wrong. Not all cultures or historical eras have recognized childhood needs in the ways envisaged by contemporary Euroamericans. In these circumstances, are children's 'true' needs going unrecognized and unmet? Making Euroamerican conceptualizations of childhood the basis for *all* childhoods can be read as a form of cultural imperialism, in which only 'we' know the 'truth' (Woodhead, 1990).

'Needs talk' around children's needs, then, is not the transparent, apolitical talk it might represent itself as being. Rather, it is political, theory-laden talk which obscures the political and social preoccupations which underwrite its production through its claims to be describing something inherent within the child's 'nature'. Further, when children's needs remain unexamined, there is no space for a radical conceptualization of motherhood (Lawler, 1999a).

While some feminist analyses have problematized the linkage between mothering and children's needs to the extent that they have proposed equal parenting between women and men (Dinnerstein, 1976; Chodorow, 1978; Benjamin, 1988; Ruddick, 1990), 'mothering' as a category largely remains intact. Walkerdine and Lucey argue:

> [I]mplicitly the argument remains: children have needs and mothering is necessary as a *function* to meet them. … [W]hile it is not coincidental that the ideal mother embodies all the characteristics of nurturant femininity, and while the bonds between the universal, ungendered 'mother' just happen to be made virtually unbreakable by the 'love bond' … between the baby and the woman who gave birth to her, the notion stands that, in principle, 'anyone can mother', but that mothering *must* be done by someone.
>
> (Walkerdine and Lucey, 1989: 19–20; emphasis in original)

Christine Everingham's (1994) study of mother–child interaction is a rare example of work which does problematize children's 'needs'. Everingham provides a useful critique of work which takes children's needs to be a (biological or psychic) 'given' and which proposes that mothers naturally 'recognize' those needs. She argues, rather, that:

> [A]n infant's needs cannot be known objectively. Nurturing activity must therefore consist of interpretive acts, which refer and feed into a particular socio-cultural milieu, as well as the caring activity that is defined as necessary by those interpretive acts.
>
> (Everingham, 1994: 49)

Drawing on Habermas' notion of 'intersubjectivity', Everingham maintains that children's needs are constructed by the mother through a process in which she both 'takes the attitude of the child' and asserts her own perspective. Through vacillating between these two perspectives, mothers can, potentially at least, foster in their children a 'relational autonomy', in which the child both exercises her/his own autonomy and recognizes that of others. The creation of this type of subjectivity in children is, according to Everingham, emancipatory for both mother and child.

However, Everingham seems in danger of reifying children's needs at the same time that she criticizes perspectives which do so. For example, although she argues that children's 'needs' are not objectively knowable, her analysis suggests that the child's perspective, or the 'attitude of the child' is. This leads to a situation in which some women are described as 'misunderstanding' their children's perspectives. Further, Everingham argues that mothers interpret their children's behaviour through reference to their 'social milieu', but not all social milieux seem equally satisfactory. It is working-class women who are most frequently described in terms of their 'misunderstanding', and this lack of understanding is linked to their 'coercive' control of their children:

> In the main, these mothers did not make the extensive efforts to understand their child, so that their child would avoid becoming distressed. Neither did they attempt to understand their child so that confrontation between themselves and their child would be kept to a minimum. Instead, they tended to console their children *after* distressing situations, and relied on more coercive means of directing their child's behaviour.
>
> (Everingham, 1994: 76; emphasis in original)

Here, the class-based knowledges of developmental psychology and, more broadly, of the psy professions and social policy is replicated in another form.

As well, Everingham's argument is voluntaristic, in two ways. Firstly, she suggests that *feelings* of autonomy in the child will result in her/his *being* autonomous. Hence, she does not adequately address the social factors which militate against most persons' achievement of autonomy; nor does she consider the ways in which 'autonomy' might consist in *self*-regulation. In proposing certain types of mothering as emancipatory for children, she places her theory within the perspective which leaves mothers responsible for the production of a particular type of 'self' in that child.

Secondly, while Everingham argues that mothers refer to their 'social milieu' in their interpretations of their children's needs, she does not address the ways in which knowledges about children's needs are socially constructed, forming the 'truth' of what we 'know' about maternity. Neither does she consider that not all interpretations of need are equally 'true'; some have a normative status, while others are outside of 'sense'.

Mothering and gendered selves

> While 'parenthood' is the term often used, in practice sensitivity is perceived as a key element of mothering rather than fathering. … Lack of sensitivity is considered to have different consequences depending on whether it is part of mothering or fathering. Insensitivity in mothers would be viewed as pathological and as having a negative impact on children's development. In fathers, however, the same behaviour is often seen as beneficial, providing children with a context in which they can learn about unpredictability and how to express themselves explicitly.
>
> (Woollett and Phoenix, 'Psychological views of mothering')

As Woollett and Phoenix indicate, mothering is a gendered activity. Despite the argument that 'anyone can mother', the characteristics of 'good' mothers are also 'feminine' characteristics. So, for example, sensitivity, responsiveness to the emotions of others, and so on, which are held by developmental psychology to be displayed by good (enough) mothers, are associated with women, rather than men, which, as Walkerdine and Lucey (1989) point out, is no accident. Katherine Gieve (1987: 44) comments:

> If childcare was the only area of a woman's life where she was called upon to be responsive, patient and tolerant, the issue would be less troublesome for women. It is because the quality of motherhood mirrors so exactly the role of women and the idea of femininity not only at home but elsewhere that it is so difficult to deal with.

Writers like Chodorow and Benjamin reinforce this point in their argument that women's 'relational selves' make them well equipped for the tasks of mothering. These theorists propose that there is the possibility of change in arguing that changes in parenting arrangements could make men, as well as women, grow up with more relational 'selves': but, as things stand, women are theorized as having 'selves' which are congruent with the emotional tasks appropriate to mothering.

Most of the women in the study did not share this view; they believed that men were just as well equipped as women to care for children, and that some men might make better 'mothers' than women. In practice, however, they acknowledged that men rarely did do this work. In their own lives, with few exceptions, this was work which they had to do alone. The only exceptions to this were Hazel and Frances, who did not or had not lived with their children for some period of their lives (see below), and Dawn, whose husband stayed at home while she worked full time.

Women who were married at the time of the interviews were most likely to say that they and their husbands *theoretically* shared out domestic tasks, including the tasks of caring for children, equally.[6] But in practice, the women themselves almost always seemed to shoulder this burden. All of the women had given up paid work for some period after their children were born, and most, when they returned to the labour market, worked part time. Although all of the women had lived with their children's fathers at some time, none of the fathers left work to care for the children when they were babies, although Dawn's husband (not, incidentally, her children's father) stayed at home when the children were older.

Although some women said that their husbands (or ex-husbands) did *nothing* in terms of child-care, most said that these men had done some practical tasks for the children, such as changing nappies or bottle-feeding when the children were small, or taking them from place to place or helping with homework later in the children's lives. However, as we have seen, the women discounted these tasks, so that they hardly counted as 'mothering' at all. It is emotional care which they saw as most important in mothering; and it is this emotional care in which men were least likely to engage. Hence, despite most women's avowal of 'equality' in parenting, it is they who do what they actually count as 'mothering'.

Married women usually justified their husbands' lack of engagement in emotional work by explaining this in terms of their commitment to paid work, or in terms of personal characteristics which they did not see as marked by gender. For example, Pauline's husband has spent long periods of time away from the home on business trips, so that she was largely left with the responsibility of bringing up her children alone. Her own job as a schoolteacher meant that her paid work 'fitted in', as she put it, with child-care – an arrangement which she saw herself as 'very lucky' to have had. In the following extract, Pauline apparently presents her husband as providing emotional support for their daughters, while also making it clear that this work is almost always hers. But her *explanation* – her husband's frequent absences – also seems to underplay his relative lack of involvement:

S.L.: Do they [daughters] rely on you for advice, or just to talk to?

PAULINE: Oh yes, definitely – both of them.

S.L.: What about emotionally?

PAULINE: Erm, yes. I think the younger one particularly, because she knows I understand – 'cause that's how I would feel [laughs]. Anyway, she's more emotional. She needs more, erm, support, emotionally, because she gets more involved, for instance in her job. But when I say it's me, it's both of us really. Whoever happens to be in at the time, when they ring. It's usually me ...... just 'cause I'm there, I finish work earlier. I don't go away weeks on end, things like that.

S.L.: So they're very close to their father as well?

PAULINE: Oh yeah. I don't think they're as close to him as they are to me, simply because all through their lives I've been the one that was always there ...... and he hasn't.

Barbara's explanation for her own greater emotional labour centres on what she sees as her husband's dislike of 'confrontation'. She clearly does not see this trait as gendered, since she describes her daughter as sharing it. Nevertheless, it means that she has to take responsibility for sorting out any problems in not only her own, but also her husband's, relationship with their daughter. It also means that she has been the one to take responsibility for disciplining their daughter:

BARBARA: He is a softy ... and I felt I was the one that had to say, you know, no sweets, or, no, she mustn't go out, or she mustn't do that. So I've always been the one who's laid the rules down. And I'm always the one who talks to her, if there's any situation like this, any problem, he always leaves it to me to do it. So I'm always the one who sits down and says, 'Look, Julia, we are unhappy about this.' He will never ever sit down and say this to her. So all that turns on me. But I don't mind. Because she is a daughter, I think we have the closer relationship anyway. He's a softy and we always say that fathers adore the daughters and the daughters can twist them round their little fingers, and to a certain extent it's true. She can get away with blue murder where her father's concerned [laughs]. ... so I'm the authoritarian figure in the house, as far as she's concerned.

But what underlies both Pauline's and Barbara's accounts here is the extent to which their husbands' decisions structure the women's own involvement in 'maternal' work. That is, their husbands are only *able* to do as little as they do because the women themselves are there to do the work.[7] These women's greater involvement in child-care is part of a general pattern in which women generally do more emotional, as well as practical, work in the home (Delphy, 1984; Delphy and Leonard, 1992).[8] However, these gender divisions are frequently naturalized, so that women's greater emotional labour is seen to derive either from their greater capacity for this work, or, as in these accounts, from the practical exigencies of women's family lives, which is not then linked to wider gender structures. As a result, women's responsibility for this work may be seen as inevitable. 'Anyone can mother', but, not only does *someone* have to do it, that someone is almost inevitably female.

For some women, their male partners not only absented themselves from emotional work, but also represented an extra emotional burden for the woman in that these men seemed to require 'looking after' by their wives. Men were very frequently ascribed 'child-like' characteristics such as petulance, jealousy and attention-seeking, and some women expressed a feeling that they had to manage these emotions in their male partners in order to ensure their children's well-being; for example:

CAROLINE: I didn't realize for a long time how angry I did feel towards him [her husband]. Erm ...... anger with him has always been over the children ...
S.L.: What do you do with that anger?
CAROLINE: Well I used to feel very uneasy about it, because I kept hearing things – reading things that said the most important thing in family life is that both partners should agree [laughs]. ... And I suppose it's, er, I feel he's very hard on the children. And I couldn't let that pass. ... He's very inclined to be negative, to think the worst of the children. And I think especially as they were getting older, I got very worried about ... a negative attitude to life being passed on. ... I sometimes felt he was like a fourth child, that complicated things.
S.L.: So did you have to look after him as well?
CAROLINE: Yes, and often had to sort things out with whatever child or children were having problems, difficulties, tempers, and then sort things out with him.

Women's position as 'mothers', then, may inscribe them as carers in a more general sense than simply caring for children.[9] It is not just that women are required to undertake a more generalized caring (though they often are). It is also that the act of mothering one's own children might involve micro-managing their environment, including the people in it. And this can involve women having to 'mother' their male partners in order to fulfil their felt obligations, not directly to their partners, but to their children. Caroline's dilemma centres on this obligation: on the one hand, both parents should agree; but agreement here would mean that her husband speaks for both of them, and her commitment to the children, and her interpretation of their best interests, will not allow this. This leads to a situation in which her mothering of her children *intrinsically involves caring for her partner*, so that he will be 'better' with the children.

Women who lived without male partners did not have this problem, but usually faced the additional burden of having to do everything (practical as well as emotional) for their children. Of the eight women who were, or who had been, single parents at some point in their lives, all but two had at least one child living with them. The exceptions were Frances, whose daughter had lived with her until she was 14, and Hazel, who had lived with her children until they were aged 9 and 12; so even these women had done most of the 'mothering' work during their children's childhood.

But, not only is 'mothering' highly gendered, but also, constructions of children's needs *rely* on assumptions about the nature of mothers. For example, the tenet, found in work like Winnicott's and Bowlby's (Winnicott, 1956, 1958, 1964, 1965a; Bowlby, 1953, 1978a and b), and retained by many more recent analysts (Ainsworth *et al.*, 1971; Kellmer-Pringle, 1975, 1980a; Leach, 1988), that infants need the total (and joyful) attention of the mother relies on the assumption that there *is* a mother (or mother substitute) around, who is both able and willing to devote herself totally to the infant. Hence this tenet is rooted in specific social relations, in which infants are nurtured by an adult, who, ideally, is financially supported by another adult.[10] Yet this specificity is obscured by the presentation of the 'needs' which are produced through these theories as 'natural' and universal.

A construction of maternity which defines it only in relation to the needs of children must necessarily occlude maternal subjectivity. Although mothers are constructed as having an individuality in that they 'uniquely' understand and respond to their children's needs (Winnicott, 1958; Kellmer-Pringle, 1975, 1980a), this individuality is no more than a *response* to the individuality of the child.[11] As Woollett and Phoenix argue:

> The invisibility of mothers in much psychological work is probably linked with the lack of a conceptual framework for analysing mothers' feelings and experiences as distinct from those of their children. It is not surprising, then, that conceptualizations of motherhood and of good mothering merely reflect ideas about children. What children are considered to need for development is generalized to define good mothering.
>
> (Woollett and Phoenix, 1991a: 40)

Having been brought in to theories of child development as the nurturer of the child's 'needs', then, the mother is simultaneously written out, as all other aspects of her subjectivity are obscured. In nurturing the child's 'self', the mother's self threatens to disappear.

Rather than seeing 'needs' as constructed by the mother through her relationship with the child and with reference only to her localized community and kin group, what has to be addressed is the political dimension of children's 'needs' – the ways in which understandings of children's 'needs' are discursively, rather than, as in Everingham's analysis, 'intersubjectively', produced. Further, these constructed needs are the defining feature of motherhood and that their imperative nature results in a subjugation of mothers, so that any exercise of their own perspective can only be an act of resistance. To pursue this argument, the next section will use Nancy Fraser's (1989) concept of the 'politics of need interpretation' in order to analyse the social and political dimensions of children's needs.

Children's needs

> What was it we needed?
>   Not much. Perhaps only the mothers and fathers with which we started. Perhaps to own and to disown us. Mothers to love us, and put themselves out on our behalf. To relinquish life as we grabbed hold of it. And smile as they did so.
>
> (Fay Weldon, *Female Friends*)

Nancy Fraser (1989) argues that talk about 'needs' inevitably implies a relationality: 'A needs x in order to y.' However, she argues, this structure occludes the complexity of needs talk; exactly how should needs be met? in what form? and by whom? These questions underlie discussion of needs, and it is this 'thick' analysis of needs which forms the basis of Fraser's analysis of need interpretation. Fraser argues that conventional accounts of needs have tended to focus on the *satisfaction* of need. Hence these accounts obscure a number of important questions. Fraser herself identifies four main problems arising from a focus on 'need satisfaction', rather than 'need interpretation':

> Firstly [theories which focus only on need satisfaction] take the interpretation of people's needs as simply given and unproblematic ... Secondly, they assume that it doesn't matter who interprets the needs in question and from what perspective and in the light of what interests ... Third, they take for granted that the socially authorized forms of public discourse available for interpreting people's needs are adequate and fair ... Fourth, such theories ... neglect such important political questions as, Where in society, in what institutions, are authoritative need interpretations developed? and What sorts of social relations are in force among the interlocutors or co-interpretors?
>
> (Fraser, 1989: 164)

So, accounts which focus on need satisfaction obscure a number of important questions: they obscure the political and contested nature of need *interpretation*; they fail to investigate *who* gets to establish authoritative definitions of needs; they fail, too, to investigate the *means* in which public discussion of needs can occur, and thus whether these means of interpretation are skewed in favour of dominant groups; and they neglect the institutional bases of needs interpretation, and the social relations which exist between various groups in contestation of 'need'. They take 'need' as a 'given', even as a natural, property, rather than subjecting it to a social and political analysis.

Fraser's focus, then, is on the discursive construction of needs, rather than on their satisfaction. However, it should be noted that she sees discourses about need as more than simply representations. 'Needs talk' in what she terms 'late capitalist' societies is a site of political struggle between publics with different interests and unequal resources:

> Dominant groups articulate need interpretations intended to exclude, defuse, and/or co-opt counterinterpretations. Subordinate or oppositional groups, on the other hand, articulate need interpretations intended to challenge, displace, and/or modify dominant ones. In neither case are the interpretations simply 'representations.' In both cases, rather, they are acts and interventions.
>
> (Fraser, 1989: 166)

According to Fraser, there are two principal axes around which needs struggle takes place in late capitalist societies. The first is the struggle to establish a need as a 'political' matter, or, conversely, to enclave it as a domestic or economic issue. The second axis represents the struggle around the interpreted content of needs, once they have been established as political. This is a struggle for hegemony – for what will constitute the authoritative 'thick' definitions of needs. And this struggle, Fraser argues, anticipates the future involvement of the state. Hence, needs become the focus of administrative procedures, and, therefore, the object of 'expert' discourses which are 'the vehicles for translating sufficiently politicized runaway needs into objects of potential state intervention' (1989: 173). These expert needs discourses tend to be depoliticizing; they remove the need in question from its social structural context, recasting it as a (potentially) universal need. Further, when expert needs discourses are incorporated into state apparatuses (for example, in 'social services') they tend to become normalizing procedures. This is especially so when they incorporate a therapeutic dimension. The effect of the intervention of these expert discourses, then, is that users of services become positioned both as the targets of administrative, bureaucratic procedures, 'rational utility maximizers … causally conditioned, predictable, and manipulable objects' and as the targets of therapeutic procedures – 'a deep self to be unravelled therapeutically' (1989: 174–5).

Fraser's analysis of need foregrounds the social mechanisms by which definitions of 'need' become authoritative, as well as the contestation which goes on around these definitions. It also draws attention to the ways in which definitions of 'need' are not free-floating, but tied in with institutional mechanisms of hierarchy and inequality. In relation to children's needs, her analysis provides a lever with which to go beyond what she calls 'thin' descriptions of need, to 'thicker' descriptions – the knowledges and 'truths' which underpin need statements. It draws important attention to the ways in which categories of 'need' arise out of political preoccupations and the ways in which what counts as 'need' is forged on the basis of specific, expert or 'authoritative' knowledges.

In Fraser's terms, children's needs have successfully become defined as a 'political' matter.[12] The state takes an explicit interest in ensuring that the needs, or 'best interests' of children are met. Through the institutional procedures of child welfare, social services, education, and the law, welfare state societies monitor children's needs and interests. Within these procedures, it is the mother/child dyad which is the primary focus of the regulatory gaze of state agencies, and hence, the defining feature of good (enough) mothering is how adequately the mother meets the children's needs.

What must be addressed, then, is how children's needs are defined. As Fraser argues, needs talk tends to become colonized by 'expert' needs discourses, and the salient 'expert' discourse here is clearly that of developmental psychology. The knowledges and truths produced through psychological discourses tend to 'leak' into mechanisms of the state such as social services, education and the law; they are also more directly available through child-care advice manuals (Ehrenreich and English, 1979; Urwin, 1985; Marshall, 1991) and they are also reproduced in popular representations – for example, films (Kaplan, 1992; Walters, 1992) and in newspaper and magazine articles. Hence these knowledges extend their domain and, by virtue of their frequent repetition in a range of different social sites, contribute to notions of 'common sense' about childhood and maternity. The next section will consider authoritative 'thick' descriptions of children's needs which are produced through the expert knowledges of psy.

What do children need? the voice of the expert

It is within the knowledges generated by psy disciplines that descriptions of children's needs become most explicit. The Royal College of Psychiatrists, for example, defines the following as the most important needs of children:

> physical care and protection;
> affection and approval;
> stimulation and teaching;
> discipline and control which are consistent and age-appropriate;
> opportunity and encouragement gradually to acquire autonomy.
>
> (Quoted in Adcock, 1990: 16)

This list is similar to the four basic needs outlined by Mia Kellmer-Pringle: for love and security, for new experiences, for praise and recognition, and for responsibility (Kellmer-Pringle, 1980a).[13] One problem with both lists is that they tell us very little: in Fraser's terms, the needs are too 'thin'. For example, what is 'age-appropriate' discipline? (and, indeed, what counts as 'discipline'?); how should children be encouraged/given the opportunity to 'gradually acquire autonomy'? And who should provide for these needs? An almost endless list of questions could be proliferated.

In order to get at 'thicker' definitions of authoritatively defined children's needs, it is necessary to look at the theories on which contemporary knowledges draw. Contemporary developmental psychology in Britain owes a tremendous debt to Bowlby and Winnicott, whose work has been modified, rather then rejected (Bradley, 1989; Riley, 1983; Singer, 1992). Bowlby's work emphasized the need for the infant to develop a firm attachment to its mother, a need which she had to meet by being constantly available. If she does this, the child will develop a deep love for her, and out of this love will come the child's self-regulation (Bowlby, 1978a and b). Adaptations of Bowlby's work have suggested that infants can form 'multiple attachments' (Rutter, 1972), suggesting that the mother's constant availability is not a 'need'. But they have also suggested that the mother's physical presence is not enough; she must be 'sensitive' (Ainsworth *et al.*, 1971; Ainsworth and Bell, 1974). Sensitivity involves taking on the perspective of the child, interpreting correctly the child's 'signals', and responding to them promptly and appropriately. Only sensitive mothering will produce properly socialized, self-regulated children. What children need, then, is sensitive mothering. This figure of the 'sensitive mother' has become extremely important within developmental psychology (see Walkerdine and Lucey, 1989; Rose, 1991; Woollett and Phoenix, 1991a). As Woollett and Phoenix argue, 'as children are considered to need sensitivity and responsiveness, this is perceived as the key feature of mothering' (1991a: 40).

Winnicott's work, similarly, stresses the mother's absorption with the child; this 'symbiotic' relationship is one in which the mother is 'naturally' attuned to her child's needs. The Winnicottian child needs to overcome the psychic chaos which is present in infancy, but s/he can only do this through the constant devoted attention of the mother (or mother-substitute), who, through her identification with the child – her 'primary maternal preoccupation' – is uniquely able to 'do the right thing' (Winnicott, 1956, 1960).

For both Winnicott and Bowlby, then, what children need to get, mothers have to give, and, indeed, 'normal' mothers *want* to give. While contemporary theorists generally refer to 'parents' and 'families' rather than mothers, this does not change the fact that mothering is overwhelmingly done by women; nor does it do away with the gendered characteristics of the 'good (enough) parent'. It is no coincidence that the features of 'sensitivity' are quintessentially 'feminine' characteristics. The bond between mother and child remains the guarantee of the meeting of needs. In this way, there is little space for a radical analysis of either 'need' or the mothering which is supposed to meet that need. As McNay observes:

> [U]ltimately, the naturalization of the need for a mother-bond, an image shared by radical feminists and traditionalists alike, is that it hypostatizes the 'patriarchal present' as the best arrangement within which to cope with what are understood as our elementary needs.
>
> (McNay, 1992: 107)

It is not simply that mothers (and not fathers) are supposed to meet these needs: the incorporation of the father does not undo the characteristics of 'mothering'. Rather, it is that mothering is built on a set of assumptions about children's needs.

Through the emphasis on 'child-centredness' which work like Bowlby's and Winnicott's, and that of their successors, has induced, the subjectivity of the mother is entirely effaced. While she has to be there, she is only in the picture as both the embodiment and the fulfilment of the child's needs. That is, she is only considered in relation to the child. Although Winnicott (1964) argues that infants should not be considered in isolation from their mothers – that we should talk of the 'nursing couple'[14] – the person of the mother is collapsed into that of the infant.

These knowledges contain assumptions about the correct ordering of society, the proper relations between women and men, and so on. Yet their political content is obscured by the constant enclosure of children's needs, and the making of children's 'selves' within the mother–child dyad. The involvement of the state is ruled out by the tenet that it is the 'family' which most effectively meets those needs, since the interests of family members are all merged:

> So long as the child is part of a viable family, his [sic] own interests are merged with those of the other members. Only *after* the family fails in its functions should the child's interests become a matter for state intrusion.
> (Goldstein *et al.*, 1980: frontispiece; emphasis in original)[15]

Because of the political assumptions embedded in knowledges about children's needs, different meanings are attached to different forms of maternal behaviour; it is white, middle-class mothering practices which tend to be understood as 'normal'. It is when defined negatively – in descriptions of the ways in which children's needs are *not* met – that this becomes most explicit. For example, Cooper (1990) acknowledges that there is considerable cross-cultural variation in definitions of 'good-enough' parenting, but goes on to argue that 'change comes with education and knowledge' (1990: 62), suggesting that non-western cultures simply have to be brought up to scratch. Similarly, she argues that there are no significant class differences in good-enough parenting; yet scale after scale of indicators of potential child abuse contain features which refer explicitly to the parents' social class (Hanson *et al.*, 1978; Kempe and Kempe, 1978; Kellmer-Pringle, 1980b; Polansky, 1981).[16]

Needs and wants

One significant feature of 'sensitive' mothering is based on the child's 'need' to feel that s/he controls the mother. Hence 'sensitive' mothers arrange their lives so that they rarely have to reprimand their children. If they do have to do so, they induce in the child a feeling that s/he *wants* to do what s/he is being asked to do; in other words, children should be given an illusion that they are acting 'autonomously', even when they are being persuaded to do what the mother wants (Stayton *et al.*, 1971; Newson and Newson, 1976). In this way, children (should) come to be governed by self-regulation, but this is only achieved by the manipulation of their own desires.

In this way, too, the mother's subjectivity is further effaced: a woman with desires of her own is effectively excluded from the definition of the 'sensitive mother'. As Elly Singer argues:

> A mother's own (career) wishes, activities and thoughts are usually placed in a negative light, as characteristics of a non-sensitive mother. Conceptualized in this fashion, *self-confidence* is something received passively by the child, and based on an illusion; the mother must act as if she has no power. If her power becomes visible it will damage [the child's] self-confidence.
>
> (Singer, 1992: 136; emphasis in original)

But of course, mothers do have desires, and being a sensitive mother does not make those desires go away. Rather, they must be repressed; in not (seeming to) control her children, the mother must control *herself* (Walkerdine and Lucey, 1989). This is not considered in the literature on meeting needs; but, among the women I spoke to, this issue surfaced in discussions of conflict, or potential conflict, between themselves and their children. For example, Gina's son wants to buy a motor bike, but Gina is worried for his safety:

GINA: I want to say, 'Don't! Don't you dare get a motor bike!' And I might still do it. You know, *I might not be able to control myself* (emphasis added).

There is another issue which arises from this discourse of sensitivity, however. If the child 'needs' to be autonomous, then her/his demands should not be thwarted. Wants and needs become conflated; demands become manifestations of 'need' and needs must be met. This can leave mothers in an extremely vulnerable position *vis à vis* their children's demands. The adaptation of psychoanalytic theory on which much contemporary developmental psychology is based has moved a long way from the conceptualization of infancy and childhood described by Freud and Klein, in which desires and demands are not realizable. Now, children's desires have an inherent legitimacy. The casting of 'wants' as 'needs' makes desires all the more compelling (Woodhead, 1990).

These discourses are fundamentally depoliticizing in their simultaneous inclusion of, and denial of, class, gender and 'race'. In theory, they propose, anyone can meet children's needs; it is 'parenting skills', rather than social (dis)advantage, which counts. In practice, only certain, socially advantaged, families are understood as adequately meeting their children's needs. There is no consideration that the very *definitions* of 'parenting skills' might themselves be class- and race-specific.[17] Further, these discourses contain the needs of children within 'families' in which conflicts of interest can only indicate abnormality. In claiming to describe 'normal' mother–child interaction, they construct an idealized figure of the mother, presenting her as 'natural' and 'normal'.

These knowledge relations contribute to the 'normalizing' project by which publics are governed principally by the presentations of certain, approved types of behaviour as normal and desirable. For this to happen, these knowledges have to escape from their specialist enclaves (Fraser, 1989). Such knowledges constantly find a place within wider public discussion and representations of children and mothers, where there is a tremendous emphasis on meeting children's needs.

This emphasis on child-centredness might seem at odds with contemporary 'moral panics' about juvenile crime, for example. But both of these preoccupations are two sides of the same coin; it is when children's needs have not been met during infancy that children become out of control, and have to be regulated by coercion. Media representation of juvenile crime (see, for example, Carvel, 1991; Pilkington, 1994) owes a great deal to this understanding of the aetiology of delinquency,[18] as do many government interventions. This contemporary theme has hardly changed since the work of Bowlby and Winnicott, for whom delinquency was a product of inadequate maternal care.

Further, the 'out of control' children who are the subjects of moral panics are the 'abnormal' children against whom normality is defined (Rose, 1991). 'Delinquent' children and their 'bad' mothers, become the obverse side of normality, marking out the boundaries of the normal. These understandings form schemata through which mothers can understand and regulate their own behaviour and that of their children. Nikolas Rose (1991) argues that the family has come to be governed, not, principally, through threats and sanctions, but through the self-surveillance of family members themselves:

> At least in its ideal form, [the socializing project] inheres in each of us, maintained and reactivated constantly by the images that surround us – in advertising, on television, in newspapers and magazines, in the baby books. No longer do experts have to reach the family by way of the law or the coercive intrusion of social work. They interpellate us through the radio call-in, through the weekly magazine column, through the gentle advice of the health visitor, teacher, or neighbour, and through the unceasing reflexive gaze of our own psychologically educated self-scrutiny.
>
> (Rose, 1991: 208)

As Chapter 1 showed, however, 'expert' discourses still do reach the family through more coercive mechanisms such as the law and social work; and, indeed, law may be extending its domain through what Carol Smart (1989: 20) has called the 'symbiotic relationship between law and the "psy" professions'. Mechanisms for ensuring the normality of families and children within them are, then, contained within statutes and activated by those whose work is governed by those statutes. Techniques of the self are grounded in both juridical and regulatory mechanisms, and processes of 'normalization' are found in both types of mechanism. Yet what largely, and at least 'ideally', dictates the ways in which mothers relate to their children are the processes of self-government and the manipulation of one's own desires. This is not achieved through any straightforward link between advice given to mothers and the actions of mothers themselves, but through specific understandings of selfhood, of the nature of children and of the functions of maternity. After all, child-care advice, for example, can only 'work' by appealing to shared assumptions; for example, advice which proposes the nurturing of the child's autonomy can only work if mothers understand the self as (at least potentially) autonomous.

Knowing the self

Further, it is not even necessary that mothers use child-care advice books in order to gain access to 'expert' understandings of childhood. All of the women in the study had had access to some form of child-care advice, even if this was only in the form of leaflets given out at the ante- or post-natal clinic. However, only half of the women said they had actually *used* advice manuals, in terms of following the advice given or monitoring their babies' development through them. The majority of the women who had not used manuals had made a definite decision not to do so, usually because the advice given was seen to be at variance with 'what it's really like', or because it was too general and 'every child is different'. Women who rejected this form of advice were usually highly critical of the hidden expectations of maternity contained within it. For example:

S.L.: Have you ever used baby-care books?

LYNNE: Oh they're hilarious! Oh they are hilarious. And of course when you have your babies they give you a pack with lots of things in. And of course you're so passionate about this new baby, this first child, that you read every single one. … But I was quite annoyed and amazed at this image that they were putting forward of what I was supposed to be when I'd had this baby, what I was as a pregnant woman. Actually pregnant woman is not a word they generally use – it's 'Expectant mum' which, you know, oh, it was dreadful. No I didn't like them at all.

S.L.: So what kind of image was that?

LYNNE: It's very much, you know, roses round the door, pretty little cottage, wonderful husband with a job, you know, who supported you. And you kind of blossomed with this pregnancy and floated … into this glorious experience. And actually that's all you were supposed to do. You were not supposed to engage with the processes or with the treatment.

Lynne identifies what she sees as the maternal passivity connoted within these works and uses this to mount a critique, not only of the books and leaflets, but of wider representations of maternity. Like most of the other women who eschewed child-care advice, she has a clearly worked out position from which to criticize the voice of the experts; her own experience, her own knowledge of her children and her mechanisms for coping with the exigencies of her life, give her a means of resisting the representation of motherhood as the ultimate fulfilment of her life (cf. Marshall, 1991). As the next chapter will show, this has implications for her sense of self.

It would be tempting, then, to see women who actively and consciously did use child-care advice as being more trapped by hegemonic, expert definitions of 'good' motherhood. However, the picture is more complicated than this. Firstly, women who used manuals were just as likely to be critical of representations of motherhood, and of the conditions of motherhood, as those who did not (although, not surprisingly, they were not so critical of advice books). Secondly, women who had not used these books used concepts of child-centredness, of meeting needs, and of sensitive mothering – the most important themes of developmental psychology – *more* than most of the women who had followed child-care advice. For example, in this extract from Lynne's account, she uses these themes to criticize the advice she was given by 'health-care professionals' after the birth of her first child:

LYNNE: I decided they just didn't know what they were talking about [laughs] and that the only person who was gonna know what to do with this baby was really the baby. And I gave him a fairly equal power in the decision-making about what happened and, er, decided that, you know, that he knew as much as I did about what was needed, and if I fulfilled his needs, then it'd all work.

An important point is that almost all the middle-class women in this study had been trained in the 'caring professions' (teaching, social work, nursing). This training, and especially that of teaching and social work, relies on psychological understandings of 'normal' children and 'normal' mothers. In addition, five middle-class women and one working-class woman had had contact with some form of psychotherapy, either as practitioners or as clients (or both). These women 'knew' the understandings of selfhood and of mother–child relations generated by the 'psy professions', but did not see them as something imposed on them. Rather, they actively participated in these discourses (cf. Urwin, 1985). They gained pleasure from these understandings, seeing themselves as knowledgeable about the best way to bring up their daughters, and therefore as able to do this well. In this way, these women participated in the construction of themselves (as mothers) as *uniquely* able to understand and respond to their child's needs (Winnicott, 1958; Kellmer-Pringle, 1980a) – a theme found in the advice books they criticized (Marshall, 1991).

Women who made heavy investments in these knowledges, whether or not they had used advice manuals, expressed the most anxieties around their relationships with their daughters, and their role in nurturing their daughters' selves. Because they saw their daughters as 'deep selves', 'superficial' indications that all was well could be seen as masking 'deeper' problems. Further, because most of these women saw their relationships with their own mothers as determining a great many of the problems in their own lives, they feared causing similar (or worse) problems in their daughters. So Caroline, for example, worries about her youngest daughter's continued involvement in 'family' activities, since she feels she should be more 'separate'. In marked contrast, Janet and Margaret, women who had neither been trained in the 'caring professions' nor had had contact with psychotherapy, expressed hardly any anxieties about their relationships with their daughters. Janet's account expresses, as Caroline's does, a close and companionable relationship with her daughters, but, unlike Caroline, she sees this as an entirely desirable state of affairs. Further, although she describes her earlier relationship with her youngest daughter as having been 'a nightmare', she also, as we saw in Chapter 3, describes this daughter's frequent absences from school and her running away from home at 14 as 'normal teenage problems'.

Yet whatever the women's psychological knowledge, it was extremely rare for anyone to link this knowledge directly with the way they brought up their children. That is, although many of the women were extremely knowledgeable about psychological theories, no-one saw this as *determining* her mothering. Indeed, this knowledge was consistently downplayed in most of their accounts, as for example, in the following extract from Hazel's account:

HAZEL: I wonder if it's because there are so many books written on childcare and how to bring up your kids that we suffer so much more than other generations did. I mean mothers just used to get on with it. And they did it well, or they did it not so well. ...... I mean when my daughter was born, I didn't read any books, deliberately. I just decided – and I did everything I could by intuition. I read a book about the pregnancy and how it was developing and all that sort of thing. And I had got some child development knowledge from when I was trained as a teacher, but very little.

When I asked women how they knew how to mother, most said that they did not know. They often suggested that it might be instinct, or things picked up from their own mothers. Even those who had deliberately used child-care advice did not cite this as the source of their knowledge of how to mother. For example, Barbara, who said that she had brought up her daughter 'by the book', also said:

BARBARA: You can't say it's instinct, can you? I mean you look up – I learnt how to bath the baby in hospital, and then I read as much as I possibly could. And she was brought up by the book [Spock], I suppose [laughs] and what I thought – I've got a certain amount of common sense. ... I don't know, I don't know. Yes, it's an interesting question, actually, because I was so unprepared, not having wanted to be a mum until the last couple of years [before the birth] and not having anyone around to help me.

Kate, too, had used Spock's *Baby and Child Care*, and, like Barbara, does not present the book as determining of her behaviour with her children. This extract from her account illustrates the paradox of normalization in this context: the ways in which the expertise of advice books is obscured through an appeal to the mother's *own* (innate) 'reason' or 'common-sense':

KATE: Well Spock was like a bible when they were little. Whenever they cried, we looked it up. ...... But as I said, after a bit – I think Spock does advocate being reasonable and thinking things through and what is the reasonable thing to do and that sort of thing. And I think, you know, after a bit we started doing that and, er, using the book far less. You know, tended to just, er, decide what seemed reasonable to us.

A few women, however, suggested that the culture was filled with cues about appropriate behaviour:

ELIZABETH: You've just asked me if I read any books – I hadn't consciously read Dr. Spock or any other book. But I must have read – or heard people talking. I think you pick up more than – on everything, one picks up more than one realizes.

GINA: I guess I remembered what my mother had said and [what I] saw all around me – television and books I'd read.

Theories of children's needs have become so naturalized, so much part of 'common sense' that they cease to be recognizable *as* theories. This can make them particularly intractable; they are not part of a debate, but authoritative knowledges through which 'normality' is constructed. Yet, very often, these knowledges mask their own authority by appeals to 'common sense', 'nature' or 'reason' (especially in child-care manuals). They resonate with wider understandings of selfhood, and their use in welfare state services means that, even if women fail to understand themselves according to these knowledges, there is always the back-up of professionals who monitor the development of children, though, as Rose (1991) comments, this generally (and at least initially) takes the form of 'gentle advice' rather than coercion. Margaret related the following account of her move from a disciplinarian model of child-rearing to one based on 'reason':

MARGARET: I found it hard when I'd had Anthony [first child] and then I got Nicola, 'cause I was – I didn't get much sleep. I found it hard to control my temper. I used to shout a lot then. But it wasn't at Nicola, who was a baby – Anthony got all the – I used to shout a lot at him. But after – I looked at myself, and, you know, the Health Visitor talked to me about it. I sit back, if I feel like I'm getting annoyed, or, you know, something's upset me, I sit back and think about it for a minute or two, and, er, weigh it up, and then discuss it. I don't shout and scream at them any more.

Indeed, an understanding of these theories *as* theories, rather than as 'truths', may give mothers a platform from which to reject them. Only Pauline discussed knowledges of child-rearing in these terms; her training as a teacher meant that she saw the Piagetian theories popular when her own children were young in the context of a wider debate. She also sees her work with older children as giving her a privileged standpoint from which to assess these theories:

PAULINE: I read that [Spock's *Baby and Child Care*] and decided that I wasn't all that keen on it. ... And I can remember saying to someone, 'Well it's all very well letting them please themselves and find their own way completely now, when all they want is a biscuit or a toy or something. But what are you going to do when they're sixteen, and they want things that are either dangerous or anti-social? How can you change then, and say, "Well no. You've got to have some sort of self-restraint"?' ... And then of course when they [her daughters] went to primary school, I think it was a continuation of that really, 'cause Piaget was all the rage, and they were discovering all the day, instead of ... The discipline was really quite bad. And my older daughter came home one day and said, 'We had to do what we liked today, and I don't know what I like, 'cause nobody told me what you could do'. And so I thought, you know, you've got to have some sort of restraint and explanation about life before you can make your mind up. ... I suppose having worked a lot with older children, you can kind of see the end result of what happens when they're smaller. And perhaps I was thinking further ahead than some people ...... because I knew what teenagers – what sort of things they came up against and had to cope with.

'Techniques of subjectification' construct mothers as subjects who are *subjected* to the norms of maternity (Foucault, 1983). So expert discourses are not just representations, but interventions into the lives of mothers and children (Fraser, 1989; Foucault, 1992). My contention, then, is that mothers do not simply interpret their children's needs with reference to their social milieu, as Everingham argues, but that they interpret these needs in the light of hegemonic understandings of childhood, and of the mother–child relationship: and that, moreover, they interpret childhood and motherhood themselves in terms of (children's) 'need'. This does not mean that mothers do not resist these understandings: indeed, resistance is built into the power relations which inhere in these understandings. But there are certain frameworks which can be used, and others which cannot. While there may be some contestation around the exact components of children's needs, these needs are the point around which mothering revolves. Women as mothers can and do resist, but the prescriptive, imperative nature of children's 'needs' means that there is very little space in which to do so.

Further, not only mothers themselves, but also their children, may participate in these understandings of the mother–child relationship, and children's adoption of these understandings may further reinforce the demands made on the mother. That is, as children grow older, they may themselves become subject to schemata of understanding which propose that their demands are inherently legitimate, and, further, that they should be met by their mothers. As Woollett and Phoenix comment:

[C]hildren's assumptions about mothers' functions and responsibilities influence how children may come to see their mothers and the extent to which they get involved in mother-blaming. ... The feedback children provide as they grow up is an increasingly important part of women's experience of motherhood.

(1991b: 221)

On this basis, daughters may expect almost total devotion from their mothers: as I suggested earlier, many of these women's daughters did make considerable demands on them. Caroline, for example, feels that her daughters resent her writing because, when writing, she is unavailable to them:

CAROLINE: They've said things about, you know, we'd come in and you'd be at the type-writer, and ...... it was perhaps a time when they wanted to talk, and I was busy.

In circumstances like these, how are mothers to sort out needs from desires?

Needs and rights

Children's needs are constructed out of particular 'knowledges' which reflect political interests and preoccupations, but these political dimensions become occluded through various depoliticizing mechanisms within the discourse. Although children's needs have become politicized, they are also enclaved within the domestic realm. Within this sphere, mothers stand in a particularly vulnerable position, since their maternity only exists in relation to children's 'needs'. This discourse proposes that needs *can* be met, and that, in the main, it is mothers who should meet them. While there is contestation around the exact components of children's needs, mothers always stand in this relationship to them. Further, discourses of 'sensitive mothering', which suggest that children's demands should not (ostensibly) be thwarted, result in a translation of 'wants' into 'needs'. Since 'need' has a more powerful impact than 'want' or 'demand', the 'good mother' is subjected to her child's demands.

Given these problematic features of needs claims, their replacement by 'rights claims' might seem more politically useful. Nancy Fraser (1989) adopts this line, arguing that claims to rights 'avoid the forms of paternalism that arise [in social welfare policies] when needs claims are divorced from rights claims' (Fraser, 1989: 183). Fraser claims that rights claims are not *inherently* individual, bourgeois or androcentric; they become so, she suggests, only when such values are enshrined as 'rights'.

Sophie Laws (1994b) explicitly adopts a 'children's rights' perspective as a platform from which to contest contemporary right-wing attacks on single mothers. She points to the ways in which government policy in respect of single mothers contravenes the right of children enshrined in the 1989 United Nations Convention on the Rights of the Child. Laws argues:

The great strength of the children's rights perspective is that it reminds us that children have rights as persons. So often children are seen only as potential adults and their present reality disregarded. Focusing on the rights of children can bring an interesting perspective to debates which are generally conducted in terms of conflicts of interest between different adults.

(Laws, 1994b: 13)

Laws' analysis usefully points up the contradictions between the UN Declaration (to which the UK is a signatory) and current British social policy. In this, it reveals the ways in which government attacks on, and discrimination against, single mothers, contravenes the rights of these mothers' children. And certainly, if the Convention were to be fully implemented, the lives of many children would change immeasurably for the better.

Nevertheless, it seems to me that the replacing of 'needs talk' with 'rights talk' has to proceed with extreme caution. Needs and rights are not so easily separable as they might appear. Rights – and, in particular, children's rights – are formulated *on the basis of* need. The UN Convention on Children's Rights, for example, although ostensibly dealing with children's rights, frequently fudges the line between rights and 'needs' (or 'best interests').[19] Further, the Convention's assertion of children's rights is framed in the context of their needs (which, it suggests, they may not recognize) and, indeed, their 'development'. This means that rights are always vulnerable to obliteration by 'needs'. So, for example, the obligation to ensure free access to information, enshrined in Article 17 of the Convention, is offset by the obligation to protect the child from 'information and material injurious to his or her well-being' (Article 17 (e)).

But more fundamentally, claims to rights are caught between increasing individualization (which would rule out state intervention) (Smart, 1989) and increasing scrutiny and governance. Hence, on the one hand, children's rights would be framed in terms of the obligations of their parents[20] – as in the UN Convention's stated conviction that:

> [T]he family, as the fundamental group of society and the natural environment for the growth and well-being of all its members and particularly children, should be afforded the necessary assistance so that it can more fully assume its responsibilities within the community,

and that

> the child, for the full and harmonious development of his or her personality, should grow up in a family environment.

(Preamble)

These clauses place the child firmly within the context of the family, whose task it is (albeit supported by the state) to provide physically, emotionally and psychologically for the child.[21] On the other hand, states are able to override the wishes of parents[22] (and, indeed, of children themselves.[23])

'Rights' do not exist in a social and institutional vacuum, any more than 'needs' do; and claims for children's 'rights' would not, in themselves, alter contemporary Euroamerican constructions of childhood. Invoking 'rights' would seem unlikely to place any obligation on the state to provide resources which might benefit children or the families in which they live. It might, indeed, lead to a situation in which both children and parents are tied more closely in to relations of expertise.

Concluding remarks

'Needs talk' assumes a tremendous significance in defining childhood and in inscribing the obligations of mothers. While 'children's rights' perspectives represent an important attempt to cut across some of the shortcomings of needs talk, they run into similar shortcomings themselves. In practice, needs, wants and rights are bound up with each other, but needs remain the bedrock which validate wants and which underscore rights. And here we have the crux of the difference between mothers and daughters: while daughterly identities are built on the basis of (fulfilled or unfulfilled) 'need', maternal identities can only be built on the basis of responsiveness to that need. Mothers could only escape from this positioning by being bad mothers, and who would want to be a bad mother?

The point is *not* that women – either as mothers or as daughters – are 'cultural dupes': rather, it is that they inhabit a social world in which their identities *as mothers and daughters* are forged within relations of power/knowledge which it is impossible to simply walk out of. They cannot simply 'escape' these understandings. They can, however, subvert hegemonic understandings of the mother–child relationship, as the next chapter will show.

7 Children's needs and mothers' desires

Need is also a political instrument meticulously prepared, calculated and used.

(Michel Foucault, *Discipline and Punish*, p. 26)

Nobody within a discourse of meeting needs talks about the mother; what effect being 'constantly available' might have on her. No one talks about how she must constantly struggle to maintain the rich environment of which she is guardian or how much hidden effort is made; while the child is enjoying 'liberation' and autonomy, this to some extent depends on the mother's oppression.

(Valerie Walkerdine and Helen Lucey, *Democracy in the Kitchen*, p. 106; emphasis in original)

I argued in the preceding chapter that, whatever the exact constituents of children's needs, it is primarily mothers who are positioned as having to meet them. This chapter will explore some of the consequences, for mothers, of this relationship between maternity and children's needs.

Fraser (1989: 165) argues that claims about needs are always 'internally dialogized', in that they invoke resonances of other, competing, need interpretations. Although Fraser does not develop this point, it is clear that part of this process also involves allusions to the competing needs claims of other *persons*. For example, in recent 'moral panics' about the numbers of young, single mothers living on state benefits in Britain, needs claims were frequently cast in terms of the needs of 'the taxpayer' as against the needs of these women and their children.

The most obvious competing claim, however, in discussion of children's needs, are the needs claims of the mother. So what happens to the mother's needs claims in discourses of children's needs? First of all, it is important to note that the needs of the mother are rarely explicitly considered in discussions of children's needs. In Winnicott's work, for example, the mother is reduced to the child's 'facilitating environment' (Winnicott, 1965b). But, as this chapter will show, even when potential needs claims on the part of mothers are alluded to, these needs claims are occluded by those of the child. There are two main types of movement involved in this process; the invoking of a congruence of needs between mother and child, and the translation of claims of maternal 'need' into maternal 'desires'.

The 'congruence of needs' model

One type of construction of maternal 'needs' is that they are the same as those of the child. This construction is implicit or explicit in much child-care advice: it achieves an emphasis on child-centredness which comes close to proposing that child-centredness is, for the mother, the same as self-centredness. Winnicott's 'ordinary devoted mother' has a 'need' to behave in exactly the way that is good for the baby. And, more recently, Penelope Leach advises that:

> taking the baby's point of view does not mean neglecting your, her parents' viewpoint. Your interests and hers are identical. You are all on the same side, the side that wants to be happy, to have fun. If you make happiness for her, she will make happiness for you. If she is unhappy, you will find your-selves unhappy as well, however much you want or intend to keep your feelings separate from hers.
>
> (Leach, 1988: 8)

As Cathy Urwin (1985: 193) notes, this argument that the baby's and the mother's needs are identical only works by 'totally discounting the needs of the mother as an independent person altogether'. And as Marshall (1991) comments, Leach's argument is 'ingenious' in that it encourages mothers to give up aspects of their lives (particularly any aspects other than those as wife and mother[1]) without resentment. As well, this type of account contributes to a 'normalizing' process in which 'normal' (or 'good-enough' or 'sensitive') mothers are constructed as without any needs or desires of their own. Their 'interests' are valid only in so far as they coincide with those of the child – an extremely restricted sphere.

Needs versus desires

The second movement in the effacing of maternal needs claims which I want to explore here consists in the denial of those needs *as* needs. 'Normal' mothers are constructed as having no desires, beyond the (biologically or socially impelled) desire to have children (Warnock, 1985). However, this desire is only appropriate in married, heterosexual women ('normal' mothers), in whom it is translated into a 'need' (Stanworth, 1987). In women who fall outside of this category of 'normality', though, the reverse process occurs. These mothers seem to have plenty of desires; what they do not have are (legitimate) 'needs'.

To illustrate my argument here, I want to refer to a story which preoccupied the British press in March 1991. This story concerned a woman who had become pregnant through the use of artificial insemination by donor (AID). She had received the AID through the British Pregnancy Advisory Service. What made her story into one which attracted so much attention, not only from the media, but from MPs, church leaders, counsellors and psychotherapists, were two facts: she was unmarried, and she was described as a 'virgin'.

The main focus of the representation of this story in the press was the clear unsuitability of such a woman for motherhood. What I want to focus on here is the way in which 'children's needs' were used as a means of effacing any potential needs claims which might have been made on the woman's behalf.

There was considerable consensus in the nature of the press coverage of this story: every national newspaper presented the story in more or less negative terms, and used more or less the same quotations from the same group of people, with only a few exceptions. The emphasis on the needs of the (potential) child within these accounts seems to be an example of the psychological discourse of children's needs escaping from their specialized arena (Fraser, 1989). Psychologists were in a minority among the persons quoted (although they appeared more frequently in 'broadsheet' newspapers) but the emphasis on children's needs originated from this specialism, and, as I will go on to argue, presents a particularly intractable argument.

For the sake of brevity, I will focus on just one newspaper story (Milhill, 1991), since it encapsulates both the opposition which was set up between the interests of the woman and the foetus, and the movement from maternal 'needs' to maternal 'wants'. This story appeared in *The Guardian*[2] under the headline, 'Child's needs before mother's desires'. After a general introduction, and a discussion of the ethics of offering AID to single women, the story moves on to children's needs, quoting Dame Mary Donaldson (chairwoman of the Interim Licensing Authority):

> I am old-fashioned enough to believe that a child needs two parents. In these cases it seems that the needs of the women are being seen as paramount.
>
> (quoted in Milhill, 1991)

Later in the story, these needs become translated into 'wants' in the following quotation from John Habgood, the Archbishop of York:

> A child wanted because the parent [*sic*] wants someone to love, wanted as an act of defiance, wanted, in extreme cases, as a kind of accessory, has to carry too much of the emotional burden of its parent's needs. It can be the victim of dangerous selfishness.
>
> (quoted in Milhill, 1991)

Although Habgood introduces the concept of 'needs', it is clearly not the 'need' for a child to which he is referring, but broader emotional 'needs' which the child, once born, will have to meet. The illegitimacy of these 'needs' in mothers is signified by Habgood's contention that these needs represent a 'burden' on the child, and one which will make the child into a 'victim'. It is also clear that the 'parents' referred to here are not any parents; they are obviously not fathers (since it is not men becoming pregnant!) and neither are they married, heterosexual mothers, who are presumably free of these desires.

There is, then, a narrative closure of the women's potential needs claims, congruent with the story's headline. This contrast between children's needs and maternal desires is reproduced throughout the national press coverage: for example:

> Opponents believe women who want to exclude men are being perverse and will harm the emotional and psychological well-being of their children.
>
> (Carr, 1991)

> A spokesman [for Barnardo's] said: 'The *needs* of the child are of paramount importance and must come before the *preferences* of parents'.
>
> (Chaytor, 1991; emphasis added)

> We do not carry out assisted conception for single women except when they are in a stable relationship of, say, a year or more. I know this upsets women's rights organizations, but I do not plan any changes. We have a clinical ethical committee which ... decided that *the prime concern is for the baby – not the women* – and that it was not right deliberately to create children, in addition to those produced accidentally, in an environment that might not be ideal.
>
> (Peter Brinsden, medical director of Bourne Hall, which pioneered in vitro fertilization, quoted in Doyle, 1991; emphasis added)

Throughout the press coverage of this story, then, a hierarchy is set up between the (imagined) child and the woman. Within this hierarchy, the child is attributed a set of needs which are the absolute priority, while any possible needs of the woman are pathologized. This powerful contrast is an important feature, too, of discourses of 'foetal personhood', in which the potential child is afforded a subjectivity, while that of the pregnant woman is wholly effaced (Petchesky, 1986; Stanworth, 1987; Franklin, 1991).

This story illustrates one way in which the mother's potential needs claims can be discounted and rendered illegitimate. The construction of children as having 'needs' while (bad) mothers only have 'desires' means that any claims made by the woman as mother on her own behalf can be rendered as no more than 'dangerous selfishness'. I want to emphasize that I am not arguing that 'needs' are more 'real' or imperative than 'desires': rather, I am arguing that 'need' implies both a more objective reality and a greater legitimacy than 'desire'. Desires can be met, or not. Needs *must* be met, or dire consequences will result (Woodhead, 1990).

Losing the self

> The child-centricity of most feminist and nonfeminist accounts of mothering deflects feminist attention from central questions: What are the effects of current

conditions of mothering on *mothers*? And how might *mothers* benefit from a revisioning of motherhood?

(Daly and Reddy, 'Narrating mothers', p. 3; emphasis in original)

If maternal needs claims are occluded in favour of those of the child within authoritative understandings of the mother–child relationship, how is this lived out? How do the women themselves understand it? None of the women in this study considered that their own needs/desires were the same as those of their daughters in the sense that writers like Winnicott and Leach suggest. Clearly, then, there is a conflict of interests here which must be negotiated.

All of the women presented their position as mothers as one in which their daughters' (and sons') needs 'came first'. But what did they come before? The women tended to cast this situation in terms of their children's needs versus their own desires. In other words, what mothers want should be subordinated to what children *need*. Most women saw putting one's own desires or interests first as the mark of a 'bad mother'. For example:

ANNA: I suppose if she consistently puts her own interests first, then, yes, that's bad mothering.

BARBARA: I suppose you could say …… to be a good mother you have to put your children first, rather than yourself, in quite a lot of situations, circumstances.

This looks like a manifestation of the discursive construction of the mother–child relationship which I outlined above. However, there are important differences. While this construction simply obliterates maternal desires in 'normal'/'good' mothers, these women (who did see themselves as good mothers) also saw themselves as having desires. However, only one desire – the desire to be the good mother – could claim any legitimacy when faced with children's needs. For some women, this created a situation in which no other wants could be acted on. This was the situation which all the middle-class women I spoke to mentioned as a sacrifice to becoming a mother, reflecting, I think, their tremendous investment in discourses of children's emotional needs. For example:

S.L.: What are the sacrifices?
RACHEL: Well not living your own life entirely, I think, when you have the children. Because they're always there and, to me, anyway, they come first. …… I know there are mothers who manage to be good mothers and also live their own lives, but you're always reading, er, biographical books about people who have really terrible mothers, so you know what really terrible mothers are like. But I think balancing doing your own thing and being a mother must be quite difficult. I think I've not really tried to balance it very much. I think I've, er, – I feel I know what I should be doing as a mother, so I do that, but I maybe don't do a lot of what I want to do.

For some women, however, the sacrifice of their own desires had repercussions beyond simply not doing what they wanted. These women conceptualized their maternity as involving a loss of self. In the following extract from Lynne's account, this situation arises from her positioning during her pregnancies. She feels herself to have been positioned as no more than the child's environment – what Oakley (1987) has designated an 'object-container':

LYNNE: You're imaged as – as just this carrier of this – this thing that is actually possessed by the doctors and the medical services, so that the pregnancy isn't your own. Although it's within you, it's actually nothing to do with you. It's the responsibility of the health-care professionals. And your duty – it's quite often stated that your duty is to give your baby the 'best chance', which, you know, is – just makes you into something that transports this thing that is not yours. … And I resented that, because, being a trained nurse, I wanted to engage with the process. I wanted to engage with – you know, make decisions about what was going to happen to *me*. … I did not want to be seen as a mindless kind of, you know, transporter of this more important ……. thing that was inside me.

Lynne, like Pauline in Chapter 6, uses her own expertise, in this case as a 'trained nurse' to reinsert herself as a knowing subject, as someone capable of 'making decisions', of actively engaging with her own pregnancy. It is this expertise which, at least in part, enables her to mount a critique of the medicalization of pregnancy. She is able to draw a distinction between the doctors' perception of her as a pregnant woman – a mere 'transporter' of the foetus – and her own perception of herself as an active, knowing subject. For other women, though, the loss of self arose not only from others' perception of who they were as 'mothers', but also from their own consciousness of themselves. In other words, their *sense* of themselves became lost:

S.L.: What are the sacrifices to being a mother?
HAZEL: I think when they're young, it's a real giving up of self. … [A]ny women who've had an education – even those who haven't, possibly, but certainly those who've been educated to expect something else, and want something else – and then they're thrown into this motherhood thing. … I think the sacrifice is giving up like your own ambitions, your own self, and putting those on the shelf for a while, and concentrating on those issues that are to do with you, not to do with you in your role as mother. I mean when I started studying … it was brilliant to just be me, not to be Joe's partner or the children's mother, you know. … I was either Leah's mum or Joe's wife. To be just me was brilliant. It was like, oh yeah, I've forgotten about this. So, for me, that's the biggest sacrifice women make.

ELIZABETH: I think even then [when children were younger] I was aware that there was a lack of identity. I wasn't fully my own person.

Both Hazel and Elizabeth (see below) mark this loss of selfhood/personhood contrastively with work outside the home. Several women spoke of the world outside the home in this way – as one in which selfhood could be realized in a way not possible within the home. Despite the oppressively gendered nature of paid work, for these women it affords a realization of themselves which they do not see as available within the home (cf. Boulton, 1983). This characterization of paid work is class-based; Hazel talks of 'educated women' and Elizabeth of 'careers' – and indeed, none of the working-class women saw their paid work in this way. For the working-class women, it was at home, rather than at work, that they felt most 'themselves'.

It may be, though, that there is an element of a loss of selfhood for mothers of all classes, in so far as it seems to be difficult for children (even adult children) to see their mothers as having a 'self' outside of the subject-position 'mother'. Barbara, for example, said of her (working-class) mother, 'It's only now that I'm beginning to see that she wasn't mum and nothing else'. Or, as Gina ironically says:

GINA: Mothers ... shout, and mothers love you, and are there for you, and they're always there when you come home from school, and they're there when you get up in the morning. They're *there* for *you* (original emphasis).

And, as Caroline says of her middle-class mother:

CAROLINE: I can imagine that if my mother'd decided to ...... take on some career, go off and do things which meant I didn't get my tea on the table, I can imagine I would have resented that tremendously [laughs]. I thought the other day, if my mother suddenly decided she wanted to get married again, how would I feel? ... And at first I just thought, oh that's too ridiculous to contemplate [laughs]. And then I thought, that's awful. Why shouldn't she have relationships? You know, at 76, why shouldn't she meet someone and fall in love with someone? And I don't know at all how I'd feel if she did. Although, you know, [laughs] I would think it was – I mean I can't imagine anyone else in the world that it would worry me, their having a relationship. ... Which, you know, says something. ... I don't think I'd find it ridiculous about *anyone* of 76 – it's because it's my mother (original emphasis).

For me, the most poignant example of the effacement of the mother's self was contained in a letter written to Frances by her mother. Frances spoke of her relationship with her mother as one marked by conflict and mutual misunderstanding. The gulf between them widened further when Frances went to university and later embarked on a prestigious career, leaving behind her working-class origins. Despite brief periods of rapprochement, the difficulties of the relationship continued until her mother's death. The letter from which this extract is taken seems to have been written in response to some attempt by Frances to forge an understanding between herself and her mother:

I was very touched at what you said to me, and felt that at last my prayers were answered after all the years gone by, you'll never know how I felt, it was a revelation to me, because I've always felt as if I was pushed away from you, but which I now know isn't at all true, and which I'm so sincerely pleased about.

It's funny Fran, how one person does not *really know* another, no matter how long they may have known one another. Deep down in me is a lot of affection which I would give to people (and at which I'm now doing) but all through my life it seems as if I've been on the defensive all the time and not shown my true self.

...

I hope this letter doesn't sound selfish as it's all about myself, but I'm just pleased to be able to write for once without wondering what to say and to let you know how I feel and the real person I am. (original emphasis)[3]

This extract seems to me to encapsulate the difficulties, for a mother, in bringing her own sense of herself – 'the real person I am' – into the mother–daughter relationship. If maternal subjectivity is effaced in favour of childhood 'autonomy', then to take up the subject position 'mother' is to both position oneself, and be positioned by others, as having no desires and no subjectivity.

If, as Judith Roof (1991) argues, narrative inscribes desire, then the maternal story can be particularly hard to relate, since maternal desires are always problematic. Indeed, there seems to be an absence of a cultural framework into which the mother's story could be fitted. In psychoanalysis, as in literature, it is the daughter's story which is paramount (Hirsch, 1989).[4] Not only is the mother's story an absence, then, but the daughter herself may narrate motherhood as involving the loss of control and autonomy, as do the girls in Steedman's *The Tidy House* (Steedman, 1982). As I will argue later, it is only by positioning themselves outside of the signifier 'mother' that women are easily able to assert a sense of themselves. First, though, I want to consider the contradiction between the belief in an ideal of autonomy and this apparent loss of the self.

Although some women expressed, as Lynne (above) does, a sense of resentment at their positioning by others as nothing more than a mother, it was extremely rare for any women to express any resentment at the loss of their own desires/self which they saw as a feature of motherhood.[5] This is all the more surprising since the women who spoke most of this loss were also those who most stressed the importance of 'autonomy' as a feature of (full) personhood, as we saw in Chapter 4. These women related the importance of their own autonomy from their mothers, and of that of their daughters from themselves. How is it, then, that the autonomous self apparently disappears when the selves of mothers are being discussed?

If motherhood is tied to a form of femininity based on relationality, rather than autonomy, then autonomy is impossible from within this position. And because autonomy is held to be a normal and substantive state of personhood, then the take-up of the subject position 'mother' – a position tied to relationality – evokes the sacrifice of personhood. If persons are centrally and fundamentally autonomous, mothers, existing only in relation to and in response to children's 'needs', are going to have difficulty counting as persons.

A commonplace understanding of mothering in this respect would have it that, in the early years of a child's life, mothers might lack some autonomy, but with a good job (and preferably a 'career'), and possibly, a supportive partner, they can at least gain some autonomy as the children become more independent. At one level, this is a compelling argument, and it is a viewpoint that was shared by many of the women. For example:

PAULINE: I think, personally, going out to work and doing your own thing gives you your own life, whereas my mother – in those days, mothers lived their daughters' lives because they weren't doing anything themselves. And that made it much harder to be a daughter, because you've got this person sort of on your back all the time. Whereas I haven't time to be fussing about them. Although they think I fuss, but I don't really.

DAWN: I would like to feel that I've absorbed some of the things I admired about my mother. I feel that we were very similar and that might have been a problem when I was a teenager. ... But I also think that I perhaps learnt from the negative bits of her, that was perhaps very domesticated, give everything up for the children, you know. Erm, her whole life was lived through us. So that was something that I deliberately, erm, set out not to do in my relationship with my own daughters. You know, to be from the start a little bit emotionally detached from them. But I mean having said that, my mother didn't stay as an unchanging mother-figure. Because as I grew older and her horizons widened a bit – we all went off and came back again. So my parents changed, you know. ... I mean I am aware that she didn't stay as that sort of mother – controlling. Yes, she might have been at one stage, but she changed, as we did.

A life outside of the home is characterized here as good for both mothers and children. And certainly to have an identity outside of 'mother' can be important and rewarding for women. However, to leave the analysis there works to detract attention from mothering *itself*. Certainly, as children grow, they may demand less of the mother's time and attention. This means that she may have more time to do other things, aside from being a 'mother'. Indeed, as later sections of this chapter will show, the category 'mother' cannot sum up the entirety of a mother's subjectivity. However, *as mother*, her self is defined *in relation to* that of the child. 'Mother', *in its very definition*, is a relational category.

Motherhood, in this context, can be seen to represent a rupture in these women's selfhood, a breach of the autonomy which is held to be constitutive of the person. Unlike daughterhood, which is more closely aligned with autonomy, and hence with personhood, motherhood *as motherhood* is relational. Hence, maternity marks a breach in the self-narrative through which lives are understood and constituted as coherent (Ricoeur, 1991b; Somers and Gibson, 1994; Ewick and Silbey, 1995). Paul Ricoeur's (1991b) analysis of identity may cast some light on this rupture. Ricoeur distinguishes between two principal uses of the concept of identity: identity as selfhood (*ipse*), and identity as sameness (*idem*).

Ricoeur argues that identity as sameness implies continuity: identity as selfhood is also understood on the basis of this feature of continuity; hence, he argues, persons are understood as being continuous, in terms of being the same entity, from foetus to old age. Here, both understandings of identity – as selfhood, and as sameness (continuity) coincide.

However, Ricoeur argues, identity as sameness also implies permanence, and it is here that identity as selfhood may not coincide with identity as sameness. If the self changes over time, then it is not an identity based on permanence. When this permanence is lost, as in a breach of the 'self' which went before, the subject may experience the self as 'nothing' – as lost: 'Who is "I" when the subject says that (s)he/it is nothing? Precisely a self deprived of assistance from sameness – (*idem*) identity' (Ricoeur, 1991b: 198).

Hence, although there is still a speaking subject, still an 'I' to say, 'I am nothing', the loss of sameness-identity may precipitate a 'dark night of personal identity' (Ricoeur, 1991b: 199), in which the self *feels* as though '(s)he/it is nothing'.

If women experience motherhood as a loss of the self, then, this may be because the self of the mother is distinct from the pre-maternal self. The maternal self is constituted on the basis of a response to children's 'needs'. In contradistinction to the autonomy of 'normal' personhood, maternity is constituted on the basis of relationality. Although autonomy is militated against by the fact of a woman's *being* a woman, it is in motherhood that autonomy seems most difficult to achieve. Hence, women may experience maternity as a rupture in the self, a lack of permanence with what went before.

The transition from daughterhood to motherhood, then, involves a rupture in the self-narrative through which, as Ricoeur (1991a) suggests, we understand ourselves. According to Carolyn Steedman, 'children are always episodes in someone else's narrative, not their own people' (Steedman, 1986: 122). But, although children may not have their 'own' narratives, they are centrally inscribed within narratives (and particularly within 'child-centred' narratives) of the mother–child relationship. The overwhelming emphasis on meeting the child's 'needs' within child-centred discourse positions the mother as little more than both the embodiment and the fulfilment of her child's 'needs'. Hence *her* story can be colonized by that of the child. The period of children's dependency may mark a suspension of women's own story – a period during which children become the heroes of both their own and their mothers' stories.

However, as Ricoeur argues, there *is* still a 'self': still an 'I' to *say* 'I am nothing.' Hence, it is possible for this self to find ways of reinscribing itself. The women in this study did find ways in which to reinscribe the lost self, to reinstate a maternal story. I want to turn now to an examination of the ways in which the women did this, and to look at the ways in which the women negotiate the tensions between their own desires and those of their children, and between their belief in the 'ideal' self as autonomous, and the expressions of their own lack of autonomy in their positions as mothers. Women used a number of mechanisms to contain this contradiction. Most often, the 'sacrifice' of their autonomy was transformed into 'choice'; or they engaged in processes of redefining 'need'; or they distanced themselves from the very category 'mother'.

The discourse of choice

> Don't expect gratitude; your child did not ask to be born – the choice was yours.
> (Mia Kellmer-Pringle, 'Ten child care commandments')

In the enterprise culture, according to Strathern, 'Choice has become the privileged vantage from which to measure all action' (Strathern 1992a: 36). Further, Strathern (1992b) suggests that choice has come to be definitive of personhood: not to choose is to be less of a person, and, conversely, personhood is secured through the exercise of choice. So, if mothers' personhood is threatened through their relationship to children's 'needs', the language of choice may provide a means of reinstating that personhood:

RACHEL: I feel that I chose to have them and, you know, therefore it's a relationship that I chose to have and therefore it's a very necessary one. ...

S.L.: When you say that it's a necessary relationship with your children, what does that mean?

RACHEL: Well because I feel they need me.

S.L.: What are the sacrifices of being a mother?

ELIZABETH: Erm, I suppose you sacrifice your identity, to a large extent. Maybe it's different nowadays because so many more women go out to work and have a career as well as a family. Whereas I was at home for twenty years. ...... I certainly don't regret it. I felt I did the right thing in being there, particularly when the children were young. We were desperately hard up a lot of the time, but I still think it was the right thing for us. And I don't consider I've sacrificed a career or anything because I made a choice. So I had my – my job there, really. ... Sacrificed is the wrong word, really, because it was a choice.

But what both Elizabeth and Rachel also express in the passages quoted is the very rigidity of this system of 'choice': having made the choice to have children, having expressed and fulfilled their desires in this way, there is no room for complaint. Their choices, and hence their desires, are literally embodied in their children, whose imperative needs must then structure the mother's life. As Strathern (1992a) argues, reproduction, especially in the wake of the new reproductive technologies, is now supposed to (ideally) be a 'choice':

> However one looks at it, procreation can now be *thought about* as subject to personal preference and choice in a way that has never before been conceivable. The child is literally ... the embodiment of the act of choice.
> (Strathern, 1992b: 34; emphasis in original)

Choice, in other words, brings with it a responsibility, and mothers must carry in themselves the responsibility for exercising this choice. Once the choice has been made, and the desire for a child satisfied, there can be no expression of discontent. Thus, for Elizabeth, choice wipes out any potentiality for understanding her life in terms of sacrifice. For Rachel, her choice sets up a chain of causation ('and therefore ... and therefore ... ') the end result of which is her children's neediness. It is choice which induces need. In a sense, she has exercised choice *on behalf of* her children (since they did not choose to be born). Therefore, her children's choices, or desires, must be reinstated, in the form of 'needs'. So Rachel relates her life in terms of not doing what she wants to do, since her children largely dictate her activities. But there is no resentment towards her children in her account, and, indeed, it is characterized by the pleasure she derives from her relationship with them.

Both Keat (1991) and Strathern (1992b) link the exercise of choice with consumption: so what, if anything, is being consumed here? It seems to me that consumption in this situation centres around a form of self – not directly the enhancement of the selves of the women, but the enhancement of the selves of their children, which is mothers' principal task. The responsibility for producing children's properly socialized selves lies with mothers and, conversely, if there are any problems, it is mothers who are likely to be blamed (Caplan and Hall-McCorquodale, 1985; Bradley, 1989). The choice to produce children carries the injunction to produce (emotionally and psychologically) *perfect* children. Since the only way to do this is to meet children's 'needs', mothers should subordinate themselves to those needs. Their desires are harnessed to this aim; having made the choice, and having had their desires fulfilled, mothers should not expect anything *else*. As in Kellmer-Pringle's 'child-care commandment', the language of choice erases any possibility of further desire on the mother's part.

Yet Rachel, who presents herself as a mother whose life is totally organized around the desires of her children, speaks of her younger self as a girl who consistently wanted and demanded (and got) her own way, to such an extent that her mother's nickname for her was 'Rachel-Wanting'. But now she hardly seems to express any wants at all. Of all the women I spoke to, Rachel was the most critical of the nuclear family, yet she remains within it because she does not want her children to experience the insecurity of marital breakup. When she quarrels with her husband, she feels guilty if her children hear, again because she fears their becoming insecure; and she does not engage in pursuits she enjoys if her children veto them. How did this wanting and demanding girl become the woman who seems to give her own wants hardly any legitimacy at all? Where did Rachel-Wanting go? The language of choice hardly seems sufficient to contain all this desire. As I will discuss below, Rachel uses humour to express a sense of herself outside of the position 'mother'. She also defers her longings onto a time in the future when she will not have to be the one who meets her children's needs. At this time, she will not have to live in a marriage, which she sees as only viable 'in terms of bringing up kids':

RACHEL: I think the nicest old age I can imagine for myself would be living in some-where like Knightsbridge, with a cat or two, and just tottering around … tottering off to Harrods for your half pound of mince [laughs]. But not with a man about. I mean what use are they by then?

Rachel's projection of the fulfilment of her desires into the future renders her narrative of herself as one in which her desires are not so much lost as deferred. In the interim however, her exercise of choice inscribes her as a person, since only persons can 'choose'. Similarly, Elizabeth considers that now, having divorced her husband and with both children having left home, she now has her 'own life': but her (in her case, retrospective) invocation of 'choice' situates her as a person, rather than as merely the embodiment and fulfilment of her children's needs.

Redefining 'need'

Several women were also able to assert a sense of themselves through a process of defining their children's needs, such that they (at least at times) coincided with their own. This seems to be a form of 'the congruence of needs model' discussed earlier, but with the crucial difference that, rather than the women's own needs being subsumed under those of their children, women presented their children as needing to recognize the (separate) needs of the mother:

KATE: I think [to be a good mother] you've got to have endless supplies of love and concern about the needs of the other person, but at the same time you've got to be able to set boundaries so that you're not totally washed out by it all. You've got to be able to provide yourself with time and some kind of nurturing from someone else, or perhaps from the child, even, erm, so that you can get refreshed. I think you can be a very bad mother if you put so much into it that you're left drained yourself and left with nothing. It's a matter of, erm, setting limits, I suppose, both in time and space.

S.L.: How do you set those boundaries?

KATE: Erm …… partly to do with organization. You know, deciding, I'm going to have so much time off or whatever, a week, and getting someone else to take care of the chil-dren. And getting the children to understand that you have rights as well, and that sometimes you need half an hour of peace and quiet to read or whatever. It doesn't always work, but it's worth a try.

HAZEL: [Children] need nurturing. I think at times, certainly when they're very young, you have to be completely unselfish. Their needs have to come first. I mean that's it, you know, they just do. ……. I think you have to be honest. I think a mother has to be real with her children. I think it's pointless for her to pretend to be something she's not. If they're irritated, they have to be irritated. Erm, I think they can apologize afterwards, but, you know, to have this ideal – a good mother is somebody who never shouts and never smacks and never – I think that's crap. Crap, and I think it makes it almost impossible for women to live up to, and that's why women feel so much guilt. I

think any kind of mother is fine, as long as they're not actually abusing their children.
...

S.L.: Why d'you think it is so important to be real?

HAZEL: How do they learn to be themselves, if you don't act like that? I mean it's no good, erm – a woman who doesn't go out to work and stays at home, when she wants to be out at work, is gonna be frustrated, pissed off, unfulfilled, unhappy, and the kids aren't gonna get any good out of her. ... I mean that's what I mean by being real, it's not pretending to be something you're not, and not trying to – to be the perfect mother. ... I think a lot of mothers try to protect their children from life and you can't, you just can't. And I think the earlier you acknowledge that, the better ...... the easier it is for the kids.

The authentic, autonomous self reappears in Hazel's account, and, unusually, it is ascribed to the mother, as well as to the daughter. What is particularly note-worthy about both extracts above is the way in which the manifestation of maternal needs is framed in terms of the benefits to the children. Both Kate and Hazel use the imperative constitution of children's needs to make claims about maternal needs. In other words, maternal needs-claims (which might otherwise be delegitimated as 'desires') are legitimated on the basis that they meet chil-dren's needs. In a reversal of more customary discourses, these women are able to inhabit the category 'good mother' at the same time as asserting their own separate existence.

Several women presented their own and their children's needs as congruent in this way, most often in accounts of divorce and separation. All of the women who had been divorced expressed feelings of guilt in relation to their children. For a woman to end a relationship with her children's father may, after all, be an undeniable manifestation of her own wants. Seeing the situation in terms of benefits to the child is a means of minimizing the tensions which must inevitably occur as a result of this exercise of wants. But not all women were able to see their divorces in this light. The extract below is taken from a group discussion; the women present had been talking about the difficulties of being a single parent, of having to provide *everything* for the child[ren]. While Lynne presents her own needs and those of her children as congruent, Dawn is clearly not convinced:

LYNNE: When I don't come up with the ironed shirt, or the cake, or whatever it is I'm supposed to come up with as this perfect mother, I just say, 'Well, failed again!' Because I just will not try and be this perfect person, for them or for anybody. You know, they have to learn that I have limitations and not expect everybody else to be perfect. ... But I think it makes them into better people. Recognition of the parent's need, I think, makes them into more understanding people, so I don't feel guilty about it.

DAWN: Well, I suppose it was a constructive learning for them, but I can't say it's one I would have chosen.

(GD)

Even women who did seem convinced by this marrying of needs, however, did not sustain this position throughout their accounts. Bringing together children's and mother's needs in this way, then, represents some resolution to a sensed loss of self, but only a partial and temporary one.

Escaping motherhood

> You might believe that Daisy has no gaiety left in her, but this is not true, since she lives outside her story as well as inside.
>
> (Carol Shields, *The Stone Diaries*, p. 123)

I want to finally consider another technique used by the women to recoup a sense of self which they saw as 'lost' during motherhood. This was the assertion of a self which 'escaped' from the subject-position 'mother'. Their accounts here are a reminder that 'mother' did not constitute the whole of these women's subjectivities or selves: they lived outside of the maternal story, as well as inside it. These women are daughters, lovers, friends, sisters. Some of these positions sit more easily with contemporary Euroamerican conceptualizations of personhood than the position 'mother'.[6] So, some women straightforwardly dissociated themselves from the signifier 'mother' at various points in their accounts. Anna, for example, sees 'all mothers' as having to mediate between family members. Yet she does not see herself as having to do this. In our first interview, she said:

ANNA: Mothers are always in that awkward position in the middle, aren't they? Having to balance all kinds of loyalties.

In the second interview I asked her:

S.L.: You know last time, you said mothers are always in a difficult position, balancing different kinds of loyalties?
ANNA: Yeah.
S.L.: Well, have you ever been in that position?
ANNA: Erm, no ...... I honestly don't think I have.

Is Anna not a 'mother' then? Her account strongly suggests that her self-identity is bound up, not only with the category 'mother', but with the category 'good mother'. She is confident about her motherhood and clearly considers she has done it reasonably well. At the same time, Anna wants to dissociate herself from what she sees as conventional motherhood, which she associates with her own mother, and also with more 'stereotypical' (as she puts it) mothers. Anna, then, both is and is not a mother: she refuses to align herself with what she sees as a 'stereotypical' type of motherhood; but, like the other women here, she considers that maternal wants should be subordinated to childhood needs, and that to do so is the mark of a 'good mother'. What is important, though, is that Anna represents her maternity as not encapsulating her self. Lynne goes further, in representing her mothering as almost antithetical to her self:

LYNNE: The time that those responsibilities [of child-care] take up is time that's taken away from me to be myself.

Like Anna, Lynne considers herself to be a good (if imperfect) mother. And, like Anna, she represents her self as 'escaping' the category mother. There is an excess to the self in these women's accounts, something which cannot be contained within the position 'mother'. And at the same time, this excess – something *outside* of the category 'mother' – is what can constitute these women as *good* mothers. A movement occurs in which women are able to take up the assigned category 'mother' and use it as a source of individuality: a kind of nonconformity of motherhood. The (real or imaginary) existence of other/ed mothers provides the 'constitutive outside' (Hall, 1996) to this specific take-up of the assigned category 'mother'. The following extract from the group discussion gives some indication of the ways in which some women, at least, used this movement:

S.L.: How much do you feel that the way you are as mothers is different to the socially acceptable 'good mother'? I don't mean your perceived inadequacies, but the way you've consciously – or unconsciously – chosen to mother?
HAZEL: Chalk and cheese. ... I mean my kids ... might as well be from a different planet, because they're so unlike the other children in the school, because their background is so different. They're very different. ... I think a lot of the kids there, their upbringing is, you know, twenty years ago. I mean their upbringing is twenty years behind in a lot of ways –
CAROLINE: Yeah, yeah.
HAZEL: – so that the children's horizons are much more limited than mine [children's]. Their horizons are much narrower.
    ...
LYNNE: ... My daughter thinks I'm weird, and all her friends think I'm weird, which makes me quite pleased [laughs]. I'm quite pleased with this image that I'm weird. 'Cause I wear leggings and I go to university, and their mothers all sit at home and bake cakes [laughs]. I think she's secretly quite proud of me for being different. I'm certainly quite proud of myself for being different [laughs].
    ...
DAWN: I think I do remember my daughters making the odd comment like, 'You're not like other mums' or something like that. Er, but it might have just been a fleeting comment. But I know she certainly sees my – they both see my new husband, who they like very much, as being weird, and so both of us together are fairly weird. But again, I think they quite like that.

(GD)

Here, 'conventional' mothers are characterized as the 'others' who give meaning and definition to 'different' mothers. And, for Hazel, at least, conventional mothers are associated with a prior generation. There is clear pleasure to be derived here from being 'different', and a strong suggestion that in this difference lies a way to be a good mother which is outside of convention. In some ways, this, too, involves a redefinition of children's needs, so that living outside the maternal story as well as inside it is deemed to actually enhance maternity itself, not only for the mother, but for her children.

For some women, though, this dissociation from the category 'mother' was more partial. Caroline, for example (who was part of the group discussion but who did not express any particular pleasure or pride in being 'different') splits herself to account for her competing desires:

CAROLINE: I got a letter today from someone who's being paid to spend two months writing in a castle in Scotland [laughs]. I have a problem in that I have many things I'd like to do with my adult life, which aren't compatible. Part of me would like to go off and ...... be completely on my own, and write for however long it took to complete things. ... In a way, I would like to do more for her [eldest daughter]. ... And I would like in future to take – to be there to take him [her daughter's baby] sometimes. But that also ...... that gets me further and further away from this time of going off [laughs].

S.L.: To a castle in Scotland.

CAROLINE: Yes.

For other women, it was the intervention of an alternative category – that of 'child' – which assisted their dissociation from motherhood. The category 'child' is characterized by both its neediness and its personhood, so the taking up of childish/like behaviour can be a way of reasserting selfhood, at the same time as establishing oneself as a good mother. For example, Margaret presents herself as an unconventional mother in her 'childish' behaviour:

MARGARET: We'll go and have a game of football on the street, you know. Or we'll get the big skipping rope out and go and have a skip on the street, and people think I'm mad [laughs]. I don't care.

Although children may welcome this kind of behaviour, it may also be a source of difficulties to them. When mothers display non-maternal behaviour, children may be forced to confront the fact that there are aspects of their mothers' selves outside of anything to do with them. This response may in itself be pleasurable to women. Rachel, who, as we saw earlier, presented herself as without desire in her relationship with her children, found ways of breaking out of this maternity, by behaving in ways which her children (and especially her daughter) found out of place with Rachel's position as 'mother'. Rachel draws attention to herself, asserting a presence within a category which is otherwise marked only by its responsiveness. And, in doing so, she seems to relish her daughter's discomfort:

RACHEL: I embarrass her a lot, she says [laughs]. I think she probably thinks I'm a bit, erm – a bit immature for my age. She says I don't act like other mothers.

S.L.: What d' you do that's so embarrassing?

RACHEL: Well, I go round town singing and that's no good. I laugh too much and that's no good. Erm, I take my clothes off too happily. ... I embarrassed her terribly in the summer. ... I was wearing a bikini top and boxer shorts and, erm, I said [laughs], 'I haven't sunbathed my bottom much this summer', so I took my shorts down. And Olivia suddenly said, 'Ma!' and I thought, she's just being proper now. ... And I turned round, and there's this man coming up the path with a video camera. ... And this went on for days – she kept saying, 'I bet that man was from England. You'll be on Beadle[7]' [laughs]. So that kind of thing is totally embarrassing. ... She's often said, 'Why don't you act like other mothers?' ... That's the thing – 'So-and-so's mother would never do that'. That kind of thing. ...... And perhaps I do it all the more then.

If the subject position 'mother' is one in which selfhood is eclipsed, and experienced as 'lost', then by placing themselves outside of this category, however, temporarily, women may be able to regain the lost (pre-maternal) self. But it is important to reiterate that there is no doubt that any of these women consider themselves to be 'good mothers'. Within their accounts of dissociation, then, they are engaged in a process of redefining 'good motherhood' in ways which enable them to *exceed* the category 'mother'.

Concluding remarks

> We can tell other stories. These stories can be very frightening because they appear to blow apart the fictions through which we have come to understand ourselves.
>
> (Walkerdine, *Schoolgirl Fictions*, p. xiv)

Despite their heavy investments in a discourse I have argued to be problematic – the discourse of childhood and its imperative 'need' for autonomy – these women do not simply absorb these knowledges: their investments are more complex than this. While their maternal narratives indicate a loss of the self, the self is reinstated through other narratives within their accounts – narratives which inscribe them as persons. In this way, the assigned category 'mother' can be taken up and used as a source of individuality, and these women can become mothers who are not 'really' mothers, but who, nevertheless, are 'good mothers'. That the women find ways of negotiating the tension between a belief in autonomy and a perception that autonomy is lost during maternity, and that they find ways of resisting the occlusion of the maternal self, is an indication of their unwillingness to wholly participate in 'expert' understandings of motherhood, which would place them as little more as the passive nurturers of the child's autonomous self.

In their resistance to these expert understandings, the women use the tools they have to hand – the schemata of understanding through which childhood is produced and on the basis of which 'good mothering' is defined. But they use them in creative and subversive ways which enable them to assert a self for themselves. In effect, they are redefining the constraints under which they, as mothers, are placed. And they are doing so in ways which force a recognition of the exigencies of their lives. It is not that they have free rein to define motherhood, or the mother–daughter relationship, in any way they want. But neither are they wholly determined by the discourses which position them. They are rewriting the story of motherhood, albeit in partial and fragmented ways. They are telling other stories (Walkerdine, 1990).

8　Telling other stories
Refiguring motherhood and daughterhood

> My point is not that everything is bad, but that everything is dangerous, which is not exactly the same as bad. If everything is dangerous, then we always have something to do. So my position leads not to apathy but to a hyper- and pessimistic activism. I think that the ethico-political choice we have to make every day is to determine which is the main danger.
>
> (Michel Foucault, 'On the genealogy of ethics', p. 343)

My aim in this book has been to discuss some of the dangers inherent in what have become commonplace and common-sense understandings of motherhood, of daughterhood and of selfhood. Throughout it, I have considered the ways in which the mother–daughter relationship is enmeshed in relations of power/knowledge. I want to end the book by considering the ways in which resistance is built into those relations. This is not an attempt at a heroic saga from darkness to light – from the darkness of power to the light of resistance. Rather, it is an attempt, firstly, to explore the very concept of resistance in this context, and, secondly, to make some tentative suggestions for alternative ways of understanding the mother–daughter relationship.

Resistance and refusal

It has become a truism that subjugated groups resist the conditions of their subjugation, and indeed, it does remain politically and theoretically important to understand the ways in which social actors really do subvert, negotiate and refuse the identities and the positionings which are produced for them. The women in this study, for example – even those who make very heavy investments in maternal discourses – do not wholeheartedly or straightforwardly embrace the maternal positionings which would construct them only in terms of a child-centred responsiveness.

However, the notion of 'resistance' is, for me, a troubling one, suggesting, as it often does, a revolutionary stance, a sort of guerrilla warfare against 'dominant' values. These women are not revolutionaries: their opposition, where it arises, takes place in the 'cramped spaces' talked about by Rose (1999), 'within a set of relations that are intolerable, where movement is blocked and voice is strangulated' (Rose, 1999: 280). Maternal resistance, as such, is indeed 'blocked': for how could one oppose the notion of 'good mothering'? It would be like arguing against virtue. Further, to cast the women in such a light would be to ignore their own desires, for incorporation as well as for subversion. Certainly, they can, and they do, negotiate the terms of motherhood: and they carve out a space for themselves *outside of* the maternal story. But within it, they (as mothers) are meeters of their children's needs. To fundamentally redefine those needs would be to redefine a whole social conceptualization, not only of childhood, but of selfhood. Meanwhile, they are getting on with the unheroic task of being mothers.

But heroism and courage, as Rose (1999) reminds us, are redundant here. The image of the social actor as revolutionary resister in her everyday life is a romanticized picture which has little to do with most of what goes on in the social world: it is also an image which relies on a view of power-as-domination. As such, it cannot deal with the complexities of power – the ways, for example, power induces and creates pleasure and meaning; the ways in which it appeals to a normality or a fulfilment; the ways in which it can be hard to disentangle what is power and what is resistance.

In this, I am not arguing that the two are impossible to disentangle, or that there is no difference between them. But the differences are less straightforward than they may appear. This is another troubling aspect of conventional notions of 'resistance': *who decides* what is domination and what is resistance? on what basis? As Pamela Fox has observed, notions of resistance tend to approve only certain forms of behaviour – those which are approved by the bourgeois observer:

> *Contestation, disruption, opposition, subversion* – all have become keywords in our profession for describing practices by which a range of marginalized groups can suggest some sense of both action and refusal. But refusal of what? Despite their attentiveness to … class-based cultural differences, resistance theorists tend to answer that question by proceeding from what are essentially dominant assumptions and values. Experiencing as well as sacrificing privilege, they can afford to accept the premise that incorporation is equivalent to defeat or regression. The Left stamp of approval thus falls on those behaviors, tendencies and gestures which not only resist domination but do so for decidedly progressive aims.
>
> (Fox, 1994: 8; emphasis in original)

As Fox suggests here, most notions of resistance to date betray an unwitting collaboration with the very workings of power they ostensibly criticize. In the case of classed resistance (the focus of Fox's argument) working-class people have been made the repositories of middle-class desires for social change (Skeggs, 1997). Hence, only some of their actions are approved, while others are pathologized. More broadly, definitions of what counts as domination, and as resistance, are often assumed rather than demonstrated. And these definitions inevitably bear the marks of the desires, fantasies and hope of the writers themselves.

Power and danger

In an era of self-management, self-regulation, self-government, relations of power can be particularly obscured. Power, after all, is not very power*ful* when it is apparent, when it is saying 'No' (Foucault, 1980). The discourses of psy promise, not domination, but freedom, actualization and fulfilment. They promise a self which knows the truth, and is thus made free. My contention throughout this book has been that this is not freedom but a means of power working on and 'in' the human subject, producing a subject tied to the workings of its own subjectivity, striving towards a 'normality' which is manufactured for it. More than this, these 'liberating' psy discourses rest on an exclusion of 'outsider' groups: groups who mark the boundaries of the normal, or who can be blamed for the current state of affairs.

The identity of these 'outsider' groups varies according to the identity/ies under discussion (though working-class people are usually in there somewhere). In the case of the mother–daughter relationship, they may be, simply, mothers. That is, daughterly identities may be founded on a radical expulsion and disavowal of (the daughter's image of) the mother, and daughterly resistance forged on a pathologization of the mother. It is in the accounts of the women when they were speaking as daughters that the complex nature of resistance becomes most apparent.

In these daughterly stories, there are numerous moments in which women resist their positioning as, for example, 'feminine' subjects, or as working-class women. For instance, many of the women resisted their positioning as 'feminine' by representing their selves as autonomous, as (potentially) able to achieve anything. But this resistance was usually directed against the mother, who was related as holding the daughter back from her achievement of autonomous self-hood. In this way, mothers could be held *individually* responsible for the effects of *social* inequality. Similarly, in resisting their positioning as working class, some women (those who had experienced 'upward' class mobility) constructed a self which was *really* middle class. Hence, their working-class mothers are the 'others' against whom their own selfhood is defined. Their anxieties about their class origins often lead these women to constantly state and re-state the differences between themselves and their mothers, usually in ways which position the mother, not only as 'other', but as a *negative* 'other'. Again, social relations of inequality, in which working-class existence is pathologized, are both obscured and reinstated.

Psy discourses, so ubiquitous and so apparently liberating, can be a way of feeling empowered for people who might otherwise feel 'trapped' by the exigencies of their lives. Yet they involve a relentless scrutiny of the self, and they involve, too, a further subjugation to regimes of normalization in which only some selves are 'healthy'. Against these 'healthy', 'normal' selves, the patholo-gized 'others' mark out the boundaries of health and normality.

Resistance on the part of oppressed groups can seem inevitably positive, but, not only can such resistance involve being caught up in regimes of power/knowledge, they may also rest on a further subjection and pathologization of other groups, who are also oppressed. Specifically, in this context, the daughter's resistance may involve a reinstatement of the discourses which position her mother as responsible for nurturing the daughter's self, and as culpable if the self fails to 'achieve'. These discourses rest, ultimately, on the subjugation of the mother who is, as Walkerdine and Lucey observe, 'the price paid for autonomy, its hidden and dispensable cost' (1989: 116).

In this context, it is only a daughterly position from which 'resistance' is possible. Daughters can assert their claims to needs, their autonomy, and so on, and in the process, apparently resist the conditions of their subjection. But mothers cannot. Their very identity *as mother* is built on responsiveness, on meeting needs, on relationality. As we have seen, there is more to the subjectivity of women who are mothers than 'mother'. But, insofar as they *are* (being) mothers, there is extraordinarily little space for manoeuvre.

More than this, though, it seem to me that the whole notion of resistance in this arena is founded on a position, and an ethic, which is always-already middle class. The 'good mother' who encourages her child towards self-actualization; the good daughter who achieves her own individuality and autonomy – both are built on an ethic of individualism which is associated with middle-class existence, and against which working-class people are 'massified' (Skeggs, 1997). It is ironic that the discourses of psy come to be seen as 'revolutionary' – inevitably associ-ated with radicalism and with social change[1] – when they iterate and reiterate the old divisions between the self-aware, self-actualized, middle classes and their 'culturally lagging' counterparts among the working classes. Styles of being, forms of self-inspection, ways of being and of narrating being a mother – all can be used as marks of 'distinction' (Bourdieu, 1984): they can signify the ownership of newer, trendier, classier knowledge. But they can only do this through figuring the 'owner' of such knowledge as trendier, classier, and more knowing than those 'others' against whom the distinction is made.

So what is left? Not, I think, a model of the mother–daughter relationship in which mothers and daughters are automatically aligned because of their gender. Not a model of class which fails to consider the ways in which aesthetics and cultural competence are marked in ways which not only exclude certain people but render their selves wrong, incompetent, pretentious. And not a model of resistance which relies on only the behaviours approved by the middle classes. The women's accounts point up the inadequacy of all these formulations. Rather, what has to be given attention is the sheer impossibility of living out the subject positions offered within discourses of mothering and daughtering. The accounts of the women in this study expose the contradictions and tensions inherent in these discursive constitutions. They are supposed to be autonomous, free selves, yet their gender, and, for some of them, their class, militates against any easy autonomy. When they become mothers, they cannot be autonomous and free since they inhabit a position which exists only in terms of its relationality to a child who is, in turn, supposed to be autonomous and independent.

More fundamentally, though, a revisioning of motherhood must entail a revisioning of daughterhood/childhood. And this in turn entails a re-visioning of selfhood so that selves need no longer only be understood as the autonomous, bounded, rational self which underwrites most current Euroamerican thinking. But this would involve (to change from a visual to an aural metaphor) listening to a plethora of voices, and doing so without offering some the approbation of 'rightness' and 'appropriateness', and some the opprobrium of 'wrongness' and 'inadequacy'. Thus, it requires those positioned as 'right', as 'in the know' listening to those marked as 'wrong', as lacking.

This work would entail a continued politicization of the politics of self and subjectivity, for childhood as well as for adult selves. These are too easily conceptualized as essential, transcendent phenomena. Where they *are* politicized (as in 'identity politics') they often bring in their wake a replication of exclusionary mechanisms, where some groups claim their 'freedom' by pitting themselves against others; or they propose an essence to the self, replicating normative constructions of the self. In both cases, also, only certain 'identities' seem amenable to identity politics.[2]

A politicization of self and subjectivity would entail, I suggest, continuing attention to the ways in which selves are made through the workings of power; how some selves are marked as 'better' than others; how the 'good society' is assumed to be an amalgam of 'good selves'; and how mothers are understood as producing these selves. To do this, we have to use the tools we have to hand – the meanings, the practices, the contradictions, which make up all these categories and our understanding of them. We can, however, use them in different ways, moving away from prescriptions for good (enough) mothering and towards, instead, a radical scrutiny of how the figure of the good (enough) mother has been constituted in the way she has. There is no space 'above' or 'beyond' power: no space in which a pre-social form of subjectivity or of social relations could be found. There is no neutral, asocial space, in which mothers and daughters could reclaim a 'true' relationship. But there *is* space for a refusal and a questioning of the ways in which we are positioned.

This is no collapse into political apathy. Foucault's comment that 'everything is dangerous' alerts us to the ubiquity of power relations, to the fact that nothing can stand outside of the social relations in which we are all embedded. But it also alerts us to the task of determining, over and over again, 'the main danger' – not an easy task, but a necessary one.

Appendix I

The women and the research

I interviewed the fourteen women who took part in the research for between three and nine hours each. Interviews took place in the women's houses, in my house, or in an office at the university. Most women were interviewed three times, although in one case I carried out only one interview, and in two others, I carried out four. In addition, I organized a group discussion when I was about half way through the interviews, in which five women participated (see Appendix II for an edited transcript of the group discussion).

I asked the women about their relationships with their mothers and their daughters; I wanted to attempt to uncover how they saw their relationships with their mothers as inflecting their own mothering. I only interviewed women whose daughters were 10 years of age or over, since I considered that by this age, the daughter would be seen as having a 'self' separate to that of the mother, and that issues of dependence/independence would have begun to arise. I was interested, in any case, in the ongoing relationship between mother and daughter, rather than in the 'transition to motherhood'. The only other criterion for selection was that the women should live in or around the city in which the research was based.

Because the research method was to consist of repeated interviews with each woman, and because I thought (rightly, as it turned out) that the research would touch on sensitive and even painful memories, it was very important that any woman interviewed should definitely want to participate in the research. The first six women interviewed were contacted through friends or colleagues. I had originally anticipated using a 'snowball' technique, asking the women I interviewed if they could suggest anyone else who might be willing to talk to me. However, this proved to be something of a dead end – either the women did not know anyone else who fitted the criteria, or the women they knew who did were reluctant to be interviewed. In the end, only two other women were contacted in this way. My aim was to interview at least twelve women, but at this point I had interviewed only eight – Anna, Caroline, Dawn, Gina, Hazel, Janet, Lynne and Margaret. I asked the local newspaper to run a short article which outlined my research and asked anyone interested to contact me at the university. Following this, six women – Barbara, Elizabeth, Frances, Kate, Pauline and Rachel – wrote to me; all of these women subsequently took part in the research.

Clearly, there are drawbacks to both of the methods of selection I used. Contacting women through friends and colleagues was likely to yield a particularly homogeneous group. This group of eight women ranged in age from 36 to 45; all were white English, Welsh or Scots; three were working class and had working-class birth families, three were middle class, but had been born into working-class families, and two were middle class, with middle-class birth families. Two women were married and living with their husbands, one was separated, and five were divorced. Although this group was relatively homogeneous in terms of age and ethnicity, it was less homogeneous in class terms than the second group (i.e. women who responded to the newspaper article).

This second group consisted of six women, ranging in age from 44 to 55; all were white and English, Scots or Welsh; and all were middle class. Three of these women had middle-class, and three working-class, birth families. Five were married and living with their husbands, and one was divorced (see Tables 1 and 2). So the women in this group were almost all older than those in the first group, they were all middle class, and they were more likely to be married. It may be

Table 1   Class (self-defined), parents' class (self-defined), educational qualifications and ages

name	class	parents' class	ed. qualifications	age	age of daughter(s)
Anna	middle	middle	postgraduate	41	16
Caroline	middle	middle	postgraduate	41	20, 19, 13
Margaret	working	working	CSE[a]	38	10
Lynne	middle	working	degree	42	13
Dawn	middle	working	postgraduate	38	13, 11
Janet	working	working	'O' levels	42	22, 21, 17
Gina	working	working	'O' levels	45	19
Hazel	middle	working	prof. qualification	43	17
Elizabeth	middle	middle	'O' levels	52	29
Rachel	middle	middle	postgraduate	44	13
Kate	middle	working	postgraduate	47	19
Pauline	middle	middle	postgraduate	55	28, 26
Barbara	middle	working	prof. qualification	50	20
Frances	middle	working	postgraduate	48	23

Note:
[a]CSE – Certificate in Secondary Education

Table 2   Employment and housing

name	employment	partner's employment	father's employment	mother's employment	housing
Anna	social work	n/a	law	housewife	owner-occupied
Caroline	education	education	music/journalism	housewife	owner-occupied
Margaret	catering	n/a	manual work	cleaning	rented
Lynne	student	n/a	textiles	computers	rented
Dawn	education	unemployed	police	housewife	owner-occupied
Janet	retail	n/a	mining	housewife	rented
Gina	welfare	n/a	armed services	housewife	owner-occupied (shared)
Hazel	welfare	n/a	plumbing (self-employed)	father's business	owner-occupied (shared)
Elizabeth	administration	n/a	education	education	owner-occupied
Rachel	education (p.t.)	education	engineering	housewife	owner-occupied
Kate	charity work (voluntary)(was employed in education)	education	textiles	nursing	owner-occupied
Pauline	teacher (f.t.)	finance	police	housewife	owner-occupied
Barbara	freelance craft work	administration	transport	housewife	owner-occupied
Frances	unemployed (ex lecturer)	education	clerical	housewife/home-working	owner-occupied

that the use of a university address for contact – which, at the time, I had felt would mark my credentials as a 'real' researcher – discouraged many women from responding to the newspaper article. Women who did respond would seem likely to value the formal knowledge-production process. In fact, most of the second group had had some contact with universities: four had degrees and two also had postgraduate qualifications. Two women had left school after 'O' Levels, but one of these women also had a non-graduate professional qualification, and the other was working towards one at the time of the interviews. Among the first group, half of the women (four) had degrees, and three of these also had postgraduate qualifications; one woman had a non-graduate professional qualification; and three had left school at 16 with three or fewer 'O' Levels, or CSEs. I asked the women to self-define both class and ethnicity. Their self-definitions of class coincided with the Registrar General's scale, which was in use at the time of the research (taking their own present or last employment for their current class position, and their father's occupation for their class position at birth). Class scales are problematic when applied to women, so self-definitions may be more meaningful.

Overall, then, the group of women I interviewed was an unusual one, and although it was never my aim to interview a 'representative' sample, this fact still needs to be noted. It may, in part, be an effect of the geographical location of the research: higher social classes are over-represented in the city in which the research was based; in particular, there is a higher than average proportion of women with higher educational qualifications.

However, the nature of the research itself may have had a greater bearing on who did and who did not agree to be interviewed. The women's self-selection means that they had to have some interest or investment in the subject of the research and/or the research process itself. For all of them, their relationships with their mothers and daughters was clearly very significant in their lives. Most of the women also evidently valued the processes of academic knowledge-production. As well, women who have been trained in the 'caring professions' (as nine of these women were) may be more likely to be attracted to research of this sort; 'talking through' issues may make more sense if this is the practice in which you have been trained.

The fact that only white women volunteered to be interviewed also seems to indicate that black women may have felt that the research had little relevance to their lives. The city in which the research is based has a very large majority of white inhabitants: nevertheless, to have had no response from black women is a fact which has to be noted and taken into account in evaluating the analysis.

Appendix II

The interviews

Interview schedule (individual interviews)

Inheritance

- How would you describe yourself?
- Who do you 'take after' (i.e. – what have you inherited from other family members)?
- Who does your daughter 'take after'?

Relationships

- What is the most important relationship in your life?
- What is it about it that makes it so important?
- What is/are the most important relationship(s) in daughter(s)' lives?
- What is/are the most important relationship(s) in mother's life?

Mother–daughter relationship

- Do you feel a special bond or link with your mother?
- (If so) can you describe what's different or special about it?
- What (if anything) do you have in your relationship with her that you don't have with anyone else?
- In what ways has the relationship changed?
- How happy was your mother as you were growing up?
- Do you feel a special bond or link with your daughter(s)?
- What (if anything) do you have in your relationship with her/them that you don't have with anyone else?
- In what ways has the relationship changed?
- How would you describe your mother?
- How would she describe you?
- Do you rely on her (in what ways)?
- How would you describe your daughter(s)?

- How would she/they describe you?
- Do your daughters rely on you? (in what ways)?
- How did you feel about being pregnant?
- How did you feel when your daughter(s) was (were) born?
- How did you feel when your son(s) was (were) born?
- Do you like your mother?
- What do you particularly like about her?
- What do you particularly dislike about her?
- Do you see your mother as your friend?
- What kind of things can you/can you not talk to your mother about – now and in the past?
- What kinds of things has your mother talked to you about – now and in the past?
- Do you ever wish you could talk to your mother more – now and in the past?
- How often do you see your mother?
- How often do you see your daughter(s)?
- Did (does) mother do any child-care for you?
- Did she come to stay after child(ren) born?
- Does your mother ever upset you?
- (In what ways) does your mother upset you?
- Do you feel your mother ever tries to control you – or has she?
- What happens?
- Does your mother have any influence over you?
- Does anyone else have influence over you?
- What are the main problems in your relationship with your mother?
- How do you deal with them?
- Do you like your daughters?
- What do you particularly like about them?
- What do you particularly dislike about them?
- Do you see your daughters as your friends?
- What kinds of things can you/can you not talk to your daughters about?
- How has this changed as they have grown older?
- Do you ever wish you could talk to your daughters more?
- Or do you ever wish that they would talk to you more? – now and in the past?
- Do your daughters ever upset you?
- In what ways do they upset you?
- Do you try to control your daughters?
- What happens?
- What are the main problems in your relationships with your daughters?
- How do you deal with them?
- Do you have a mother–daughter type relationship with anyone else?
- Do you think men are ever excluded from the mother–daughter relationship?
- Do you share any secrets with your mother/daughters – that other family members wouldn't know about?

Intergenerational transmission

- What did your mother teach you?
- Was any of it valuable to you?
- Was any of it harmful to you?
- Do you think women generally can learn from their mothers?
- What sorts of things can women learn from their mothers?
- What did you learn from her – from watching her life, and not just what she taught you?
- Would you say your mother is/was a role model (positive or negative)?
- Has anyone else been a role model in your life?
- In what ways are you/are you not the woman your mother wanted you to be?
- What have you tried to teach your daughters?
- What do you hope they've learned from watching your life?
- Do your daughters see you as a role model?
- Have you consciously tried to pass on to your daughters any of what you learned from your mother?
- Or have you tried *not* to pass on any of it?
- In what ways are your daughters the women you wanted them to be?
- In what ways are your daughters not the women you wanted them to be?

Mothering

- What does it mean to mother someone?
- Can anybody else do it, other than the birth mother?
- What qualities do you think make a good mother?
- What qualities do you think make a bad mother?
- What qualities of a good/bad mother do you have?
- What qualities of a good/bad mother does your mother have?
- What (if any) are the rewards attached to being a mother?
- What (if any) are the sacrifices attached to being a mother?
- Are you the type of mother you expected to be, before you had children?
- Are there any areas in which you'd say you'd failed as a mother?
- (If not) – what would make you feel you'd failed?
- What would the ideal relationship with your daughter be like?
- What would the ideal relationship with your mother be like?
- Do you think the mother–daughter relationship is generally a problem?
- Or do you think the mother–daughter relationship is generally good?

Representations of the relationship

- Who do/did you go to for advice on child-care?
- Was any of this advice useful?
- Was any of this advice harmful?
- In what ways was the advice useful/harmful?

- Is there anyone you would specifically not ask?
- Did you use babycare books when children were small?
- Who/where would you now turn to for advice on relationship with mother?
- Who/where would you now turn to for advice on relationship with daughter?
- Are there any images of mothers and/or daughters you can remember seeing or reading about – e.g. on TV, films, soaps, in books or magazines – that have particularly struck you?

General

- Who do you think has/will have the better life – you or your daughter(s)?
- If you could start again, what would you do with your adult life?
- Would you still have children?
- How many?
- What did you think of the interviews?
- Is there anything else you want to say?
- Or is there anything you want to ask me?

Group discussion: edited transcript

The group discussion took place at my house. As well as myself, five of the women in the study were present – Caroline, Dawn, Gina, Lynne and Hazel. The interview was tape recorded. The women had not met before the group discussion, except for Gina and Hazel, who were friends.

This edited transcript is included to give readers some idea of the interaction between the women, and the women and myself, during the interview process.

S.L.: Did anybody have any feelings after the interviews? ...... you know, like 'I haven't said what I meant', or –

HAZEL: I think I thought about a few things a bit more ...

S.L.: I was thinking about the issue of how far our mothers make us who we are ... how far our mothers can actually do that – can they make us who we are?

HAZEL: I think they can try. I don't think they have much success [laughs].

S.L.: So looking at the person you are now, do you think any of that is made by your mother?

HAZEL: I think the way I am is influenced by my mother. I'm diametrically the opposite of the way she wanted me to be, basically. I suppose that was influential.

S.L.: So did your mother make you what you are, then? – in going the opposite way?

HAZEL: No I don't think so. No, I don't agree with that, actually.

CAROLINE: I don't think my mother had any aspirations for me. I mean I don't think she attempted to try to ......

S.L.: D'you think, though, you formed your identity as a result of the way she –

CAROLINE: I think as I get older, I do more and more things like her. Which I might not want to do.

HAZEL: I think an awful lot of that's just genetic though, isn't it? I mean we are half of –

CAROLINE: No, I don't agree with that.

HAZEL: Oh I do. I do. ...... Don't you think there are inherited traits then, that we get from our mothers or our fathers? I mean I hear my mother's voice sometimes. It's not particularly what she would say, but I think, gosh that's really like my mum – the tone of voice is – . And observing as well.

CAROLINE: Yes. I can even sometimes feel my face looking like – although I don't look anything like my mother – I can feel an expression that's like hers.

HAZEL: D'you think it's acquired, rather than –

CAROLINE: I think so.

DAWN: I would like to feel that I've absorbed some of the things I admired about my mother. I feel that we were very similar and that might have been a problem when I was a teenager, you know, to be so similar – we're the same star sign and so on. Erm, but I also think that I perhaps learnt from the negative bits of her, that was perhaps very domesticated, give everything up for the children, you know. Erm, her whole life was lived through us. So that was something that I deliberately, erm, set out not to do in my relationship with my own daughter. You know, to be from the start a little bit emotionally detached from them. But I mean having said that, my mother didn't stay as, er, an unchanging mother-figure. Because as I grew older and her horizons widened a bit – we all went off, and came back again. So my parents changed, you know. My dad left work early and started to do things round the house. They started to go off and do different things. So I don't think erm, – I think certainly at one time she was much more influential. But I think she changed as a person, as I did, you know. So we did some sort of circular thing, going away and coming back more as an equal, more as somebody who'd be, er, a little bit detached from her and not so influenced by her. Because I was also thinking that it's a little bit – it might be different for me because my mother's dead. I'm less likely to pick up negative aspects. You know, it doesn't quite seem right now, to do that. I mean I am aware that she didn't stay as that sort of mother – controlling. Yes, she might have been at one stage, but she changed, as we did.

S.L.: So when you came through that circle, were you still alike, but you had both changed?

DAWN: Well, when I say alike – perhaps in small ways, or perhaps in some ways but not in others. You know, we're separate people ...... Thinking about aspirations – I don't see my mother as having separate aspirations, I see my parents as having aspirations which were very difficult to achieve, you know. They did want all the children to do – not just well, but the best.

HAZEL: It's the 50s, isn't it? Children of the 50s and 60s – the conditioning was very much –

DAWN: Yes, you know, it was a lot of pressure.

HAZEL: – was very much sort of upward.

DAWN: Upwardly socially mobile, and that was a lot of pressure. Er, it's certainly difficult to cope with failure on any level because of those pressures at home. And as a result again. I've – I feel that I've gone to perhaps the other extreme with my daughters. I don't push, er, academic achievement as a main factor. But I might well have strong aspirations in another area, you know, which could be just as – just as bad.

LYNNE: My experience was almost opposite to that, really. I think my mother tried very hard to make me [unclear]. And in doing that, she made life very difficult for me because I had to overcome all these kinds of problems that she'd created to do with my emotional ability to do what I wanted to do, she completely squashed. And she still does to a great extent, things that I'm interested in, and I'm doing. And I found that growing up in the 50s and 60s, in the working-class community that I grew up in, there wasn't those aspirations to education for girls. It was still very much, go out to work as soon as you can and get a good marriage and that's it. That's the best that you can get, and I've had to break away from all of those kinds of restrictions. So I think that, in getting older, the influences were my parents, but as one of the major obstacles, rather than one of the things that's impelled me forward.

S.L.: So d'you ever feel any identification with your mother? And d'you ever feel that thing, 'Oh I sound like my mother?'

LYNNE: Yeah, but it's something not to do [laughs]. I mean I do with the children. You know, you come up with the sayings that – and it trips off your tongue. And you think, oh no, I must stop saying that, because they're controlling sayings which you use when, you know, the children are getting too much for you, or it's a difficult situation you're having to deal with, and instead of thinking it through and working it through, you come up with whatever comes instinctively to mind. And it's at that point I think, you've not thought this through and you're just reacting, and I kind of pedal back.

HAZEL: You know that it's your mother's tape and not yours.

LYNNE: That's right, yeah.

GINA: I think I've come to understand my mother more as I've gone through the same situations. I've handled them differently to her, but I've realized where she was coming from. And in a funny way, that's made me feel a lot closer to her, 'cause I've blamed her a lot in my life. You know like, if it wasn't for her, if it wasn't for the way she brought me up I wouldn't be like this. And, er, I think the interviews for me sort of brought that home to me. Like at the end I felt like I really came out thinking she did the best she could with what she had, and although I don't agree with it, and certainly early on in life I just rebelled against her terribly, it's like I really came to love her through that. Because I could feel myself going through the same situations, and maybe I handled them differently because I had the opportunity to do that. And, er, and she didn't.

HAZEL: Yeah, I think I judge my mother less than I used to, certainly. I think I used to blame my mother for everything. You know, it was just like it was her fault I was like I was [unclear]. And I stopped blaming her and I think I forgave her. And then I've been able to forgive myself, actually, and therefore not continue a cycle with my own daughter. But there again, my mother's dead as well and it's easier for me in that case, I can stop – because if I met her again tomorrow, all the old things would be triggered off again, you know [laughs]. I'd go into reaction, I'm sure.

CAROLINE: I never blamed my mother when I was young. I don't think I ever thought about it. And I think only about five years ago did I start to feel angry with her, and she's 77 now [laughs]. ...... I think the interviews brought that up didn't they?

S.L.: Yes.

LYNNE: I went through a period of being really angry with my mother and having to come to a decision that I really didn't like her very much. And that was quite a big step for me, erm, because I'd been brought up to accept her implicitly and to not question her. And to say that you didn't like her or that you didn't love her was, you know, the ultimate sin. And to come to that acceptance that I didn't like her, but you know, because she was my mother I was going to choose a relationship, then it was quite a freeing thing, to choose that relationship. So I now see it as a relationship on my terms, rather than on hers, which means we've got two different relationships, with a big gap in the middle [laughs].

S.L.: D'you mean in terms of time, you've got two relationships?

HAZEL: Or she's got one and you've got one? [laughs]

LYNNE: Yeah, that's right, but then I've got to accept her world view as her world view and must not argue with her when she comes up with these things that she needs to believe which are patently not true. You know and I just think, well she needs to feel that if she need to feel that, and I just let her go on about them. I don't argue with her, because I can think, well, that's just her, and not connected emotionally to me.

HAZEL: I think for me there came a point when I realized that I didn't like my mother, but also that she didn't like me, and it was actually fine [laughs]. It was like, okay, so it's on a totally different ground. You know I can choose, and really chose not to have a lot to do with her. I didn't visit her very often, and I certainly didn't choose to confide in her, which is what she wanted.

S.L.: Do you two then feel that it's a big loss?

HAZEL: I sometimes hear – one of the women in my house, I hear her talking to her mother on the phone, and she laughs and she talks to her and they gabble away, and I think, aaah. There's a pang, a sort of aaah, it's a shame that I never had that. Or I had it when I was younger. I mean it wasn't all black, and we did have some good times together. But, er, yeah, there's a slight sort of pang and I think, oh what a shame, perhaps if she was still alive it'd be all right, and I know damn well if she was still alive it wouldn't be any different at all [laughs]. It would be the same. But yeah, there's the odd pang like that. You know, what a shame I didn't have a better relationship with her.

DAWN: I get quite a few pangs because she's not around and she hasn't been there to sort of support me at times. Because she really was only around when everything seemed rosy and wonderful. You know I only had that nice social kind of arrangement. Except, erm, when she died, that wasn't rosy and wonderful. I mean in that position, I was the mother-figure, and she was – it was a sort of role-reversal, because she was going through a lot of pain and agony after a car accident, and operations and so on, so I mean perhaps I saw her in a different light as very vulnerable, but a very strong, admirable character, because of the way she coped with all of that, with very little self-pity or negative – you know. So that her weak points – her stubbornness, which I came up against, erm, as a teenager, you know, and at home, was actually, er, used in that situation as a very strong – as a ...... became her strength, her stubbornness. You know, she was hanging on and trying hard and so on. But I do miss my mother, quite a lot. Erm ...... not every day; I don't pine or anything, but you know, at times.

HAZEL: How long ago did she die?

DAWN: Erm, seven years ago. And she does seem very close sometimes. You know, particularly if I'm doing activities which I associate with her, like sewing at the sewing machine, I really do feel sometimes that she's there, and she's ...... doing things. You know, it's odd [laughs]. The feeling you [Caroline] feel where it's almost your mother's face, I do feel that sometimes, that she's actually there. Yes, and if I'm at the piano, I do hear her singing and things, so – [trails off].

S.L.: How does that feel?

DAWN: Well, I feel there's a sort of link there. I feel emotional. And I imagine that she would be emotional, because she was an emotional person as well. You know, I'm not gonna talk about life after death or that sort of thing, but there is a certain element of frustration that you can't communicate as you probably did once. So ...... I mean it's interesting to hear other viewpoints and, er, ... I mean really you've only inter-viewed eight women and it'd be interesting to find out – well you said you can't come to conclusions.

S.L.: Well I have to try [laughs].

CAROLINE: What you find out is how unique everyone is, don't you? That's what I always find.

   ...

HAZEL: I think one of the things that our generation find difficult is that, brought up in the 50s, as I think we all were, is that right? – 50s and 60s – is that we had this dual thing. I think for women these days it's slightly easier in that they do have more – there's less propaganda to be the perfect housewife and the perfect mother, isn't there? I mean, that's my observation – it's not quite as strong.

GINA: I don't know –

HAZEL: 'cause in the 50s, there was a tremendous amount of pressure to get women back into the home.

GINA: But there's pressure – I feel like there's pressure to be the perfect housewife and the perfect –

DAWN: – working mother.

GINA: – business woman.

DAWN: There's more pressure! [laughs]

GINA: – and not to actually juggle them – to detract from them. I noticed that over the Christmas period, that that conditioning is still – through the media –

DAWN: A wife, a mother, a lover, all that sort of stuff.

HAZEL: So it's been added, rather than taken away, d'you think?

DAWN: Yes.

GINA: Yes.

DAWN: I think there's far more stresses on you in a way.

GINA: At times I think it must be quite nice to be my mother and just be – just! [laughs].

HAZEL: But my mother wasn't happy, that was the thing. Her bitterness was so intense that it poisoned everybody around her. There wasn't the options then for women. I mean she didn't have the choice of working the way that she wanted to work – well she did I suppose, but she didn't think she had any choices.

DAWN: I felt particularly when I gave up work, erm, to have my children, that I felt guilty that I wasn't at work. You know, it took me a long time to come to terms with being at home and just being a mother, despite the fact that I felt I'd had a good example from my mother, to go on. I thought, 'Well, what else can I do?' You know, 'Is this all?' [laughs].

S.L.: D'you think that historical period in which all of us grew up is unique in the sense that bringing our daughters up now is inevitably going to be different? Or d'you not think it makes such a difference?

HAZEL: I think we're a product of our environment in which we're brought up. I mean I agree with you [Caroline] on that. I think you learn what you see around you. I think that that is a very strong influence. Now obviously our children's environment − my children's environment is extremely different from mine − extremely. But I think that there still are some threads in relationships that are the same. There still are. I see things with my daughter that I saw in my mother. And I see differences with my son. It's really interesting. It'd be interesting to know what it would be like if I had two daughters.

DAWN: I've got two daughters.

CAROLINE: I've got three. But also I see similarities in − although they're very different people − in my partner and my father. Which − I have recognized scenes with my daughters as being similar to things which happened in my past. I don't know quite how that happens. He wasn't like my father when I met him [laughs].

LYNNE: I think my daughter's got a lot more opportunity to be herself than I had.

HAZEL: Absolutely − so has mine.

LYNNE: − and she's not actually got so much of femininity imposed on her because she's been given the freedom to choose [unclear]. And I think because she's growing up in a different environment and without the family pressures that I had − we had a very close-knit family, and my aunts and cousins were very keen to give their opinion on what you should be doing as well, which Naomi doesn't have, she's very much got the choice to make her own way and her own decisions, and to wear her own clothes and to not conform to anybody else's idea of femininity, er, which I think is very freeing for her.

HAZEL: My daughter I think is allowed to be herself far more than I ever was.

S.L.: How much of that is because you've done that and how much is the times we live in?

LYNNE: Well I think it's there in society; I think the differences are there. Er, because I mean she can study what she wants at school, which I mean I never could. I was limited. You know, if you were a girl, you studied certain subjects, boys studied certain subjects. So she gets to choose. And, erm, because it's a deliberate effort on my part to not impose the kinds of problems on her that my mother imposed on me. So I think it's both.

HAZEL: I think it's − well I don't know if you're a single parent −

LYNNE: I am at the moment.

HAZEL: Yeah. My children live with their dad, so that's another dynamic, if you like. The fact that he also lets them be who they are. I had a lot of input and have a lot of input, but I think choosing the right father for your kids, in a way [laughs] – or choosing the right person to be – to have the influence from, is equally important.

LYNNE: Yes. My ex-husband does try and influence her femininity and now criticizes her clothing and her behaviour, and her behaviour changes to a somewhat more simpering attitude when she's with him, which is a constant source of irritation [laughs].

GINA: Yeah, I've just recently been accused of being an irresponsible mother, which has been quite – [trails off].

S.L.: Why?

GINA: [laughs] It's over one of my sons. He's totally rejected [his father]. The eldest son well, he's totally alienated him because he [father] thinks he has too much freedom.

S.L.: And this is somehow your fault that he's rejected his father?

GINA: Yes, it's my fault because I have provided an environment where he can explore his boundaries. I think his father thinks that I've put the boundaries far too far away. Yeah, he's semi-threatened me with … I don't know what, over it. I mean it's very implied threats, but, er, it was interesting that he didn't do that with my daughter.

DAWN: I must admit I feel a bit schizophrenic about what you were saying – about my 13-year-old. On the one hand, I feel pleased that she's trying things out, and certainly looks unconventional, and on the other hand I feel peeved that it doesn't suit her, you know. And I know what would suit her [laughs].

HAZEL: My mother used to say that to me.

DAWN: Yes, that's right. And this is where I'm very lucky, and my husband, being a non-parent and having that sort of non-parental attitude, can say, 'Oh, it's good that she's experimenting'. You know, he can instantly put water on my sort of – I don't know what it is – illogical reaction to her, erm, dress. And I think, 'Oh yes, that's right', so mum's the word.

HAZEL: My daughter is just starting to go through the process of finding out who she is separate from me. You know, she is – she's stopped being a vegetarian. She's really starting to look at who she is aside from me. I mean she'll probably come back to being a vegetarian. You know, it's the little things – I think she's never learned how to rebel, because I've given her – she's had so much freedom, she's had so much choice that it's like, "What can I do to be different from her?" So she's having to find her way – find out who she is.

DAWN: How d'you feel? What do you feel?

HAZEL: I fell absolutely fine about it, absolutely fine. I think she's beautiful, I think she's absolutely fine the ways she is, you know.

S.L.: That can be difficult, though, can't it? To acknowledge your daughter is different.

HAZEL: My daughter looks a lot like me, as well. I find it difficult because I don't want her to be – I want her to be her own self, because it was so difficult for me to be my own self, away from my mother. Because she looks so much like me, people keep saying 'Oh you're like your mother' and I have to keep saying 'Well she's not. She's who she is'.

S.L.: When you feel this identification with your mother, do any of you feel, that's great? [laughter]. Do any of you feel pleased?

CAROLINE: I think it's quite funny. Because I feel so – actually so very deeply different from her, it's not a problem. I don't feel any worry about an identification with her. Not seriously.

S.L.: So you don't feel you will ever turn into your mother?

CAROLINE: No. That was never something in the past, and it's not now. ...... And she certainly didn't want me to be like her. She didn't want any of us to be like her.

S.L.: How do you know she didn't?

CAROLINE: Because she felt very negative about herself, and I think if she did have any aspirations for any of us, it was that we didn't.

GINA: What happens to me now is that I think, oh that's why she did it. If I do something, or react in some way, I think, oh my mother used to do that. It's quite analytical, I suppose. It sounds analytical, but it happens quite quickly. I think, oh yeah, that's why she did it. For me, it seems to be a process of understanding, and not immediately thinking, oh shit, you know, I'm acting like my mother, I must stop immediately, and doing exactly the opposite, whatever that was, but I can understand why she did it. And maybe I'll, you know, I'll end up doing something differently. I can't actually think of anything to illustrate it. Especially round – I suppose control. You know I think my mother tried to control me, and I think I tried to control my children ...... in a kind of benign dictatorship [laughs]. And I honestly didn't know I was doing it, but I was. And that's the other thing that came out of the interviews for me; it really hit me in the face how much I was controlling. And since then I've really tried to let go, and it's been quite hard. But I really understand why she did it. And why I do it.

CAROLINE: What sort of control?

GINA: It's really hard – when I talked to Steph about it, it took up quite a long time. I most probably recognized something in myself. ...... Erm, I might have even possibly controlled them to be the opposite way to what I was. Like I set up all this freedom and environment and things, and I tried so hard with it. I almost really tried so hard to do something differently to my mother, in a way that was kind of control because it was something that I wanted to do. It might not necessarily have been something that they wanted. It's quite kind of ... obscure, the train of thought in my head, but it's also the kind of thing I'd say, oh I don't wanna think about that, because that would make me like my mother, you know ...... I knew – I recognized that I did try to hold on to them, by being quite over-protective like my mother was, but in a different way. I did it in a different way, but I did the same things. ...... And this sort of holding on, which was the big thing with me and my mother, when I left home and she didn't want me to go. And I really understood when my daughter left home, what my mother must have felt like, and how sad that must have been. But we never talked about it. And I think that's the difference between me and my mother – in my relationship with the kids, we talk about it, communicate – as much as possible, our feelings round things. But I'm also aware that it's like, *I* want you to be like this, *I* want you to have this freedom, *I* want you to have it. And it's – have I kind of checked it out with them? Was that okay? Was that what they wanted?

CAROLINE: I feel that I wanted mine to be self-disciplined. And maybe that's a very hard thing to be. I still insist that they do it, that they make their own minds up. ...... You know, sometimes I think it's really being tough.

HAZEL: It is hard.

CAROLINE: Yeah.

HAZEL: But I think if you can give that to your kids, then it's one of the biggest gifts you can give them. If you can empower them to be like that. But they might resent that in the future. That's what I think, that my kids'll turn round in the future and say 'But you made me make all the decisions!' [laughs]. 'You didn't give me any guidance, or any clues.' That's not true, cause I do, but –

GINA: I think I gave them my perfect childhood.

HAZEL: You've tried to do that.

GINA: I tried to give my children what I wanted in my childhood.

HAZEL: I think that's what all mothers do, actually.

GINA: Yeah, my mother did the same with me. She came from such a poor background, really really poor. And so what she gave me was her idea of – she had nine brothers and sisters, and I only had one sister. You know I had a lot more than she had. And so she gave me that. And I might not – [laughs] – I might not have liked it. I would probably have liked my mother to be a lot more kind of irresponsible. Not irresponsible, but sort of more alternative, or whatever, you know, and a lot more liberal and free. Cause her mother didn't give a fuck what happened to her. This is the story that she gives me. She was lost in all these children. And she did care about me, and so she was constantly behind me all the time. And so I tried to kind of redress the balance.

HAZEL: Don't you think that was a bit like my mother? It was that she had never experienced what it was to be loved. I mean she never knew what it was like to be – she never felt loved – and she wanted me to love her. Having children was her way of being loved, and she hadn't learned how to love, really, because she'd never had that experience.

CAROLINE: That may be true; my mother wasn't loved, and she was an only child. And she had five children. Maybe that was exactly what she was trying to do.

HAZEL: It took an awfully long time for me to realize that I didn't know how to love, either, because I'd not felt loved. And so it was the whole process that was passed on. And I think – I hope that I've broken that with my daughter in that I think she feels loved by me. One of my goals is that my children feel loved by me. And if they learn nothing else from me, that's what I want that I didn't have, if you like. You know, that I'll always –

CAROLINE: I thought the most important thing with my kids was that they should feel that whatever they did, they wouldn't be rejected. And I think I must have grown up feeling that I could be rejected.

HAZEL: Well I was.

GINA: I feel – I feel loved by my mother in retrospect, almost, because now I feel like I understand her more. Erm, through various things. I think she did what she did because she did love me, but it was her way of loving me, and I certainly didn't understand it. ...... You know, and I think she probably did do those things because she loved me. But it's just a funny way of showing it sometimes [laughs].

LYNNE: I know my mother loves me, but I never feel it.

GINA: Yeah.

HAZEL: I would say my mother loved me at some level, but I didn't feel it.

LYNNE: I always wanted to be somebody else's child. I thought they'd got mixed up in the nursery. I used to imagine I was some princess. I never felt as though I fitted.

HAZEL: I've always said I felt like a cuckoo in my family. Like, this isn't my nest! What am I doing here?

LYNNE: But I'm still finding reasons why I'm not her child. I watch her now, and I can see her mother in her older years, and I can see my mother getting more like her mother, and behaving the way her mother behaved when she got older, in this kind of petulant, demanding manner. And this kind of matriarchal do this, do that, do the other, kind of attitude. And I think, I am never, ever going to do that. You know, this is a reason not to be like her, that I do not want to kind of continue this pattern, of how you get to be when you're 60. I would do anything to avoid it [laughs].
...

DAWN: I'll put another ...... viewpoint on it. I have to say that I do remember really admiring my mother. I mean I think one of her best qualities that I admired then was that, erm, I have three brothers and whenever any of them brought any friends home, she would instantly be warm and friendly with them and the kettle would come out and there'd be something on the table. You know, anybody who came in the house, she would drop whatever she was doing and give them her attention. You know, she was just a very warm and giving sort of person. ... So I do feel that that – that is something that I try to, er, emulate myself a little bit. I mean obviously it's more contrived and it's not just as natural as she was, but, erm, that's definitely an example of something that I'm always aware of being grateful for seeing her in operation just with people. You know, she really was interested in people. You know, she'd ask them about their brothers and sisters and how they were doing at school. And kids very often are ignored by adults. And as far as feeling loved, I know in retrospect that she did love us each differently and that she had her favourites. Her favourite was my eldest brother and she told me all this when she was poorly, and she said, 'I really tried never to show this.' You know, she talked to me about this. And I don't think I was aware of this – you know that she had different feelings of love for us.

HAZEL: How did you feel about it when she told you?

DAWN: I felt okay, really. In a way. Erm, ... I felt grateful that she was able to say something like that. ... I don't feel – I feel that my mother and father were happily married and that together they were giving -. I mean perhaps my father loved me more, I don't know. I couldn't tell that either. But there was love coming from both of them, slightly different amounts, in different directions, but the sum total was, erm, you know, great. Which is why I took it rather badly when my husband left. You know, I felt this happy family relationships I had ...... at home – I thought then I wasn't ever able to offer to the kids, because it was denied me when their father decided that was it, he was going. I mean I know you've – it sounds as if you've all – or some of you have had this sort of experience, but it really was one of the worst disappoint-ments, that that – my happy family background seemed impossible at that point. Since then I don't feel that it has been too much of a problem. ...... Because my, erm, new-ish husband is someone I would have chosen to be their father anyway, yet he doesn't behave like a parent. As I said before, that's quite positive. And they see their father regularly ... So it's not too bad, is it? There must be some advantages. Double holidays, and double family, providing it's okay. ...... I don't think mums should get all the flak for giving love, you know. If there are two people then they can share it, which is perhaps my idea of an ideal family unit. I have been a single parent for several years and it was [laughs] bloody hard. You know, I don't think you can give two lots of love when there's just one of you.

LYNNE: Oh yes, I don't try [laughs]. I don't try. I give them what resources I've got, when they need it, if I can. And if I can't, I just say, 'Well I'm sorry kids, I'm too tired. Talk to me a bit later on.'

HAZEL: They have to learn that you're not an inexhaustible supply, because if you do, you're falling into the trap that our mothers' generation fell into, of trying to be everything.

LYNNE: When I don't come up with the ironed shirt, or the cake, or whatever it is I'm supposed to come up with as the perfect mother, I just say, 'Well, failed again!' Because I just will not try and be this perfect person, for them or for anybody. You know, they have to learn that I have limitations and not expect everybody else to be perfect.

DAWN: I found when I was in that situation that my eldest daughter particularly was being very motherly towards me, actually, from time to time, and I maybe always felt guilty that the children were sort of supporting me emotionally. And I never hid from them that there was a problem and that I wasn't coping, you know, when I wasn't coping. But, er, it's just exhausting. I mean if you've got somebody else there and you don't feel up to it, you can go away and let them get on with it for a time, you know. You can share it.

LYNNE: But I think it makes them into better people. Recognition of the parent's need, I think makes them into more understanding people, so I don't feel guilty about it.

DAWN: Well it was probably a constructive learning for them, but I suppose it was one I wouldn't have chosen.

HAZEL: I was very clear I didn't want to be a single parent. I was very clear. I didn't want to take that on at all. And I think it's – for me now, when my children come [here], they're bathed in love because they get it from so many people. Not only from me, but from the people who I live with, and from the people who I see. You know, they have more hugs and more cuddles and more – certainly more physical affection than they'd have if I was living in the usual nuclear family. They get a lot of positive input. It's not just up to me, or up to their dad. There's loads of people.

CAROLINE: Because that's always a problem, isn't it? That there aren't enough parents to go around in any family. ...... Mine don't have happy memories of commune life.

HAZEL: No, I suppose it's very different when they're young.

CAROLINE: Although actually Jocelyn who's nearly 19 came back from Glastonbury festival saying, 'I think I'm gonna live in a commune.' [laughs]. She's always said, 'D'you remember that birthday I had with 15 adults and no children?' [laughs]

HAZEL: I think that I feel, you know like you were saying, Gina, about your mum, that she did her best. And I feel that about my mum, that she did her best. She didn't do a very good job, but she did her best. She did all she could do. And I know that's certainly true of me, is that I've done all I could do. I do everything that I can do. But you know like you [Lynne] were saying, there are some things that I'm just not able to do at that point and they have to accept that, and they have accepted that. Although they might not like it.

GINA: I did find that very difficult in the beginning, being a single parent, you know just wearing myself out, trying to be everything to them. And I've reached a point now, like you said you [Lynne] had, where I can say, 'Look, I can't do this.' ...... And allowing myself to be looked after. ...

S.L.: D'you feel, Dawn, that your mother recognized you for what you were and accepted you for that?

DAWN: ...... Erm, I think so. Er, it's very difficult to know what goes on inside somebody else's head.

S.L.: Yes, but was that your feeling?

DAWN: ...... I think so. I mean there's nothing springing to mind in either direction. I felt closer to her, really the last months of her life, when we were on this more one-to-one, equal kind of relationship. And she was going over things in her childhood and, er, about her marriage and her different feelings about all of us, so I think for her to be able to speak to me like that, she must have accepted that I was somebody that she could say that to, you know, and I wouldn't judge her, er, for saying those things. So on the evidence of that, I would say, yes. ...... I mean there are bits of myself that I find difficult to accept. You know, I'm perhaps – I find it easier to accept other people as they are than myself as I am. But I know that and it's something I try to – . And somebody else said – you [Caroline] said you felt your mother felt negative about herself, and I think mine did, so perhaps there is some thread of continuity – that I don't want to particularly recognize that she wasn't happy about herself in this way, and maybe I'm not happy about myself in that way. But I can't prove it's down to that. Erm, perhaps at a different level – . I mean with your children you communicate love not just with words, but with feelings. It's there, isn't it? It's all the feelings that are going around that are sometimes difficult to pin down or remember – or put into words.

CAROLINE: I'm very scared of upsetting people, and I know my mother was very very scared of upsetting people. Which I think is part of feeling negative about yourself. I was just thinking about that today, because there's somebody who I thought was avoiding me because I'd upset her today, and I felt terrible. And she's probably thinking about something totally different [laughs]. ...... I am like her in that respect.

S.L.: Do you think it's – inasmuch as we want to mother differently to the ways our mothers cared for us – do you think that's an easy thing to do, or are there processes which work against it? I mean how easy have you found that to do, if you've wanted to do it?

HAZEL: I think once I'd realized how many of my needs I was projecting onto my children, and actually took them back as being owned and as being my needs, I was able to – I found mothering much easier. Once I realized that I was trying to compensate for my unhappiness through my children, you know, that I was trying to – projecting my needs onto them. Once I'd realized that, it was different. It was a very big difference. I was able to allow them to be who they are, and to see them as individuals in an equal relationship.

GINA: I think I found it quite difficult. Probably still find it relatively difficult, because somewhere there's a sort of conditioned response in me, oh my mother wouldn't have done it that way. I sometimes feel that I really do believe the perfect mother has the meal on the table when they come home, and you know, there is a part of me that still thinks that's the way you should do it. You know, and get up and make the breakfast.

HAZEL: Oh Gina!

GINA: I know, I've never done it. But somewhere there is this little nag that says, ooh, your mother wouldn't have done that. You're not doing it properly. And that really came home to me at Christmas. I really allowed the feeling to come through – that there was a little bit of me that believed you couldn't be a good mother if you didn't do these things, and once I'd actually allowed that, I could let it go. But it nagged at me for ages, you know, that I didn't do the things that she did. But I consciously didn't do them, just because I wanted to do other things – that she didn't do ...... that I wanted her to do [laughs]. But still, I like that, myself. I like the idea that I come home from work, and somebody's got a meal cooked for me.

S.L.: Oh yes!

GINA: You know, and when that happens, it's great. Somebody says, sit down, have a cup of tea, the meal'll be ready in half an hour, and you can sit down and eat it, and I'll wash up, and it's brilliant! You know, so I can see the attraction of the perfect mother. It's just that I want one too. I think everyone should have one.

CAROLINE: Especially when you're ill, that's when you need the perfect mother, and the perfect mother's never there.

GINA: Yeah! The one that does fluff up your pillows and brings you nourishing drinks and reads to you. Really looks after you.

S.L.: How much do you feel that the way you are as mothers is different to the socially acceptable 'good mother'? I don't mean your perceived inadequacies, but the way you've consciously – or unconsciously – chosen to mother?

HAZEL: Chalk and cheese. I mean my children go to X school in [neighbouring county], and they might as well be from a different planet, because they're so unlike the other children in the school, because their background is so different. They're very different. ... I've always been aware that I was very different from farmers' wives and ... I think a lot of the kids there, their upbringing is, you know twenty years ago. I mean their upbringing is twenty years behind in a lot of ways.

CAROLINE: Yeah, yeah.

HAZEL: – so that the children's horizons are much more limited than mine [children's]. their horizons are much narrower.

...

GINA: I think I have tried to be different. I tried to be the same to start with – my idea of what a mother should be, especially when Abigail was born. For the first couple of years, I tried to be my idea of what a mother was, by looking around, because I didn't have any kind of peer group that had children. I wasn't involved in a kind of set up where my friends or, you know, anybody I knew had babies. So I guess I remembered what my mother did and – saw around me – television and books I'd read. And then I got bored with that, and I didn't like it any more. I didn't want to play that particular game. So then I suppose I consciously tried to do it differently. And certainly once I'd separated from their father, I really went for it. I realize that in retrospect, because there was always a clash between us and how we should bring up the children. So once he was out of the way, if you like – I remember saying this to you as well – I had a sort of realization when I was talking to Steph, that actually one of my motives for leaving him was so that I could have, you know, total free rein with the kids.

HAZEL: Total control?

GINA: Yes! [laughs]. It was like that. 'Cause he was getting in my way, where that was concerned. But I didn't feel very good about it when I realized. But then I think, yeah, I did try to be different to the acceptable ...... social sort of conditioned way of what being a mother was.

HAZEL: Yes, I set out to be different. I can remember deciding not to read books about how to bring up babies.

CAROLINE: Yes, it never occurred to me.

HAZEL: I just decided that I was going to try and do it by instinct, by how I felt it should be done, you know. From me, rather than from reading it in a book, or from taking it from what my mother had tried to do, or had done with me, or whatever. It was very much I was gonna do it my way.

S.L.: I was quite shocked, actually, 'cause none of you seemed to have read much at all about child-care.

LYNNE: I read it, and then I threw it away [laughs]. I soon realized that the babies hadn't read the books and that they hadn't got a clue what they were talking about. And if any of my children were going to survive, they had to work on what they knew and I knew and how we worked it out together, and I just went from there. But having said that, on the surface, I tried very hard to be the perfect middle-class wife and mother, while I was married to the children's father. And that was quite a struggle for me – a huge struggle, coming from a working-class upbringing and having to fit this kind of middle-class life, especially since I absolutely hate housework. And when I came to the decision that I didn't need to learn how to bake cakes, that freed me from having to be this perfect middle-class housewife. I didn't even want to learn how to bake cakes, and all the pain I'd gone through, trying to learn how to do it in the way that I'd seen other people do it, was unnecessary. And that was the kind of break-point. The other thing was ironing the knickers and the tights, you know. And then I stopped worrying about when the washing-up was done, and gradually things kind of got left.

S.L.: So it was the cakes.

LYNNE: Yes, it was the cakes, and I just refused to try ... and that's my kind of symbol of not being perfect. And my daughter thinks I'm weird, and all her friends think I'm weird, which makes me quite pleased [laughs]. I'm quite pleased with this image that I'm weird. Cause I wear leggings and I go to university, and their mothers all sit at home and bake cakes [laughs]. I think she's secretly quite proud of me for being different. I'm certainly secretly quite proud of myself for being different [laughs].

HAZEL: I think my kids have always wanted me to be different. I've heard this from other people – that their kids say, 'Oh I wish you were like everybody else's mum.' But mine have never said that.

GINA: I had it from my sons briefly – that when we moved [here], they wanted to be normal – their idea of normal. But I think that was because I started to live in a shared house, and I think it was that – you know, they didn't have me all to themselves.

LYNNE: My son wants me to be normal, and he's very impatient with the fact that I insist he does his own washing and ironing. I don't create meals of a night time and I don't cook joints cause I don't eat meat any more, and he gets very irritated with me.

GINA: My nearly 16-year-old son's broken through the barrier [unclear]. He's really enjoying it now. But his father isn't enjoying the fact that he's enjoying it.

DAWN: I think I do remember my daughters making the odd comment like, 'You're not like the other mums' or something like that. Er, but it might have just been a fleeting comment. But I know she certainly sees my – they both see my new husband, who they like very much, as being weird, and so both of us together are fairly weird. But again, I think they quite like that. So I don't know, maybe with all of us weird people in here, then we're quite normal really [laughs].

CAROLINE: My 13-year-old did point out that advert for toothpaste, and she said 'That's what proper mothers look like.' ... She was being ironic.

  ...

DAWN: I did deliberately set out not to be what was my idea of the archetypal mother – possessive of my two kids, emotionally. Erm, but the reason for that wasn't so much my own mother, although there was a strong emotional link, but one of my aunts, whose daughter was so tied to her that it absolutely ruined what would have been a sparkling musical career. Because I saw this lass – I used to go and stay with them; she could never come and stay with us because she got homesick overnight ...

CAROLINE: Yes, I feel like that. My mother – my parents were very over-protective of me, much more so than the rest of my family when I grew up. And I felt very strongly that I wanted my kids not to feel that sort of claustrophobia, and to feel they could stay in a house on their own without being scared out of their minds.

Notes

Introduction: mothering the self

1   I adapt this expression from Marilyn Strathern's 'Euro-American', and follow her usage. Strathern comments that Euro-American is 'preferable to the monolithic "Western", though needs further specification as North American/Northern European' (Strathern, 1992b: 11). She expands on this in Strathern (1996b): 'The culture in question I call Euro-American, to refer to the largely middle-class, North American/Northern European discourse of public and professional life' (1996b: 38).

2   As, for example in the work of Eichenbaum and Orbach, who see daughters' unmet 'dependency needs' as producing a specific type of self – one which is relational, in danger of being 'lost', and as rather fragile. See Eichenbaum and Orbach, 1982, 1988; Orbach with Hollway, 1997. For a critique of this kind of perspective, see Simonds, 1992, 1996.

3   It seems that, no matter what mothers say they do, they are likely to be disbelieved if they contend they do not mother in ways in which women are assumed to mother. Susie Orbach, for example, claims:

> A lot of parents will say, 'Well, I treated them [sons and daughters] exactly the same.' ... 'But did you feel the same way about them? Did you have the same kind of conversations? Did you hold them the same? Are you the kind of mother who actually fed your daughters and sons the same length of time, felt equally relaxed about their appetites, potty trained them at the same time? No, you didn't, did you? You did exactly what the whole culture does, which is you weaned your daughter early, you know you potty trained her earlier'. ... But they'll all say they did the same thing.
> (Orbach, with Hollway, 1997: 102)

Although Orbach refers to 'parents' here, since her emphasis is on maternal relationships, I assume she is actually talking about mothers.

4   The women's ages ranged from 38 to 55. Their daughters were aged between 10 and 29.

5   The method and methodology are further discussed in Appendix I.

6   This question was clearly a request for intervention in a dispute between this woman and her daughter – which made it all the more difficult to answer.

7   One of the women in this study (Janet) did in fact decide to withdraw after one interview, and said that she was too busy to participate further.

8   Throughout the book, the following are used to mark extracts from interview transcripts: three dots (...) indicate that material has been edited; six dots (......) indicate a pause; square brackets indicate non-verbal communication, e.g. [laughs]; GD indicates the extract is taken from the group discussion.

9 This does not seem to happen the other way round – i.e. I have come across no analyses in which the mother's account of the daughter is held to be a 'true' representation, and very few within which the mother's voice is privileged over that of the daughter.

10 All names are pseudonyms and some biographical details have been changed.

1 Being and knowing: the social relations of truth

1 For example, in the UK, the number of divorces per 1,000 existing marriages more than doubled between 1970 and 1987 (Roll, 1989). In the last twenty years, the proportion of lone parents as a proportion of all families with dependent children rose steeply in most European countries and in the USA. In Britain, this proportion rose from 8 per cent to 20 per cent between 1971 and 1991 (Duncan and Edwards, 1997); in Australia, it rose from 9 per cent in 1975 to 18 per cent in 1994 (McHugh and Millar, 1997); in the USA, the number of families maintained by a lone parent rose from 3.9 million to 10.1 million between 1976 and 1991 (de Acosta, 1997). The vast majority of these lone parents are divorced mothers.

It needs to be noted, however, that most children still live with both biological parents (Coote *et al.*, 1990); that most people still marry (Kiernan and Wicks, 1990); and that most single parents either marry or cohabit within five years (Roll, 1989; Byrne, 1999). The much-publicized 'teen pregnancies' in Britain and the USA remain a small proportion of all pregnancies, and, contrary to the overall tone of most representations, have not risen in either country. In Britain, the numbers have remained fairly static since the early 1980s (and, moreover, the vast majority of teenage mothers are aged 17, 18 or 19) (Norton, 1999). In the USA, births to teenage mothers declined between 1972 and 1986 (de Acosta, 1997).

2 As, for example in the 1989 Children Act (England and Wales) discussed later in the chapter.

3 And this is the crucial difference between Foucault's concept of difference and theories of ideology. While discourse is productive of social phenomena, ideology almost always presupposes a 'real' which is both beyond ideology and obscured by it.

4 Especially in his later work, Foucault considers the ways in which subjects actively participate in the formation of their own subjectivity, through 'technologies of the self' (Foucault, 1988a).

5 Foucault tends to assume an inter-relatedness between 'modern' and European (or perhaps Euroamerican) forms of government. According to Edward Said, 'his Eurocentricism was almost total' (Said, 1991: 370).

6 The 'Gillick principle' is enshrined in the Act, following the decision in the House of Lords in *Gillick v West Norfolk and Wisbech Area Health Authority* (1986) 1AC 112. This decision recognized older children's capacity for decision-making and held that the child's decisions could supersede parental rights. According to Lord Scarman, the parental right: 'yields to the child's right to make his [*sic*] own decisions when he reaches a sufficient understanding and intelligence to be capable of making up his mind on the matter requiring decision' (quoted in Bainham, 1992: 4–5).

7 The full statutory checklist is as follows:

a court shall have regard in particular to

(a) the ascertainable wishes and feelings of the child concerned (considered in the light of his age and understanding);
(b) his physical, emotional and educational needs;
(c) the likely effect on him of any change in his circumstances;

(d) his age, sex, background and any characteristics of his which the court considers relevant;

(e) any harm which he has suffered or is at risk of suffering;

(f) how capable each of his parents, and any other person in relation to whom the court considers the question to be relevant, is of meeting his needs;

(g) the range of powers available to the court under this Act in the proceedings in question.

(Children Act 1989: S. 1(3): text in Bainham, 1992)

8 See for example Department of Health, 1988; Bannister, 1990; Frude, 1990; Coulshed, 1991; Payne, 1991.

9 Though the cause of these inequalities *is* contested – as in the 'underclass' debates. See, for example Morris, 1994; Murray, 1994a; Slipman, 1994.

10 Ironically, at the same time that the death of class is being trumpeted, concern in Britain is focusing on how to enable working-class children to have access to higher education. This concern reveals an awareness of class distinctions, at least within education, at the same time that class as a distinction is deemed to have been over-turned by social and economic changes. Class moves in and out of popular discussion.

11 See, for example, Steedman, 1986; Walkerdine and Lucey, 1989; Walkerdine, 1990, 1996, 1997; Kuhn, 1995; Skeggs, 1997.

12 Skeggs (1997: 5) argues:

> [C]lass is a discursive, historically specific, construction, a product of middle-class political consolidation, which includes elements of fantasy and projection. The historical generation of classed categorizations provide discursive frameworks which enable, legitimate and map onto material inequalities. Class conceptualizations are tautological in that positioning by categorizations and representation influence access to economic and cultural resources.

13 I do not mean to argue here that class is somehow incorporated into a pre-existing self: what I am suggesting, rather, is that one of the ways in which the self *as self* is brought into being is through mechanisms of class. The work of Walkerdine (Walkerdine and Lucey, 1989; Walkerdine, 1990, 1997) provides some good illustra-tions of how these processes work.

14 See, for example, Foucault, 1990.

15 Psychoanalytic theory generally uses the spelling 'phantasy' to denote the importance of the unconscious in its formation. However, since many writers now use the spelling 'fantasy', I have used this latter spelling throughout the book in order to achieve consistency.

16 Further, by locating the aetiology of adult psychic states in childhood experiences, psychoanalysis gives these narratives a linear dimension.

17 As Mitchell (1982) points out, Lacan represented his work as a 'return to Freud'. In contrast to the adaptations of Freud's work made by object-relations and ego-psychology theorists, Lacan saw his own work as building on the 'coherent theorist in Freud whose ideas do not need to be diverged from' (Mitchell, 1982: 1). Into this framework, Lacan built Saussurean and structuralist linguistic theory.

18 Object-relations psychoanalysis can be split into two broad 'streams': that associated with Klein, Segal, etc; and that associated with the Balints, Winnicott and Fairbairn, etc. These two schools of thought offer fundamentally different approaches to anal-yses of mothering. All object-relations approaches theorize the infant's relationship

with 'objects', in particular, with the mother, or parts of the mother's body (and the internalized mother). In this way, object relations is distinct from Freud's notion of 'drive' (*Trieb*): the ego, for Freud, is formed through the workings of the drives; the object is, in a sense, arbitrary. For object-relations theorists, the ego is formed through interaction with whole- or part-objects. Where the two 'schools' of object-relations psychoanalysis part company is in their emphasis (or lack of it) on 'real' mothers. Kleinian psychoanalysis is primarily concerned with the child's unconscious fantasies around the mother (the maternal imago) (Klein, 1932, 1975). The approach favoured by non-Kleinian object relations makes the actual, social or 'environmental' mother a focus of analysis.

2 Guaranteeing the social order: good-enough daughters, good-enough mothers

1 It is not that 'the child' has not been considered; rather, that its constitution has rarely been questioned. In conventional 'socialization' accounts, for example, the child is little more than a tabula rasa on to which 'society' (for good or ill) imposes its demands. See James *et al.* (1998) for more detailed discussion of the treatment of the child in sociological work.

2 Hockey and James (1993: 60) identify four significant characteristics of contemporary Western children, as discursively constituted: the child is spatially and temporally set apart as different, as 'other'; the child is said to have a special nature, and to be associated with nature; the child is innocent; as result of this innocence, the child is vulnerably dependent. This social creation is forged on the basis of the knowledges which surround childhood and which produce the 'truths' by which childhood is 'known' (Walkerdine, 1984, 1990; Rose, 1991; Stainton Rogers and Stainton Rogers, 1992). Knowledges which claim to be disinterestedly and objectively *describing* a pre-existing category of 'childhood' can be seen as *producing* this category (Walkerdine, 1984). They generate schemata of understanding through which the individuals marked as 'children' come to be known and understood, and, indeed, come to understand themselves.

3 Butler's original formulation is:

> The moderate critic might conceded that *some part of* 'sex' is constructed, but some other certainly is not, and then, of course, find him or herself not only under some obligation to draw the lines between what is and what is not constructed, but to explain how it is that 'sex' comes in parts whose differentiation is not a matter of construction.
>
> (Butler, 1993: 11; emphasis hers)

4 Sensitivity is usually defined as involving 'an awareness of children's behaviour, a reasonably accurate interpretation of their behaviour, as well as prompt and appropriate responses' (Woollett and Phoenix, 1991a: 35). As Woollett and Phoenix point out, the situating of research within laboratory settings, together with the concentration of studying mothers with young infants, has meant that conflict is not frequently observed – and has become obscured in a focus on 'sensitivity' and on child-centredness.

5 For critiques of this perspective, see Abbott and Wallace, 1992; Braid, 1993; Laws, 1994a.

6 John Redwood was, at the time, the Welsh Secretary in the British (Conservative) Government.

7 These comments were made in the aftermath of the 'Bulger case' discussed later in the chapter.

8 Compare Foucault's comment on educational institutions, where, he argues, 'one is managing others and teaching them to manage themselves' (1983: 370).

9 James Bulger's murder was neither the first, nor the last, murder of a child by a child or children. Yet it was clearly a flash point in British culture – something happened around this murder, and its coming to trial, which was less to do with what happened than with the specific context of its reception.

In 1996, three years after the murder of James Bulger, 9-year-old Jade Matthews was beaten to death by Brian Smith, then aged 13. This murder took place only a short distance from the scene of James Bulger's murder. Neither Jade's murder, nor Smith's subsequent court appearance, received anything like the frenetic publicity which surrounded Bulger's murder and the trial of Thompson and Venables, the boys who killed him.

10 See also Sereny, 1995a and b. Sereny makes much the same kind of movement in her analysis of Mary Bell, who in 1968, at the age of 11, was convicted of the murder of two children, and of the killers of James Bulger. If anything, Sereny is even more insulting towards these mothers than Morrison is.

11 Ultimately, though, Morrison fails in this recouping. He attempts to suture the gap between semblance and substance by attempting to normalize the boys' (working-class, urban) childhoods through comparison with his own (middle-class, rural). But this very attempt at recouping establishes which childhood is 'normal' – a 'real' child-hood – and which is not. This movement simply would not work in reverse – Morrison's childhood could not be established as 'normal' through comparison with the childhoods of Thompson and Venables. Indeed, there is no need for such a move, since Morrison's childhood is always-already established as the more normal one – the 'real' childhood.

12 See also Walkerdine and Lucey, 1989. The authors comment that the same meanings are not attached to girls' and boys' behaviour in the classroom. Of the 10-year-old girls in their study, they comment:

> No matter how much their mothers prepared them, this is what the girls have to face. They can manifest the same behaviour as boys until they are blue in the face, but it will never 'mean' the same thing. If they are independent they may be a 'madam'; if they are strong, they may be 'selfish'.
>
> (Walkerdine and Lucey, 1989: 201)

13 Walkerdine (1981, 1987) argues that aggressive masculine sexuality is tolerated, and even validated, in the classroom. She argues that it is the task of the female teacher to contain expressions of this violence, transforming them into 'reason'.

14 For analyses of the place of mothers in the 'underclass' debates in Britain and North America, see Collins, 1991; Morris, 1994; Slipman, 1994; de Acosta, 1997; Skeggs, 1997.

15 Such a conceptualization of childhood and family life is also found in Murray's contributions to the 'underclass debate'. Murray (1994b) identifies eight characteristics of what he calls 'the New Rabble':

Low-skilled working class, poorly educated;
Single parent families are the norm;
Largely dependent on welfare and the black economy;
High levels of criminality, child neglect and abuse, and drug use;
Impervious to social welfare policies which seek to change their behaviour;
Will not enter legitimate labour market when times are good, and will recruit more working class young people when times are bad;
Children attend school irregularly and pose discipline problems;

Large and lucrative market for violent and pornographic films, television and music.

Against this, the 'New Victorians' (the middle classes) are represented by Murray as having a 'renewed concern for concepts such as fidelity, courage, loyalty, self-restraint and moderation' .

16 Winnicott has probably been the single most influential figure in psychoanalysis in Britain, not only because he popularized his work through a series of radio talks addressed to mothers (Winnicott, 1964), but also because he lectured to social workers, midwives, child welfare officers, and other members of the 'caring professions' (Winnicott, 1965a), as well as practising as a clinician.

17 Doane and Hodges (1992) describe its influence in the United States as 'almost hegemonic'.

18 Socialization theories have their origins in social psychology, and were adapted by sociologists, notably by Parsons, 1951; Parsons and Bales, 1956. For examples of analyses based on socialization theories, see Belotti, 1975; Phillips, 1996. For a good critique of socialization theories, see James *et al.*, 1998.

19 And here Chodorow agrees with Freud, who also argued this. See Freud, 1925, 1931.

3 (Re)producing the self

1 The effects of the mothering they have received on women's ability to mother is usually held to be particularly decisive. For example, commenting on a case-study of a woman defined as projecting her own needs on to her child, and as 'inconsistent and intrusive' in her mothering, Broussard states:

> When a woman has not experienced good mothering and a pleasurable infancy with her own mother, she may be hampered in her ability to provide good mothering for her child.
>
> (Broussard, 1982: 194)

For an example of the conflation of mothering and being mothered in child-care advice, see Jolly, 1986.

2 This is in contrast to psychoanalytic models, in which gender is ontologically contiguous with selfhood. In most 'psy' models, the self is (implicitly) theorized as ontologically prior to gender – which is conceptualized in terms of 'roles', of 'self-perception', and so on – in other words, as in some way separable from the 'real' self. See, for example, Eichenbaum and Orbach, 1982, 1988; Phillips, 1996; Lawrence, 1992.

3 I want to emphasize that I am not positing these 'models' of the self as ontological categories, as in, for example, William James' (1890) typology. Rather, they are *expressions* of (multivalent) selfhood.

4 See, for example, Dawkins, 1989, 1995.

5 This substance was not usually literally described as 'blood': nevertheless, there are links here with Schneider's conceptualization of 'blood relationships'. The substance linking kin members in the context of the 'inherited self' was described by most women in terms of a biological substance; and although, as I go on to argue, this substance was not seen as wholly determining of the self, it was usually related as an 'objective fact of nature'.

6 And also from their fathers to themselves and their daughters' fathers to their daughters.

7 However, this range is not infinite. The women only recognized inheritance from forebears whom they had known personally.

8 See Chapter 5 for further discussion of matrophobia, and of its relation to class position.

9   And it is worth noting that many women, including Barbara, saw their mothers as also lacking self-confidence.

10   When I tried to trace the women's descriptions of inherited characteristics through comparing the ways in which they described themselves compared with how they described their parents and their children, and which traits they marked as being 'passed on', I was struck by the frequency with which 'negative' traits in the self were seen as inherited from the mother, while 'positive' traits were seen as being inherited from fathers. Similarly, 'negative' traits in the daughter were more often seen as being inherited from the women themselves than from the daughters' fathers. This was not absolute: it was not that any of the women saw *only* negative traits as passing from mothers (or vice versa). Nevertheless, negative characteristics in the self and/or the daughter were more frequently seen as passing matrilineally.

11   Some of these are, of course, familial relationships, but I include them here to indicate the ways in which relationships outside of those within women's own birth families are seen as compensatory.

12   The Labour Government in Britain has extended this parental responsibility through accentuating, in the courts, parents' culpability for the offences of their children.

13   For example, a great deal of the press coverage of the trial of Robert Thompson and Jon Venables, the two 10-year-old boys discussed in Chapter 2, who were convicted of the murder of 2-year-old James Bulger, centred around the scrutiny of their mothers' mothering. Both Thompson's and Venables' parents were divorced, and were frequently positioned negatively in relation to the representations of the 'close' relationship enjoyed by the (then) married parents of James Bulger.

14   However, this dichotomy is usually collapsed within psy discourses, as what the mother does is assumed to be an effect of what her (deep) self is.

15   Although the self is processual and therefore changes over time, it is usually assumed to remain essentially the same entity (cf. Ricoeur, 1991b). Most women also considered this core self to be largely out of the control of the will: as Rachel, for example, put it, 'You can't change the way you are'. However, as I discuss in later chapters, you can become more 'yourself'. This core identity, then is capable of being either lived out or not lived out.

16   This theme runs through numerous constitutions of the mother–child relationship, including child-care advice, self-help literature, as well as developmental psychology texts, social work texts, and so on. For example, Herbert argues that 'environmental influences can determine … whether an individual achieves full genetic potential' (Herbert, 1986: 37). The argument here seems to be that uniqueness can only be acted upon through parental (especially maternal) care. The debt to Winnicott in all these kinds of formulation is clear. In 'Ego distortion in terms of true and false self' (in Winnicott, 1965c). Winnicott claimed that the 'True Self' derives from 'inherited potential'. But it is through the existence of this inheritance (the infant's likeness to its parents) that the infant is able to claim individuality (its uniqueness). For Winnicott, this True Self is primary and originary. But it can only be expressed if the mother is good enough and responds properly to the infant through identification with her/him, and through the processes of holding, handling and object-presentation (see Chapter 2).

17   In a recent radio debate in Britain, Victoria Gillick (who has campaigned widely on behalf of the conventional, two-parent family and parental authority) remarked that 'The women produce the men. If you have ignorant women, you have barbarians for men' (*Today* programme, 25.9.97, BBC Radio 4). She was referring to the responsibility of mothers for raising the next generation (presumably of women as well as men). Here we have a model of childhood as produced which might seem to sit rather uneasily with models of childhood as natural. This model also positions mothers as what Wendy Simonds, in her discussion of self-help literature, calls, 'the social construction workers of gender, for both future men and future women'

(Simonds, 1992: 178). No doubt Gillick's model of normative or ideal gender differs from that found in self-help literature, but the point is that mothers are seen as *making* children. This theme is also found in feminist versions of object-relations theories, in which the mother's unmet needs lead to her producing a feminine self in the daughter – femininity, in this case, being produced as a position in which the child defines herself as the meeter of others' needs, rather than as someone who should have her needs met. See Chodorow, 1978; Eichenbaum and Orbach, 1982, 1988, 1993; James, 1992; Lawrence, 1992.

18 This characterization of dependency as the essence of the human condition also marks work like that of Chodorow, and Eichenbaum and Orbach, all of whom locate gender as the outcome of women's unmet dependency needs.

19 See, for example, Kellmer-Pringle, 1980a, 1987; Bond, 1982; Broussard, 1982; NSPCC, 1989.

20 The enterprise culture, though closely associated in Britain with Thatcherism, is not synonymous with Thatcherism, nor is Thatcherism a necessary pre- or co-condition of the enterprise culture. Abercrombie, noting the 'remarkable agreement' about the need for enterprise between the then leaders of the two main British political parties argues:

> [T]he appearance of enterprise culture is not primarily a function of political interventions. Instead, it is produced by a set of fundamental changes in British society. In this sense Mrs. Thatcher and Mr. Kinnock are riding a wave, for their advocacy of enterprise merely reflects and accentuates changes that are happening anyway in British society.
>
> (Abercrombie, 1991: 171)

21 As Rose (1991) demonstrates, many of the themes of contemporary psy discourses have their roots in the humanistic psychology of the 1960s.

22 This is the slogan of a long-running campaign by BT (a British telephone company). The relevant advertising stresses the value, for personal relationships and for personal satisfaction, of talking on the phone.

23 For example, in a speech made in 1987, Lord Young (then Minister of Employment in the Thatcher government) asserted that:

> We are all born with enterprise. None of us would survive without enterprise. Every baby and toddler demonstrates every day ... that early in life we all have an abundance of enterprise, initiative, the ability to spot an opportunity and take rapid advantage of it. So when we are young, we are all entrepreneurs. But along the way to adult life, too many of us change.
>
> (Quoted in Selden, 1991: 63)

24 It is worth noting, however, that this conceptualization of the self, and of its relationship to nature/culture, may itself be shifting. Celia Lury (1998) argues that we are seeing a shift to what she calls 'prosthetic culture', in which the self as possessive individual is being replaced or augmented by a self which is experimental. Lury places this shift within the context of a culture in which the self comes to be defined, less by reference to an amalgam of 'nature' and 'culture' than by reference to an assemblage of '(mechanical and perceptual) prostheses' (Lury, 1998: 17).

25 I take this from Walkerdine and Lucey, 1989.

4 Girls growing up: regulation and autonomy

1 Although Kellmer-Pringle's argument explicitly invokes class, class is more usually implicit in discussions of 'normal'/'abnormal' mothering, as Chapter 2 showed. Nevertheless, it is a structuring absence: it informs the discussion.

2 See also Johnson (1988), on whom McNay draws for this part of her argument.

3 This notion is congruent with 'progressive' pedagogy, which proposes that teachers facilitate and create a 'learning environment', rather than transmitting knowledge (see, e.g. Knowles, 1983). As Beth Humphries (1988) points out, this model rests on a masculine and bourgeois notion of the individual, and makes teachers more passive than learners.

4 In some accounts, this 'inadequate mothering' is presented as not these mothers' fault: it is 'society' which has failed them (see, e.g. Adams, 1971; Ollendorf, 1971). Nevertheless, the suggestion is that any mother could (and should) mother 'sensitively' or 'democratically' given the right conditions. The model of mothering itself is not up for question.

5 The Famous Five are a group of five white, middle-class children who feature in a series of books written between the 1940s and the 1960s by the English children's author, Enid Blyton.

6 Gina, the other working-class woman in this study, however, did. Gina had had extensive contact with a therapeutic movement, and the discourse of therapy underwrote several of her views on mothering. But they also underwrote the tensions around these issues with which her account is suffused. Gina wants both to assert her authority and to refrain from asserting her authority. For example, as she says, 'I don't want my word to be law. But I do, somehow or other.' This kind of tension is explored later in the chapter.

7 For a slightly different version of this argument, see James (1992). Drawing on Chodorow's object-relations theory, James argues that the family, and, in particular, the mother–child relationship, is a potential site of the building of children's self-esteem, which, she argues, is an integral feature of the selves of democratic citizens.

8 Some accounts propose that (since mothers themselves are manifestly unable to do this properly) the therapist needs to stand in for the 'good-enough' mother (Eichenbaum and Orbach, 1982, 1993).

9 Skeggs notes a wider move towards a 'popular feminism' in which an appeal is made to the 'solitary individual'. This may, she argues, have the effect of blocking the links between the individual and the collective (Skeggs, 1997: 144–5).

10 The phrase is Giddens' (see Giddens, 1991 and 1992). He argues that social actors in the late twentieth century are moving away from relationships structured by institutional and kin demands towards relationships based on mutual desire and satisfaction. Giddens' main focus is on sexual relationships, though he also characterizes parent–child relationships as moving towards this kind of 'pure relationship'. As Jamieson notes, Giddens suggests that the 'pure relationship' is an indicator, if not a source, of growing equality between people. But it is difficult to see how his analysis can apply to how parent–child relationships are actually lived, given parents' obligations towards their children – to say nothing of the difficulties inherent in his assumption that 'pure relationships' lead to greater equality between women and men.

11 Having children at an early age (i.e. before 20) is often cited as an indicator of 'abusing parents' (e.g. Hanson *et al.*, 1978; Lynch and Roberts, 1978; Jones *et al.*, 1982). As Stainton Rogers and Stainton Rogers comment, 'Such condemnations tend to gloss over the observation that such characteristics seem not to lead to becoming an abusing parent if you are the future Queen of England' (1992: 117).

12 In English and Welsh law, the legal principle of *doli incapax* made children between the ages of 10 and 14 criminally responsible only if the prosecution could provide

evidence that they have 'guilty knowledge' – i.e. that they understood that their actions were wrong (Pilkington, 1994; Dyer, 1995). This principle was abolished in the High Court in March 1994, reinstated in March 1995, but abolished again under the Labour Government's Crime and Disorder Bill, 1996.

13 In a recent seminar on motherhood and childhood, my students identified a range of ages at which childhood might be considered to 'end' – raging from 8 to 25.

14 This naturalization of heterosexuality is an integral part of constructions of sexuality (Rich, 1980; Mackinnon, 1982; Reinhold, 1994) and has the effect of occluding the difficulties which many feminist commentators have identified within heterosexual relationships, such as sexual violence (Russell, 1982; Kelly, 1988), or the appropriation by men of women's emotional and sexual labour (Delphy and Leonard, 1992).

15 It is only at the end of her book that Friday comes close to acknowledging that the portrait of 'Mother' she has drawn may be a representation of the daughter's desires and frustrations. But the radical implications of this view are not explored, beyond a brief consideration that a view of the mother as either wholly good or wholly bad is the result of infantile fantasy. This message, however, does not form the theme of the book and is hardly explored before the final three pages.

16 Like Wylie, Friday slips from psychic to social reality. As Kaplan comments of Wylie's *Generation of Vipers*, 'the book's language indicates the transferring of unconscious hostility to the mother into a generalized depiction of a *social* mother-figure' (Kaplan, 1992: 115); emphasis in original.

17 Although it must also be noted that it has been enormously popular. See Hirsch, 1981 for a discussion of its popularity.

18 See Rossiter, 1994, for an exploration of these issues in the context of girls' first dance party.

5 Daughterly stories: matrophobia, class and the self

1 For example, Pamela Fox (1994) notes how the genre of the 'working-class novel' of the late nineteenth to mid twentieth century frequently positions women in terms of desires for respectability in the artefacts of the domestic world; desires which are constituted as disreputable and apolitical. Posed against the 'nobility' of the male manual worker, women within these plots are frequently represented as frivolous and pretentious. Walkerdine (1997) argues that, in the 'rags to riches' films of the 1950s (such as *My Fair Lady*), 'the working-class girl is given nothing to be proud of, even to like about herself' (Walkerdine, 1997: 97). Contemporary 'rags to riches' fantasies in Hollywood cinema give the working-class (or impoverished middle-class) woman little more: in *Indecent Proposal*, for example, the woman can only 'like herself' after disavowing her *haute-bourgeoise* existence and returning to her husband.

2 See Lawler (1999b) for fuller discussion of the issue of 'escape' from a working-class position.

3 The seven women were aged between 38 and 50 years old at the time of the interviews. This means that they were members of the first generation to benefit from universal, free secondary education to age 15: in England and Wales, the 1944 Education Act established compulsory, free secondary education for all children up to the age of 15. However, this Act also introduced the 'tripartite' system of education, under which all children were allocated to a grammar school, a secondary modern school, or a technical school at age 11, depending on their performance in the 'Eleven Plus' examination.

Working-class children who passed the Eleven Plus (as most of the women in this study did) have often been seen as walking a happy road to 'equal opportunities' (Walkerdine, 1997). As I will discuss later in this chapter, however, this concept obscures the pain and dislocation which many of them feel.

4 See Skeggs (1997) and Walkerdine (1997) for excellent analyses and examples of these kinds of anxieties.

5 Barbara was embarrassed to tell me this, as I am embarrassed about reproducing our discussion here: I am aware that both Barbara and I can be marked as 'pretentious'.

6 I am indebted to Mariam Fraser for this formulation.

7 Though not in all. In many working-class locations, 'posh' accents can themselves be a source of ridicule, marking pretentiousness. But in the social milieux inhabited by these women, as well as in most 'public' sites (such as the media), middle-class accents (often wrongly – and significantly – designated 'classless') are almost always preferred.

8 This representation of cleanliness signifies a further (would-be) distancing from working-class femininity. As Stallybrass and White (1986) argue, working-class existence has historically been associated with 'dirt' and pollution. This takes on a particular significance for women, because of the strong association between the category 'woman' and the banishing of dirt. Yet working-class women are frequently marked as failing here: they are often signified as *embodying* the disorder which women are supposed to banish (Skeggs, 1997).

9 Interestingly, though, and despite the association between working-class existence and 'dirt' (Stallybrass and White, 1986), Edie is represented as extremely, even pathologically, clean and houseproud. This may itself be part of the joke – another part of the (failed) attempt at 'passing'.

10 Another (rather more extreme) example is the character of Hyacinth Bucket (pronounced 'bouquet') played by Patricia Routledge in the British TV comedy, *Keeping Up Appearances* – a title that says it all.

11 Dorothy Rowe (1995) argues that comedy always involves the displacement of authority. However, what she fails to note is that particular forms of authority may be set up within the comedic structure, only in order to be overthrown or displaced. In the two programmes mentioned here (*Keeping Up Appearances* and *Last of the Summer Wine*) the women who try to 'pass' are themselves set up as figures of authority, who are 'brought down to size', either through the subversive tactics of others, or through moments of 'slapstick'. Hence, it seems to me that characters like this indicate the limitations of using concepts of 'grotesque' or 'unruly' women in celebratory or subversive ways.

12 See Fraser (1999) for an excellent analysis of the limitations of a politics of performativity in the context of class politics.

13 Hazel invokes here the familiar association between lack of 'taste' and materialism (or conspicuous consumption) – an association in which working-class people are frequently characterized as hypermaterialistic. But the middle classes, too, want things: it seems, though, that the very materiality of 'tasteful' objects can be occluded in favour of their signification of taste and refinement (Lawler, 2000).

14 As Patrick Hutton argues, 'Who we are has as much to do with what we affirm in the present as it does with what we revere in the past' (Hutton, 1988: 139–40).

15 For a feminist analysis of the family romance in literature, see Hirsch (1989), who presents a female family romance which centres around the figure of the mother.

16 This inadequate mothering is seen as having profound implications for the daughter's adult life. Within feminist accounts, there is frequently a suggestion that, if only daughters had been more loved and more valued, or if only their mothers had allowed them to separate – in other words, if only they had had better mothers – then they would be more liberated, have fewer problems, be more able to achieve their potential. In this way, women's oppression is sometimes presented as the result of inadequate mothering.

17 Recent media stories of infants in Britain and the US apparently swapped at birth and sent home with the 'wrong' parents are one indication that the certainty of the mother's identity is not so complete as Freud asserts (see, e.g. Reed, 1993). The advent of assisted procreation also shifts the meaning of motherhood and undermines the

certainty attached to the mother, in ways Freud could not have anticipated (Stanworth, 1987). More intriguingly, and as Marianne Hirsch (1989) points out, Freud seems to have overlooked the peculiar circumstances of Oedipus here.

18 Hirsch (1989) suggests that matrophobia may be the underside of the family romances she identifies in feminist texts of the 1970s, in which, she argues, relations between women are celebrated, but these relations effectively exclude the mother:

> The woman as *mother* remains in the position of *other*, and the emergence of feminine-daughterly subjectivity rests on the continued and repeated process of *othering* the mother.
>
> (Hirsch, 1989: 136)

19 Usually, these other persons were women, but some women also indicated that they had looked for (and sometimes indicated that they had found) 'mothering' in relationships with men. Marianne Hirsch (1989), describing women protagonists' search for mothering from men in literary forms, describes this as 'the fantasy of the man who would understand'; 'the man who, unlike the father, would combine maternal nurturance with paternal power' (Hirsch, 1989: 58. See also Radway, 1987).

20 But see Roschelle (1997) for a contradictory stance on this issue. Roschelle argues that African-American women are unlikely to provide care outside of the immediate family, largely because time and resource constraints render them unable to do so.

21 And, as Skeggs notes, these desires were 'the material stepping stones of escape' (Skeggs, 1997: 86).

22 There are a few, of course, including the 'rags to riches' fantasies of which Walkerdine (1997) writes, and plays like Willy Russell's *Educating Rita*. But even these position the working-class woman in troubling ways. In *Educating Rita*, for example, Rita/Susan becomes marked as 'pretentious' in a number of ways, and is, by the end of the play, re-contained within a working-class self (educated, but still – by implication – her true (old) self). See Lawler (2000) for an analysis of these issues in another of Willy Russell's plays, *Breezeblock Park*.

6 Maternal stories, maternal selves

1 Two women spoke of 'smothering' when saying that mothers could love their children too much; this phrase suggests a potentially lethal quality to maternal love.

2 There may be, however, more of a reciprocity over a lifetime, as daughters care for ageing mothers. But generally, there seems to be an assumption that obligations flow down through time (Finch, 1989).

3 While children themselves may participate in 'needs talk', formulations of childhood and knowledges around childhood and its needs do not originate with them.

4 Or, indeed, for many groups within Euroamerican cultures – see Walkerdine and Lucey, 1989; Finch, 1993.

5 However, and as earlier chapters showed, the 'truths' of psy do not go uncontested. Nevertheless, they assumed tremendous significance in the post-war period.

6 Women who were no longer married were more likely to say that their ex-husbands had *not* shared equally in child-care, perhaps because they had little investment in representing their ex-husbands in a positive light.

7 Of course, this work could just not be done at all, but this would require a redefinition of children and their 'needs'; see next section of this chapter

8 However the lines of causation are drawn, this domestic division of labour is also linked with the gendered division of labour in paid work, in which, overall, women earn less than men, white women are more likely to work part time than men, and more likely to interrupt their paid work when children are born (Westwood and Bhachu, 1988; Walby, 1990). As I indicated above, all of the women in this study had

given up paid work after their children were born, and most, when they returned to paid work, worked part time.

9 See Hochschild (1983) and Adkins and Lury (1992) for analyses of the ways in which women may be required to 'mother' in the labour market. See also Langford (1999) for an analysis of women 'mothering' men in heterosexual relations.

10 Within child-care manuals, which usually draw on the theoretical premises of the psychological accounts above, participation by fathers in child-care is often proposed. However, as Marshall (1991) points out, 'the notion of sharing [child-care] does not entail equal time spent with the child, nor equal allocation of childcare tasks' (Marshall, 1991: 78).

11 For example, Mia Kellmer-Pringle pronounces thus:

> Mothering mediates between the child's inner subjective and the outside 'real' world; it recognises and establishes his personal identity and individuality; and her loving care is unique in the sense that it is adapted to his very special, individual needs which are recognized as being different from those of any other child.
>
> (Kellmer-Pringle, 1980a: 36)

12 Although the terms on which they have been politicized are fundamentally individualistic and therefore de-collectivizing.

13 See also Herbert, 1990. Herbert specifies the following as human needs: 'security; approval; power; affiliation (companionship); sympathy; self-actualization (self-fulfilment)' (Herbert, 1990: 81).

Herbert defines these as 'secondary' (or social) needs – 'learned as a result of the unique experiences of the individual in various environments' (1990: 81).

14 Cf. Adams, 1971: Adams talks of the mother and infant during toilet-training as a 'potting couple' and suggests that the mother relives her own anal stage during this period; 'The mother is herself developing in parallel with her baby's development' (Adams, 1971: 67). Mother and infant here, as in Winnicott, seem collapsed into the person of the infant.

15 The principle that needs are contained by the family is enshrined in the 1989 Children Act. Mallinson (1992) comments that the Act

> is based upon a belief that children are best looked after within a family with both parents playing a full part and without resort to legal proceedings. Local authorities have a duty to encourage the upbringing of children in need by their families provided this is consistent with the child's best interests.
>
> (1992: vii)

16 For example, 'The family live in poor housing and on a low income' (Kellmer-Pringle, 1980b); 'Father has a manual occupation' (Hanson *et al.*, 1978). Polansky (1981) includes a 'childhood levels of living scale': part B (emotional/cognitive care) includes such items as 'Planned overnight vacation trip has been taken by the family'; 'The family owns a camera'; 'Child has been taken fishing'. Interestingly, these scales are reproduced in the same volumes as Cooper's article, without any editorial comment on the apparent contradiction.

17 Kellmer-Pringle (1980a) goes so far as to suggest that some families are poor *because* they are (socially and psychologically) inadequate.

18 For example, Pilkington (1994), writing of the public reaction to the two 10-year-old boys who murdered the toddler James Bulger, claims that:

Jamie [Bulger's] murderers suffered from a lack of attention and a failure to help them tackle their behavioural problems. Yes, they ran wild in a vacuum left by inadequate control. But they also needed the cradling and safety that only the special status of childhood can provide.

(Pilkington, 1994)

19 See Smith (1999) for a fuller analysis of this issue.
20 As indeed has been the case with 'foetal rights' (Petchesky, 1986).
21 The 1989 Children Act (England and Wales) also enshrines the principle that children's needs are to be catered for within their families – and indeed that children have a right to this.
22 A recent British case highlights this point. In September 1999, the Court of Appeal upheld an earlier legal ruling that a five-month old baby must be tested for HIV, against the wishes of her parents (the baby's mother is HIV positive). Lady Justice Butler-Sloss, one of the three Appeal Court judges, commented that 'This child has the *right* to have *sensible and responsible* people find out whether or not she is HIV positive' (Quoted in Verkaik, 1999; emphasis mine). The parents here seem to be characterized as the others to these 'sensible and responsible' people. The baby's 'rights' seem to inhere in simply adhering to expert pronouncements.
23 As in cases where children refuse medical treatment but have their wishes overridden. See Smith, 1999.

7 Children's needs and mothers' desires

1 The simultaneous roles of 'wife and mother' are, of course, a potential source of tension. As I indicated in Chapter 6, women may also have to 'mother' their male partners: and demands from men and children may be competing. However, this is not usually considered in child-care advice or in psychological texts. Where it is, it is in the context of some pathology in the woman.
2 *The Guardian* is a British centre-left broadsheet newspaper.
3 Compare this speech from a fictional mother, Ying-Ying St. Clair in Amy Tan's *The Joy Luck Club*:

> For all these years I kept my mouth closed so selfish desires would not fall out. And because I remained quiet for so long now my daughter does not hear me. …
>
> All these years I kept my true nature hidden, running along like a small shadow so nobody could catch me. And because I moved so secretly now my daughter does not see me. …
>
> And I want to tell her this: We are lost, she and I, unseen and unseeing, unheard and not hearing, unknown by others.
>
> (p. 67)

4 Kim Chernin, in her auto/biographical novel, *In My Mother's House*, suggests that it is the daughter who should tell both the mother's story and her own. With the daughter's birth, the mother's voice fades:

> [H]ere, of course, we come to Larissa's story. For me, the narrative is almost at an end. Those years, after her birth, belong to my daughter and must be told, if ever, in her voice.
>
> (p. 294)

5   Clearly, it may be that the women *felt* resentment but were unable to express it; it may be too threatening to one's sense of self as a 'good mother' to express any resentment, however oblique, in relation to one's own children. However, I am primarily concerned here with the ways in which women relate (loss of) autonomy, and the contradictions this raises for them.

6   Though, as I have already indicated, their autonomy – and hence their personhood – is militated against by the fact of their femaleness.

7   *Beadle's About*, a British TV programme in which viewers send in amusing/embarrassing video clips.

8 Telling other stories: refiguring motherhood and daughterhood

1   For example, see Gordon (1990) whose respondents (and Gordon herself) tend to equate 'feminist' with 'child-centred', without any questioning of where such knowledges come from or the effects they may have.

2   Mariam Fraser (1999), for example, argues that a politics of Queer which is based on self-aestheticization is unable to encompass working-class identities since the aesthetic used is *itself* marked as middle class.

Bibliography

Abbott, P. and Wallace, C. (1992) *The Family and the New Right*. London: Pluto Press.

Abercrombie, N. (1991) 'The privilege of the producer', in Keat and Abercrombie (eds).

Adams, Parveen (1983) 'Mothering', *m/f*, 8: 40–52.

Adams, Philip (1971) 'The infant, the family and society', in Adams *et al*.

Adams, P., Berg, L., Berger, N., Duane, M., Neill, A.S. and Ollendorf, R. (1971) *Children's Rights: Towards the Liberation of the Child*. London: Elek Books.

Adcock, M. (1990) 'Assessing parenting: the context', in Adcock and White (eds).

Adcock, M. and White, R. (eds) (1990) [1985] *Good-Enough Parenting: A Framework for Assessment*. London: British Agencies for Adoption and Fostering.

Adkins, L. and Lury, C. (1992) 'Gender and the labour market: new theory for old?', in H. Hinds, A. Phoenix and J. Stacey (eds) *Working Out: New Directions for Women's Studies*. London: Falmer Press.

Adorno, T.W. (1974) *Minima Moralia: Reflections from Damaged Life*. London: New Left Books.

Ainsworth, M., Bell, S. and Stayton, D. (1971) 'Individual differences in strange-situation behaviour in one-year-olds', in H.R. Schaffer (ed.) *The Origins of Human Social Relations*. London: Academic Press.

Ainsworth, M. and Bell, S. (1974) 'Mother–infant interactions and the development of competence', in K. Connolly and J. Bruner (eds) *The Growth of Competence*. London: Academic Press.

Alcoff, L. (1997) 'Cultural feminism versus poststructuralism: the identity crisis in feminism', in L. Nicholson (ed.) *The Second Wave: a Reader in Feminist Theory*. New York: Routledge.

Ambert, A-M. (1994) 'An international perspective on parenting: social change and social constructs', *Journal of Marriage and the Family*, 56: 529–43.

Arcana, J. (1981) *Our Mothers' Daughters*. London: The Women's Press.

Bainham, A. (1992) *Children – The New Law: The Children Act 1989*. Bristol: Family Law.

Baker, D. (1989) 'Social identity in the transition to motherhood', in S. Skevington and D. Baker (eds) *The Social Identity of Women*. London: Sage.

Bannister, D. (1990) 'Knowledge of self', in Herbert (ed.) (1990).

Barrett, M. (1991) *The Politics of Truth: From Marx to Foucault*. Cambridge: Polity Press.

Barrett, M. and McIntosh, M. (1982) *The Anti-Social Family*. London: Verso.

Bart, P. (1983) 'Review of Chodorow's *The Reproduction of Mothering*', in Treblicot (ed.).

Bates, S. (1993) 'Tory attacks fathers who reject family life', *The Guardian*, 3 July 1993.

Beck, U. (1992) *Risk Society: Towards a New Modernity*. London: Sage.

Belotti, E. (1975) *Little Girls: Social Conditioning and Its Effects on the Stereotyped Role of Women During Infancy*. London: Writers and Readers Publishing Co-operative.

Benjamin, J. (1982) 'Shame and sexual politics', *New German Critique*, 13: 35–57.

—— (1988) *The Bonds of Love: Psychoanalysis, Feminism, and the Problem of Domination*. New York: Pantheon.

Bettelheim, B. (1987) *A Good Enough Parent: The Guide to Bringing Up Your Child*. London: Thames and Hudson.

Blackman, L. (1996) 'The dangerous classes: retelling the psychiatric story', *Feminism and Psychology*, 6 (3): 355–79.

Bond, L.A. (1982) 'From prevention to promotion: optimizing infant development', in L. A. Bind and J. M. Joffe (eds) *Facilitating Infant and Early Child Development*. Hanover, NH: University Press of New England.

Bordo, S. (1990) 'Feminism, postmodernism and gender-scepticism', in Nicholson (ed.).

Boulton, M. (1983) *On Being a Mother: A Study of Women With Pre-School Children*. London: Tavistock.

Bourdieu, P. (1977) *Outline of a Theory of Practice* (translated by R. Nice). Cambridge: Cambridge University Press.

—— (1984) *Distinction* (translated by R. Nice). London: Routledge and Kegan Paul.

—— (1992) *The Logic of Practice* (translated by R. Nice). Cambridge: Polity.

—— (1993) *The Field of Cultural Production: Essays on Art and Literature* (edited and introduced by R. Johnson). Cambridge: Polity Press.

Bowlby, J. (1953) *Child Care and the Growth of Love*. Harmondsworth: Penguin.

—— (1978a) [1971] *Attachment and Loss: vol. I, Attachment*. Harmondsworth: Penguin.

—— (1978b) [1973] *Attachment and Loss: vol. II, Separation, Anxiety and Anger*. Harmondsworth: Penguin.

Boyne, R. (1990) 'War and desire', *Polish Sociological Bulletin*, 1: 33–46.

Bradley, B. (1989) *Visions of Infancy: A Critical Introduction to Child Psychology*. Oxford: Blackwell.

Brah, A. (1992) 'Difference, diversity and differentiation', in J. Donald and A. Rattansi (eds) *'Race', Culture and Difference*. London: Sage.

Braid, M. (1993) 'Return of the bogywoman', *The Independent on Sunday*, 10 October 1993.

Brannen, J., Dodd, K., Oakley, A. and Storey, A. (1994) *Young People, Health and Family Life*. Buckingham: Open University Press.

Broussard, E.R. (1982) 'Primary prevention of psychosocial disorders: assessment of outcome', in L.A. Bind and J.M. Joffe (eds) *Facilitating Infant and Early Child Development*. Hanover, NH: University Press of New England.

Butler, J. (1993) *Bodies That Matter: On the Discursive Limits of 'Sex'*. New York: Routledge.

—— (1997) *The Psychic Life of Power: Theories in Subjection*. Stanford, CA: Stanford University Press.

Byrne, D. (1999) *Social Exclusion*. Buckingham: Open University Press.

Caplan, P. and Hall-McCorquodale, I. (1985) 'Mother-blaming in major clinical journals', *American Journal of Orthopsychiatry*, 55: 345–53.

Carr, A. (1991) 'No woman should be able to have her baby the way you would buy a tin of beans', *Today*, 11 March 1991.

Carvel, J. (1991) 'The parent trap', *The Guardian*, 19 September 1991.

—— (1998) 'Labour targets lazy parents', *The Guardian*, 16 January 1998.

Chaytor, R. (1991) 'The virgin mother', *Daily Mirror*, 11 March 1991.

Chegdzoy, K. (1992) 'Family romances in Angela Carter's *Wise Children*', paper given at Lancaster University, Centre for Women's Studies.

Chernin, K. (1993) [1985] *In My Mother's House: A Daughter's Story*. New Haven and New York: Ticknor and Fields.

Chodorow, N.J. (1974) 'Family structure and feminine personality', in M.Z. Rosaldo and L. Lamphere (eds) *Woman, Culture and Society*. Stanford: Stanford University Press.

—— (1978) *The Reproduction of Mothering: Psychoanalysis and the Sociology of Gender*. London: University of California Press.

—— (1989) *Feminism and Psychoanalytic Theory*. New Haven: Yale University Press.

Chodorow, N.J. and Contratto, S. (1982) 'The fantasy of the perfect mother', in Chodorow (1989).

Clark, T.N. and Lipset, S.M. (1996) 'Are social classes dying?', in Lee and Turner (eds).

Collins, P.H. (1991) *Black Feminist Thought: Knowledge, Consciousness and the Politics of Empowerment*. London: Routledge.

Coole, D. (1996) 'Is class a difference that makes a difference?', *Radical Philosophy*, 77: 17–25.

Cooper, C. (1990) ' "Good-enough," border-line and "bad-enough" parenting', in Adcock and White (eds).

Coote, A., Harman, H. and Hewitt, P. (1990) *The Family Way*. London: Institute for Public Policy Research.

Coulshed, V. (1991) [1988] *Social Work Practice: An Introduction*. London: MacMillan.

Coward, R. (1994) 'Kids on the block', *The Guardian*, 2 December 1984.

Dally, A. (1976) *Mothers: Their Power and Influence*. London: Weidenfeld and Nicolson.

Daly, B.O. and Reddy, M.T. (1991) 'Narrating mothers', in Daly and Reddy (eds).

Daly, B.O. and Reddy, M.T. (eds) (1991) *Narrating Mothers: Theorizing Maternal Subjectivities*. Knoxville: University of Tennessee Press.

Davis, D.L. (1992) 'Feminist critics and literary mothers: daughters reading Elizabeth Gaskell', *Signs*, 17 (3): 507–32.

Dawkins, R. (1989) *The Selfish Gene*. Oxford: Oxford University Press.

—— (1995) *River Out Of Eden: A Darwinian View of Life*. London: Weidenfeld and Nicolson.

de Acosta, M. (1997) 'Single mothers in the USA: unsupported workers and mothers', in S. Duncan and R. Edwards (eds) *Single Mothers in an International Context*. London: UCL Press.

de H. Lobo, E. (1978) *Children of Immigrants to Britain: Their Health and Social Problems*. Sevenoaks: Hodder and Stoughton.

Delphy, C. (1984) *Close to Home: A Materialist Analysis of Women's Oppression*. London: Hutchinson.

Delphy, C. and Leonard, D. (1992) *Familiar Exploitation*. Cambridge: Polity.

Dennis, N. (1993) *Rising Crime and the Dismembered Family*. London: IEA Health and Welfare Unit.

—— and Erdos, G. (1993) *Families without Fatherhood*. London: IEA Health and Welfare Unit.

Department of Health (1988) *Protecting Children: A Guide for Social Workers Undertaking a Comprehensive Assessment*. London: HMSO.

Dinnerstein, D. (1976) *The Mermaid and the Minotaur*. New York: Harper.

Doane, J. and Hodges, D. (1992) *From Klein to Kristeva: Psychoanalytic Feminism and the Search for the 'Good Enough' Mother*. Ann Arbor: University of Michigan Press.

Doyle, C. (1991) 'When does a gift become a folly?', *Daily Telegraph*, 12 March 1991.

Duncan, S. and Edwards, R. (1997) 'Single mothers in Britain: unsupported workers or mothers?', in S. Duncan and R. Edwards (eds) *Single Mothers in an International Context: Mothers or Workers?* London: UCL Press.

Dyer, C. (1994) ' "Child jails" held up by local opposition', *The Guardian*, 29 November 1994.

—— (1995) 'Youth crime rule restored by law lords', *The Guardian*, 17 March 1995.

Ehrenreich, B. and English, D. (1979) *For Her Own Good: 150 Years of the Experts' Advice to Women*. London: Pluto Press.

Eichenbaum, L. and Orbach, S. (1982) *Outside In ... Inside Out: Women's Psychology: A Feminist Psychoanalytic Approach*. Harmondsworth: Penguin.

—— (1988) *Between Women: Love, Envy and Competition in Women's Friendships*. New York: Viking Penguin.

—— (1993) 'Feminine subjectivity, countertransference and the mother–daughter relationship', in van Mens-Herhulst *et al.* (eds).

Erikson, E. (1950) *Childhood and Society*. New York: W.W. Norton.

Everingham, C. (1994) *Motherhood and Modernity: An Investigation Into the Rational Dimension of Mothering*. Buckingham: Open University Press.

Ewick, P. and Silbey, S. (1995) 'Subversive stories and hegemonic tales: toward a sociology of narrative', *Law and Society Review*, 29 (2): 197–226.

Finch, J. (1984) ' "It's great to have someone to talk to": the ethics and politics of interviewing women', in C. Bell and H. Roberts (eds) *Social Researching: Politics, Problems, Practice*. London: Routledge and Kegan Paul.

—— (1989) *Family Obligations and Social Change*. Cambridge: Polity Press.

Finch, L. (1993) *The Classing Gaze: Sexuality, Class and Surveillance*. St. Leonards, NSW: Allen and Unwin.

Fiske, J. (1992) 'Cultural studies and the culture of everyday life', in L. Grossberg, C. Nelson and P. Treichler (eds) *Cultural Studies*. New York: Routledge.

Flax, J. (1990) 'Postmodernism and gender relations in feminist theory', in L.J. Nicholson (ed.) *Feminism / Postmodernism*. New York: Routledge.

Foucault, M. (1979) *Discipline and Punish: The Birth of the Prison* (translated by A.M. Sheridan). Harmondsworth: Penguin.

—— (1980) *Power/Knowledge* (ed. C. Gordon, translated by C. Gordon, L. Marshall, J. Mepham and K. Soper). Hemel Hempstead: Harvester Wheatsheaf.

—— (1981) 'The order of discourse' (translated by I. McLeod), in R. Young (ed.) *Untying the Text*. London: Routledge.

—— (1982) 'The subject and power', in H. Dreyfus and P. Rabinow, *Michel Foucault: Beyond Structuralism and Hermeneutics*. Chicago: Chicago University Press.

—— (1983) 'On the genealogy of ethics: an overview of work in progress', in P. Rabinow (ed.) (1984) *The Foucault Reader: An Introduction to Foucault's Thought*. Harmondsworth: Penguin.

—— (1988a) 'Technologies of the self', in L.H. Martin, H. Gutman and P.H. Hutton (eds) *Technologies of the Self: a Seminar with Michel Foucault*. London: Tavistock.

—— (1988b) 'The political technology of individuals', in L.H. Martin, H. Gutman and P.H. Hutton (eds) *Technologies of the Self: a Seminar with Michel Foucault*. London: Tavistock.

—— (1990) [1976] *The History of Sexuality: vol. I, an Introduction* (translated by R. Hurley). London: Penguin.

—— (1992) [1976] *The Archaeology of Knowledge* (translated by A.M. Sheridan Smith). London: Routledge.

Fox, P. (1994) *Class Fictions: Shame and Resistance in the British Working-Class Novel 1890–1945*. Durham, N. Carolina: Duke University Press.

Frankenberg, R. (1993) *White Women, Race Matters: The Social Construction of Whiteness*. London: Routledge.

Franklin, A.W. (ed.) (1978) *Child Abuse*. Edinburgh: Churchill Livingstone.

Franklin, S. (1990) 'Deconstructing "desperateness": the social construction of infertility in popular representations of New Reproductive Technologies', in M. McNeil, I. Varloe and S. Yearley (eds) *The New Reproductive Technologies*. London: MacMillan.

—— (1991) 'Fetal fascinations: new dimensions to the medical-scientific construction of fetal personhood', in S. Franklin, C. Lury and J. Stacey (eds) *Off-Centre: Feminism and Cultural Studies*. London: Harper Collins.

Fraser, M. (1999) 'Classing queer: politics in competition', *Theory, Culture and Society*, 16 (2): 107–32.

Fraser, N. (1989) *Unruly Practices: Power, Discourse and Gender in Contemporary Social Theory*. Cambridge: Polity Press.

Fraser, N. and Gordon, L. (1994) 'A genealogy of *Dependency*: tracing a keyword of the U.S. welfare system', *Signs*, 19 (2): 309–36.

Freely, M. (1996) *What About Us? An Open Letter to the Mothers Feminism Forgot*. London: Bloomsbury.

Freud, A. (1958) *The Psychoanalytic Study of the Child*. New York: International University Press.

Freud, S. (1953) *The Standard edition of the Complete Works of Sigmund Freud (S.E.)*, ed. J. Strachey. London: Hogarth Press and the Institute of Psychoanalysis.

—— (1909) 'Family romances', *S.E*, 9: 235–41.

—— (1925) 'Some psychical consequences of the anatomical distinction between the sexes', *S.E*, 19: 241–58.

—— (1931) 'Female sexuality', *S.E*, 21: 221–43.

—— (1933) 'Femininity', *S.E*, 22: 112–35.

Friday, N. (1979) *My Mother/My Self: The Daughter's Search for Identity*. London: Fontana.

—— (1991) *Women on Top*. London: Hutchinson.

Frude, N. (1990) 'The family', in Herbert (ed.) (1990).

Gallagher, J.R. and Harris, H.I. (1976) *Emotional Problems of Adolescence*. New York: Oxford University Press.

Gergen, K.J. and Gergen, M.M. (1986) 'Narrative form and the construction of psychological science', in T.R. Sarbin, *Narrative Psychology: The Storied Nature of Human Conduct*. New York: Praeger.

Giddens, A. (1990) *The Consequences of Modernity*. Cambridge: Polity.

—— (1991) *Modernity and Self-Identity: Self and Society in the Late Modern Age*. Cambridge: Polity.

—— (1992) *The Transformation of Intimacy: Sexuality, Love and Eroticism in Modern Societies*. Cambridge: Polity.

Gieve, K. (1987) 'Rethinking feminist attitudes towards mothering', *Feminist Review*, 25: 39–45.

Gilbert, L. and Webster, P. (1982) *Bound by Love: the Sweet Trap of Daughterhood*. Boston, MA: Beacon Press.

Glucksmann, M. (1994) 'The work of knowledge and the knowledge of women's work', in Maynard and Purvis (eds).

Goldstein, J., Freud, A. and Solnit, A.J. (1980) [1979] *Before the Best Interests of the Child*. London: Burnett Books.

Gordon, T. (1990) *Feminist Mothers*. London: Macmilllan.

Hacking, I. (1994) 'Memero-politics, trauma and the soul', *History of the Human Sciences*, 7 (2): 29–52.

—— (1995) *Rewriting the Soul: Multiple Personality and the Sciences of Memory*. Princeton: Princeton University Press.

Hall, S. (1996) 'Who needs "identity"?', in S. Hall and P. du Gay (eds) *Questions of Cultural Identity*. London: Sage.

Hankiss, A. (1981) 'Ontologies of the self: on the mythological rearranging of one's life history', in D. Bertaux (ed.) *Biography and Society*. Beverley Hills, CA: Sage.

Hanson, R., McCulloch, W. and Hartley, S. (1978) 'Key characteristics of child abuse', in Franklin (ed.).

Haraway, D. (1986) 'Situated knowledges', in Haraway (1991).

—— (1987) '"Gender" for a Marxist dictionary: the sexual politics of a word', in Haraway (1991).

—— (1991) *Simians, Cyborgs and Women: The Reinvention of Nature*. London: Free Association Books.

Hartsock, N. (1987) 'The feminist standpoint: developing the ground for a specifically feminist historical materialism', in S. Harding (ed.) *Feminism and Methodology*. Milton Keynes: Open University Press.

—— (1990) 'Foucault on power: a theory for women?', in Nicholson (ed.).

Henriques, J., Hollway, W., Urwin, C., Venn, C. and Walkerdine, V. (1984) *Changing the Subject: Psychology, Social Regulation and Subjectivity*. London: Methuen.

Herbert, M. (1990) 'Concepts and concerns of psychology', in Herbert (ed.) (1990).

—— (ed.) (1990) *Psychology for Social Workers*. London: British Psychological Society/MacMillan.

Hetherington, E.M. and Parke, R.D. (1986) *Child Psychology: a Contemporary Viewpoint*. New York: McGraw Hill.

Hirsch, M. (1981) 'Mothers and daughters', *Signs*, 7 (11): 200–22.

—— (1989) *The Mother/Daughter Plot: Narrative, Psychoanalysis, Feminism*. Bloomington: Indiana University Press.

Hochschild, A. (1983) *The Managed Heart: The Commercialization of Human Feeling*. Berkeley: University of California Press.

Hockey, J. and James, A. (1993) *Growing Up and Growing Old: Ageing and Dependency in the Life Course*. London: Sage.

Holland, P. (1996) ' "I've just seen a hole in the reality barrier!": children, childishness and the media in the ruins of the twentieth century', in J. Pilcher and S. Wagg (eds) *Thatcher's Children? Politics, Childhood and Society in the 1980s and 1990s*. London: Falmer Press.

Hout, M., Brooks, C. and Manza, J. (1996) 'The persistence of classes in post-industrial society', in Lee and Turner (eds).

Humphries, B. (1988) 'Adult learning in social work education: towards liberation or domestication?', *Critical Social Policy*, 23: 4–21.

Hutton, P.H. (1988) 'Foucault, Freud, and the technologies of the self', in L.H. Martin, H.Gutman and P.H. Hutton (eds) *Technologies of the Self: a Seminar With Michel Foucault*. London: Tavistock.

Ingleby, D. (1985) 'Professionals as socialisers: the "psy complex"', in A. Scull and S. Spitzer (eds) *Research in Law, Deviance and Social Control*. New York: Jai Press.

Jackson, S. (1992/3) 'The amazing deconstructing woman', *Trouble and Strife*, 25: 25–31.

Jaggar, A. (1997) 'Love and knowledge: emotion in feminist epistemology', in D.T. Meyers (ed.) *Feminist Social Thought: A Reader*. New York: Routledge.

James, A., Jenks, C. and Prout, A. (1998) *Theorizing Childhood*. Cambridge: Polity.

James, S. (1992) 'The good-enough citizen: citizenship and independence', in G. Bock and S. James (eds) *Beyond Equality and Difference: Citizenship, Feminist Politics and Female Subjectivity*. London: Routledge.

James, W. (1993) [1890] 'The self and its selves', in C. Lemert (ed.) *Social Theory: the Multicultural and Classic Readings*. Boulder: Westview Press.

Jamieson, L. (1999) 'Intimacy transformed? a critical look at the "pure relationship"'. *Sociology*, 33 (3): 477–94.

Jenks, C. (1996) *Childhood*. London: Routledge.

Johnson, P. (1988) 'Feminism and images of autonomy', *Radical Philosophy*, 50: 26–30.

Johnson, R. (1993) 'Editor's introduction', in Bourdieu (1993).

Jolly, H. (1986) *Hugh Jolly Book of Child Care: The Complete Guide for Today's Parents*. London: Unwin.

Jones, D.N., Pickett, J., Oates, M.R. and Barbor, P.H. (1982) *Understanding Child Abuse*. Sevenoaks: Hodder and Stoughton.

Jordan, J. (1993) 'The relational self: a model of women's development', in van Mens-Verhulst *et al.* (eds).

Kaplan, E.A. (1992) *Motherhood and Representation: The Mother in Popular Culture and Melodrama*. London: Routledge.

Keat, R. (1991) 'Starship Britain or universal enterprise?', in Keat and Abercrombie (eds).

Keat, R. and Abercrombie, N. (eds) (1991) *Enterprise Culture*. London: Routledge.

Kellmer-Pringle, M. (1972a) 'Deprivation and education', in Kellmer-Pringle (1987).

—— (1972b) 'The roots of violence and vandalism', in Kellmer-Pringle (1987).

—— (1974) 'Ten child care commandments', in Kellmer-Pringle (1987).

—— (1975) 'Young children need full-time mothers', in Kellmer-Pringle (1987).

—— (1980a) [1974] *The Needs of Children*. London: Hutchinson.

—— (1980b) 'Towards the prediction of child abuse', in Kellmer-Pringle (1987).

—— (1987) *Putting Children First: A Volume in Honour of Mia Kellmer-Pringle* (edited by I. Vallender and K. Fogelman). Lewes: The Falmer Press.

Kelly, L. (1988) *Surviving Sexual Violence*. Cambridge: Polity.

Kelly, L., Burton, S. and Regan, L. (1994) 'Researching women's lives or studying women's oppression? Reflections on what constitutes feminist research', in Maynard and Purvis (eds).

Kempe, R.S. and Kempe, C.H. (1978) *Child Abuse*. London: Fontana.

Kiernan, K. and Wicks, M. (1990) *Family Change and Future Policy*. London: Family Policy Studies Centre.

Klein, M. (1932) *The Psycho-Analysis of Children*. London: Hogarth Press and the Institute of Psychoanalysis.

—— (1975) *Works of Melanie Klein vol. I: Love, Guilt and Reparation and Other Works, 1921–1945*. London: The Hogarth Press and the Institute of Psychoanalysis.

Knowles, M. (1983) 'Androgogy: an emerging technology for adult learning', in M. Light (ed.) *Adult Learning in Education*. London: Croom Helm.

Kuhn, A. (1995) *Family Secrets: Acts of Memory and Imagination*. London: Verso.

Lacan, J. (1977a) *Ecrits: A Selection*, translated by A. Sheridan. London: Tavistock.

—— (1977b) *The Four Fundamental Concepts of Psychoanalysis* (edited by J.-A. Miller, translated by A. Sheridan). London: Hogarth Press.

—— (1988) *The Seminars of Jacques Lacan: The Ego in Freud's Theory and in the Techniques of Psychoanalysis 1954–55* (edited by J.-A. Miller). New York: Norton.

La Fontaine, J. (1986) 'An anthropological perspective on children in social worlds', in M. Richards and P. Light (eds) *Children of Social Worlds*. Cambridge: Polity.

Langford, W. (1999) *Revolutions of the Heart: Gender, Power and the Delusions of Love*. London: Routledge.

Lawler, S. (1999a) 'Children need but mothers only want: the power of "needs talk" in the constitution of childhood', in Seymour and Bagguley (eds).

—— (1999b) 'Getting out and getting away: women's narratives of class mobility', *Feminist Review*, 63: 3–24.

—— (2000) 'Escape and escapism: representing working-class women', in S. Munt (ed.) *Subject to Change: Cultural Studies and the Working Class*. London: Cassell.

Lawrence, M. (1992) 'Women's psychology and feminist social work practice', in M. Langan and L. Day (eds) *Women, Oppression and Social Work*. London: Routledge.

Laws, S. (1994a) 'Un-valued families', *Trouble and Strife*, 28: 5–11.

—— (1994b) 'The "lone parents" debate: a children's rights perspective', paper given at British Sociological Association Annual Conference, *Sexualities in Social Context*.

Leach, P. (1988) [1979] *Baby and Child: from Birth to Age Five*. Harmondsworth: Penguin.

Lee, D and Turner, B. (1996) (eds) *Conflicts about Class: Debating Inequality in late Industrialism*. Harlow: Longman.

Levy, A. (1994) 'The end of childhood', *The Guardian*, 29 November 1994.

Lury, C. (1996) *Consumer Culture*. Cambridge: Polity Press.

—— (1998) *Prosthetic Culture: Photography, Memory and Identity*. London: Routledge.

Lynch, M.A. and Roberts, J. (1978) 'Early alerting signs', in Franklin (ed.).

MacKinnon, C. (1982) 'Feminism, Marxism, method and the state: an agenda for theory', *Signs*, 7 (3): 515–44.

Mahler, M., Pine, F. and Bergman, A. (1975) *The Psychological Birth of the Human Infant*. New York: Basic Books.

Mallinson, I. (1992) *The Children Act: a Social Care Guide*. London: Whiting and Birch.

Mann, K. (1992) *The Making of an English Underclass? The Social Divisions of Welfare and Labour*. Buckingham: Open University Press.

Marshall, H. (1991) 'The social construction of motherhood: an analysis of childcare and parenting manuals', in Phoenix *et al.* (eds).

Maynard, M. and Purvis, J. (eds) (1994) *Researching Women's Lives From a Feminist Perspective*. Bristol: Taylor and Francis.

McEwan, I. (1998) *Enduring Love*. London: Vintage.

McHugh, M. and Millar, J. (1997) 'Single mothers in Australia: supporting mothers to seek work', in S. Duncan and R. Edwards (eds) *Single Mothers in an International Context: Mothers or Workers?* London: UCL Press.

McNay, L. (1992) *Foucault and Feminism: Power, Gender and the Self*. Cambridge: Polity Press.

McRobbie, A. (1982) 'The politics of feminist research: between talk, text and action', *Feminist Review*, 12: 46–58.

Mies, M. (1991) 'Women's research or feminist research? the debate surrounding feminist science and methodology', in M.M. Fonow and J.A. Cook (eds) *Beyond Methodology: Feminist Scholarship as Lived Research*. Bloomington: Indiana University Press.

Milhill, C. (1991) 'Child's needs before mother's desires', *The Guardian*, 12 March 1991.

Mitchell, J. (1982) 'Introduction – I', in J. Mitchell and J. Rose (eds) *Feminine Sexuality: Jacques Lacan and the Ecole Freudienne*. New York: W.W. Norton.

Moore, H. (1994) *A Passion for Difference: Essays in Anthropology and Gender*. Cambridge: Polity.

Morris, L. (1994) *Dangerous Classes: the Underclass and Social Citizenship*. London: Routledge.

Morrison, B. (1997) *As If*. London: Granta.

Murray, C. (1994a) *Underclass: the Crisis Deepens*. London: IEA Health and Welfare Unit.
—— (1994b) 'The new Victorians and the new rabble', *The Sunday Times*, 29 May 1994.
Neill, A.S. (1971) 'Freedom works', in Adams *et al.*
Newson, J. and Newson, E. (1976) *Seven Years Old in the Home Environment*. London: Allen and Unwin.
Nicholson, L. (ed.) (1990) *Feminism/Postmodernism*. London: Routledge.
Norton, C. (1999) 'Teen pregnancies "have not risen in past 20 years" ', *The Independent*, 23 September 1999.
NSPCC (1989) *Putting Children First: an NSPCC Guide*. London: NSPCC.
Oakley, A. (1980) *Women Confined: Towards a Sociology of Childbirth*. Oxford: Martin Robertson.
—— (1987) 'From walking wombs to test-tube babies', in Stanworth (ed.).
—— (1990) [1981] 'Interviewing women: a contradiction in terms', in H. Roberts (ed.) *Doing Feminist Research*. London: Routledge.
Ollendorf, R. (1971) 'The rights of adolescents', in Adams *et al.*
Orbach, S., with W. Hollway (1997) 'Mothers, parenting, gender development and therapy', in W. Hollway and B. Featherstone (eds) *Mothering and Ambivalence*. London: Routledge.
Pakula, J. (1996) 'The dying of class or of Marxist class theory?', in Lee and Turner (eds).
Parsons, T. (1951) *The Social System*. London: Routledge and Kegan Paul.
Parsons, T. and Bales, R.F. (1956) *Family, Socialization and Interaction Process*. London: Routledge and Kegan Paul.
Pateman, C. (1988) *The Sexual Contract*. Cambridge: Polity Press.
Payne, M. (1991) *Modern Social Work Theory: A Critical Introduction*. London: MacMillan.
Petchesky, R. (1986) *Abortion and Woman's Choice: The State, Sexuality and Reproduction*. London: Verso.
—— (1987) 'Foetal images: the power of visual culture in the politics of reproduction', in Stanworth (ed.).
Phillips, A. (1988) *Winnicott*. London: Fontana.
Phillips, S. (1996) *Beyond the Myths: Mother–Daughter Relationships in Psychology, History, Literature and Everyday Life*. London: Penguin.
Phoenix, A. (1991) *Young Mothers?* Cambridge: Polity Press.
Phoenix, A., Woollett, A. and Lloyd, E. (eds) (1991) *Motherhood: Meanings, Practices and Ideologies*. London: Sage.
Phoenix, A. and Woollett, A. (1991) 'Motherhood: social construction, politics and psychology', in Phoenix *et al.* (eds).
Pilkington, E. (1994) 'Killing the age of innocence', *The Guardian*, 30 May 1994.
Polansky, N.A. (1981) 'Childhood level of living scales and maternal characteristics scale', in Adcock and White (eds) (1990).
Radway, J. (1987) *Reading the Romance*. London: Verso.
Ramazanoglu, C. (1993) 'Introduction', in C. Ramazanoglu (ed.) (1993) *Up Against Foucault: Explorations of Some Tensions Between Foucault and Feminism*. London: Routledge.
Reay, D. (1996) 'Insider perspectives or stealing the words out of women's mouths: interpretation in the research process', *Feminist Review*, 53: 57–73.
Reed, C. (1993) 'U.S. girl "divorces" parents', *The Guardian*, 19 August 1993.
Reinhold, S. (1994) 'Through the Parliamentary looking glass: "real" and "pretend" families in contemporary British politics', *Feminist Review*, 48: 61–79.
Rich, A. (1973/4) 'Toward a woman-centered university', in A. Rich (1980) *On Lies, Secrets and Silence*. London: Virago.

—— (1977) *Of Woman Born: Motherhood as Experience and Institution*. London: Virago.

—— (1980) 'Compulsory heterosexuality and lesbian existence', *Signs*, 5 (4): 631–60.

Ricoeur, P. (1979) 'Psychoanalysis and the movement of contemporary culture', in P. Rabinow and W.M. Sullivan (eds) *Interpretive Social Science*. Berkeley: University of California Press.

—— (1980) 'Narrative and time', *Critical Inquiry*, 7 (1): 169–90.

—— (1991a) 'Life in quest of narrative', in D. Wood (ed.) *On Paul Ricoeur: Narrative and Interpretation*. London: Routledge.

—— (1991b) 'Narrative identity' (translated by D. Wood) in D. Wood (ed.) (above).

Riessman, C.K. (1993) *Narrative Analysis*. London: Sage.

Riley, D. (1983) *War in the Nursery: Theories of the Child and Mother*. London: Virago.

Roberts, I. (1999) 'A historical construction of the working class', in H. Beynon and P. Glavanis (eds) *Patterns of Social Inequality*. Harlow: Longman.

Roll, J. (1989) *Lone Parent Families in the European Community*. London: Family Policy Studies Centre.

Roof, J. (1991) ' "This is not for you": the sexuality of mothering', in B.O. Daly and M.T. Reddy (eds) *Narrating Mothers: Theorizing Maternal Subjectivities*. Knoxville: University of Tennessee Press.

Roschelle, A.R. (1997) *No More Kin: Exploring Race, Class and Gender in Family Networks*. London: Sage.

Rose, J. (1985) 'Dora: fragment of an analysis', in C. Bernheimer and C. Kahane (eds) *In Dora's Case: Freud, Hysteria, Feminism*. London: Virago.

—— (1987) 'Femininity and its discontents', in Feminist Review (ed.) *Sexuality: A Reader*. London: Virago.

Rose, N. (1991) *Governing the Soul: The Shaping of the Private Self*. London: Routledge.

—— (1992a) 'Engineering the human soul: analysing psychological expertise', *Science in Context*, 5 (2): 351–70.

—— (1992b) 'Governing the enterprising self', in P. Heelas and P. Morris (eds) *The Values of the Enterprise Culture: The Moral Debate*. London: Routledge.

—— (1993) 'Government, authority and expertise under advanced liberalism', *Economy and Society*, 22 (3): 283–99.

—— (1996a) 'Identity, genealogy, history', in S. Hall and P. du Gay (eds) *Questions of Cultural Identity*. London: Sage.

—— (1996b) 'The death of the social? Re-figuring the territory of government', *Economy and Society*, 25 (3): 327–56.

—— (1999) *Powers of Freedom: Reframing Political Thought*. Cambridge: Cambridge University Press.

Rose, S. (1997) *Lifelines: Biology, Freedom, Determinism*. London: Allen Lane.

Ross, E. (1993) *Love and Toil: Motherhood in Outcast London*. New York: Oxford University Press.

Rossiter, A.B. (1994) 'Chips, coke and rock-'n'-roll: children's mediation of an invitation to a first dance party', *Feminist Review*, 46: 1–20.

Rowe, D. (1995) *The Unruly Woman: Gender and the Genres of Laughter*. Austin: University of Texas Press.

Rubin, G. (1994) (with Judith Butler) 'Sexual traffic', *differences*, 6.2+3: 62–99.

Ruddick, S. (1983a) 'Maternal thinking', in Treblicot (ed.).

—— (1983b) 'Preservative love and military destruction: some reflections on mothering and peace', in Treblicot (ed.).

—— (1990) *Maternal Thinking: Towards a Politics of Peace*. London: The Women's Press.

Russell, D.E. (1982) *Rape in Marriage*. New York: MacMillan.

Russell, W. (1996) [1975] *Breezeblock Park*, in *Willy Russell Plays: 1*. London: Methuen.

Russo, M. (1994) *The Female Grotesque: Risk, Excess and Modernity*. New York: Routledge.

Rutter, M. (1972) *Maternal Deprivation Reassessed*. Harmondsworth: Penguin.

Said, E. (1991) 'Michel Foucault, 1926–1984', in J. Arac (ed.) *After Foucault: Humanistic Knowledge, Postmodern Challenges*. New Jersey: Rutgers University Press.

Sayers, J. (1984) 'Feminism and mothering: a Kleinian perspective', *Women's Studies International Forum*, 7 (4): 237–41.

—— (1986) *Sexual Contradictions: Psychology, Psychoanalysis and Feminism*. London: Tavistock.

Schneider, D.M. (1968) *American Kinship: A Cultural Account*. Englewood Cliffs, New Jersey: Prentice-Hall.

Schreurs, K. (1993) 'Daughtering: The development of female subjectivity', in van Mens-Herhulst *et al*.

Sefton Social Services Dept (1994/95) *Child Development* (training pack).

Segal, L.(1987) *Is the Future Female? Troubled Thoughts on Contemporary Feminism*. London: Virago.

Selden, R. (1991) 'The rhetoric of enterprise', in Keat and Abercrombie (eds).

Sennett, R. and Cobb, R. (1977) *The Hidden Injuries of Class*. Cambridge: Cambridge University Press.

Sereny, G. (1995a) *The Case of Mary Bell: a Portrait of a Child who Murdered*. London: Pimlico.

—— (1995b) 'The murder of James Bulger', in Sereny (1995a).

Seymour, J. and Bagguley, P. (eds) (1999) *Relating Intimacies: Power and Resistance*. London: MacMillan.

Shaffer, D.R. (1985) *Developmental Psychology: Theory, Research and Applications*. Monterey: Brooks/Cole.

Shields, C. (1994) *The Stone Diaries*. London: Fourth Estate.

Simonds, W. (1992) *Women and Self-Help Culture: Reading Between the Lines*. New Brunswick, NJ: Rutgers University Press.

—— (1996) 'Consuming selves: self-help literature and women's identities', in D. Grodin and T.R. Lindlof (eds) *Constructing the Self in a Mediated World*. Thousand Oaks, CA: Sage.

Simons, M.A. (1984) 'Motherhood, feminism and identity', *Women's Studies International Forum* 7 (5): 349–59.

Singer, E. (1992) *Child Care and the Psychology of Development* (translated by A. Porcelijn). London: Routledge.

Skeggs, B. (1994) 'Situating the production of feminist ethnography', in Maynard and Purvis (eds).

—— (1995) 'Introduction: processes in feminist cultural theory', in B. Skeggs (ed.) *Feminist Cultural Theory: Production and Process*. Manchester: Manchester University Press.

—— (1997) *Formations of Class and Gender: Becoming Respectable*. London: Sage.

Slipman, S. (1994) 'Would you take one home with you?', in C. Murray (1994) *Underclass: the Crisis Deepens*. London: IEA Health and Welfare Unit.

Smart, C. (1984) *The Ties That Bind*. London: Routledge and Kegan Paul.

—— (1989) *Feminism and the Power of Law*. London: Routledge.

Smith, B. (ed.) (1983) *Home Girls: a Black Feminist Anthology*. New York: Kitchen Table Press.

Smith, C. (1999) 'State power, children's autonomy and resistance: the juridical context', in Seymour and Bagguley (eds).

Somers, M.R. and Gibson, G.D. (1994) 'Reclaiming the epistemological "Other": narrative and the social constitution of identity', in C. Calhoun (ed.) *Social Theory and the Politics of Identity*. Cambridge, MA: Blackwell.

Spelman, E. (1988) *Inessential Woman: Problems of Exclusion in Feminist Thought*. London: The Women's Press.

Spivak, G.C. and Gunew, S. (1993) 'Questions of multiculturalism', in S. During (ed.) *The Cultural Studies Reader*. London: Routledge.

Spivak, G.C. (1997) (with E. Rooney) 'In a word: interview', in L. Nicholson (ed.) *The Second Wave: a Reader in Feminist Theory*. New York: Routledge.

Stainton Rogers, R. and Stainton Rogers, W. (1992) *Stories of Childhood: Shifting Agendas of Child Concern*. Hemel Hempstead: Harvester Wheatsheaf.

Stallybrass, P. and White, A. (1986) *The Politics and Poetics of Transgression*. London: Methuen.

Stanworth, M. (1987) 'The deconstruction of motherhood', in Stanworth (ed.).

—— (ed.) (1987) *Reproductive Technologies: Gender, Motherhood and Medicine*. Cambridge: Polity Press.

Stayton, D.J., Hogan, R. and Ainsworth, M. (1971) 'Infant obedience and maternal behaviour: the origins of socialization reconsidered', *Child Development*, 42: 1057–69.

Steedman, C. (1982) *The Tidy House: Little Girls Writing*. London: Virago.

—— (1986) *Landscape for a Good Woman: A Story of Two Lives*. London: Virago.

—— (1995) *Strange Dislocations: Childhood and the Idea of Human Interiority 1780–1930*. London: Virago.

—— (1996) 'About ends: on the ways in which the end is different from an ending', *History of the Human Sciences*, 9 (4): 99–114.

Strathern, M. (1992a) *After Nature: English Kinship in the Late Twentieth Century*. Cambridge: Cambridge University Press.

—— (1992b) *Reproducing the Future: Anthropology, Kinship and the New Reproductive Technologies*. Manchester: Manchester University Press.

—— (1996a) 'Enabling identity? biology, choice and the new reproductive technologies', in S. Hall and P. du Gay (eds) *Questions of Cultural Identity*. London: Sage.

—— (1996b) 'Gender: division or comparison?', in N. Charles and F. Hughes-Freeland (eds) *Practising Feminism: Identity, Difference, Power*. London: Routledge.

Sukenick, L. (1974) 'Feeling and reason in Doris Lessing's fiction', in A. Pratt and L.B. Dembo (eds) *Doris Lessing: Critical Studies*. Madison: University of Wisconsin Press.

Tambling, J. (1990) *Confession: Sexuality, Sin, the Subject*. Manchester: Manchester University Press.

Tan, A. (1990) *The Joy Luck Club*. London: Minerva.

Treadwell, P. (1988) *A Parents' Guide to the Problems of Adolescence*. London: Penguin.

Treblicot, J. (ed.) (1983) *Mothering: Essays in Feminist Theory*. Maryland: Rowman and Littlefield.

Triseliotis, J. (1972) 'The implications of cultural factors in social work with immigrants', in J. Triseliotis (ed.) *Social Work With Coloured Immigrants and Their Families*. London: Institute of Race Relations/Oxford University Press.

UNICEF (1990) *The Convention on the Rights of the Child*.

Urwin, C. (1985) 'Constructing motherhood: the persuasion of normal development', in C. Steedman, C. Urwin and V. Walkerdine (eds) (1985) *Language, Gender and Childhood*. London: Routledge and Kegan Paul.

Van Mens-Herhulst, J., K. Schreurs and L. Woertman (eds) (1993) *Daughtering and Mothering: Female Subjectivity Reanalysed*. London: Routledge.

Verkaik, R. (1999) 'Mother's appeal over HIV test for baby is rejected', *The Independent*, 22 September 1999.

Walby, S. (1990) *Theorizing Patriarchy*. Oxford: Blackwell.

Walden, R. and Walkerdine, V. (1983) *Girls and Mathematics: From Primary to Secondary Schooling*. London: Heinemann.

Walkerdine, V. (1981) 'Sex, power and pedagogy', in Walkerdine (1990).

—— (1984) 'Developmental psychology and the child-centred pedagogy: the insertion of Piaget into early education', in Henriques *et al.* (eds).

—— (1985a) 'Notes written after an interview for a job', in Walkerdine (1990).

—— (1985b) 'On the regulation of speaking and silence: subjectivity, class and gender in contemporary schooling', in Walkerdine (1990).

—— (1985c) 'Science and the female mind: the burden of proof', in Walkerdine (1990).

—— (1985d) 'Schoolgirl fictions', in Walkerdine (1990).

—— (1985e) 'Video replay: families, films and fantasy', in Walkerdine (1990).

—— (1985f) 'Some day my prince will come: young girls and the preparation for adolescent sexuality', in Walkerdine (1990).

—— (1987) 'Progressive pedagogy and political struggle', in Walkerdine (1990).

—— (1989) 'Fantasy and regulation', in Walkerdine (1990).

—— (1990) *Schoolgirl Fictions*. London: Verso.

—— (ed.) (1996) *Feminism and Psychology: Special Issue on Social Class*, 6 (3).

—— (1997) *Daddy's Girl: Young Girls and Popular Culture*. London: MacMillan.

Walkerdine, V. and Lucey, H. (1989) *Democracy in the Kitchen: Regulating Mothers and Socialising Daughters*. London: Virago.

Walters, S. (1992) *Lives Together, Worlds Apart: Mothers and Daughters in Popular Culture*. Berkeley: University of California Press.

Warnock, M. (1985) *A Question of Life: The Warnock Report on Human Fertilisation and Embryology*. Oxford: Blackwell.

Webb, M. (1992) 'Our daughters ourselves: how feminists can raise feminists', *Ms.* 111 (3): 31–5.

Weedon, C. (1989) [1987] *Feminist Practice and Poststructuralist Theory*. Oxford: Blackwell.

Weldon, F. (1989) *Female Friends*. London: Pan.

Westwood, S. and Bhachu, P. (1988) 'Introduction', in S. Westwood and P. Bhachu (eds) *Enterprising Women: Ethnicity, Economy and Gender Relations*. London: Routledge.

Winnicott, D.W. (1950a) 'Growth and development in immaturity', in Winnicott (1965a).

—— (1950b) 'Some thoughts on the meaning of the word democracy', in Winnicott (1965a).

—— (1956) 'Primary maternal preoccupation', in D.W. Winnicott (1958) *Collected Papers: Through Paediatrics to Psycho-Analysis*. London: Tavistock.

—— (1958) 'The first year of life: modern views on the emotional development', in Winnicott (1965a).

—— (1960) 'The relationship of a mother to her baby at the beginning', in Winnicott (1965a).

—— (1963) 'Communicating and not communicating leading to a study of certain objects', in Winnicott (1965c).

—— (1964) *The Child, the Family and the Outside World*. Harmondsworth: Penguin.

—— (1965a) *The Family and Individual Development*. London: Tavistock.

—— (1965b) 'The development of the capacity for concern', in Winnicott (1965c).

—— (1965c) *The Maturational Processes and the Facilitating Environment: Studies in the Theory of Emotional Development*. New York: International Universities Press.

Wood, N. (1985) 'Foucault on the history of sexuality: an introduction', in V. Beechey and J. Donald (eds) *Subjectivity and Social Relations*. Milton Keynes: Open University Press.

Woodhead, M. (1990) 'Psychology and the cultural construction of children's needs', in A. James and A. Prout (eds) *Constructing and Reconstructing Childhood*. London: Falmer Press.

Woolf, V. (1931) 'Introductory letter to Margaret Llewellyn Davies', in M.L. Davies (ed.) *Life As We Have Known It*. London: Hogarth Press.

Woollett, A. and Phoenix, A. (1991a) 'Psychological views of mothering', in Phoenix *et al.* (eds).

—— (1991b) 'Afterword: issues related to motherhood', in Phoenix *et al.* (eds).

Wylie, P. (1955) [1942] *Generation of Vipers*. New York: Holt, Rinehart and Winston.

Young, A. (1996) *Imagining Crime*. London: Sage.

Young, I.M. (1983) 'Is male gender identity the cause of male domination?', in J. Treblicot (ed.) *Mothering: Essays in Feminist Theory*. Maryland: Rowman and Littlefield.

Index